THE LONG
ENTANGLEMENT

Secretary of State Dean Acheson signing the North Atlantic Treaty in Washington, D.C. on 4 April 1949. President Harry S. Truman and Vice President Alben Barkley stand behind him. Courtesy of The State Department. Public Domain.

THE LONG ENTANGLEMENT

NATO's First Fifty Years

Lawrence S. Kaplan

PRAEGER

Westport, Connecticut
London

Library of Congress Cataloging-in-Publication Data

Kaplan, Lawrence S.
     The long entanglement : NATO's first fifty years
/ Lawrence S. Kaplan.
          p.   cm.
     Includes bibliographical references and index.
     ISBN 0–275–96418–3 (alk. paper).—ISBN 0–275–96419–1 (pbk.   :
alk. paper)
          1. United States—Foreign relations—1945–1989.   2. United States—
Foreign relations—1989–   3. North Atlantic Treaty Organization.
I. Title.
     E744.K177   1999
     327.73—dc21   98–37152

British Library Cataloguing in Publication Data is available.

Library of Congress Catalog Card Number: 98–37152
ISBN: 0–275–96418–3
          0–275–96419–1 (pbk.)

First published in 1999

Praeger Publishers, 88 Post Road West, Westport, CT 06881
An imprint of Greenwood Publishing Group, Inc.

Printed in the United States of America

∞™

The paper used in this book complies with the
Permanent Paper Standard issued by the National
Information Standards Organization (Z39.48–1984).

10 9 8 7 6 5 4 3 2 1

In Memory of

General Lyman L. Lemnitzer
Supreme Allied Commander, Europe
1963–1969

Contents

Preface and Acknowledgments

The fiftieth anniversary of America's long entanglement with Western Europe in the North Atlantic Treaty Organization (NATO) presents an appropriate occasion to look back on the history of that alliance. The implosion of the Soviet empire in the early 1990s left NATO seeking new reasons for its existence. Even if centrifugal forces may be greater today than were during the Cold War, none of the members wishes to abandon the alliance. While NATO has been the subject of many books, few of them have examined its history, and those few have been surveys rather than in-depth studies. The NATO archives are only beginning to be opened, but it is possible to use declassified documents in the U.S. National Archives and the presidential libraries to examine the American role. This book consists of twelve monographs and essays, most of which have appeared in conference proceedings. They examine critical issues in the organization's history and are connected by brief narratives. The result is intended to be an interpretation of a fifty-year history in which the difficulties in reaching a consensus among sixteen allies rival those dealing with the Communist adversary.

My interest in the Atlantic alliance goes back almost to the beginning of NATO, to 1951 when I joined the Historian's office of the secretary of defense. Among the duties of this office was the preparation of a monograph on the Defense Department's contribution to the Military Assistance Program in which NATO was the major beneficiary. The project was initiated by the head of the office, Rudoph A. Winnacker. It was not completed until 1980 under the sponsorship of Winnacker's successor, Alfred

Goldberg. Goldberg's encouragement revived my hopes for making NATO a major subject of research, and it has been in his office that I have continued my NATO studies. Three chapters in this book owe their origins to a larger study of the McNamara years under the auspices of the Historian's office. Goldberg's editorial skills will be evident in the final product. My thanks go to him and to the collegial environment he has provided over the years. Along with Al Goldberg at the head of the table I have received intellectual nourishment from Alice Cole, Ed Drea, John Glennon, Ron Hoffman, Ron Landa, Dick Leighton, Stuart Rochester, Max Rosenberg, Roger Trask, and Dalton West. I should like to add a special note of appreciation to Steve Rearden for his contributions to my NATO course at Georgetown.

A second source of inspiration derives from my long connection with the Lyman L. Lemnitzer Center for NATO and European Union Studies, which has extended beyond my retirement in 1993. Four chapters selected for this book were written in the course of conferences and symposia sponsored in the 1980s by the Lemnitzer Center. This is an occasion for me to express again my gratitude for the support I have received from my associates at the Center, including Bolek Boczek, Bob Clawson, Mark Rubin, Ruth Young, and, particularly, my successor as director, Vic Papacosma. A number of my former graduate students and present friends have deepened my understanding of NATO's history; Scott Bills, Lynne Dunn, Dick Grimmett, George Mazuzan, Mike Ruddy, and Tim Smith are the most prominent. Similarly, I owe a considerable debt to European colleagues for their commentaries on the United States role in Europe, including Walter Lipgens in Germany, Raimondo Luraghi in Italy, Pierre Melandri in France, Olav Riste in Norway, Nick Sherwen in Brussels, Jarrod Wiener in Britain, and, especially, Cees Wiebes and Bert Zeeman in the Netherlands. I have dedicated this book to the memory of General Lemnitzer, who devoted his life to publicizing the cause of NATO after retiring in 1969 as Supreme Allied Commander, Europe. His special interest in Kent State University energized the NATO Center.

Abbreviations

ANF	Atlantic Nuclear Force
CDE	Confidence- and Security-Building Measures in Europe
CENTO	Central Treaty Organization
CJTF	Combined Joint Task Force
CSCS	Conference on Security and Cooperation in Europe
DoD	Department of Defense
DPC	Defense Planning Committee
GDR	German Democratic Republic
ICBM	Intercontinental Ballistic Missile
IFOR	Implementation Force
INF	Intermediate-Range Nuclear Arms Reduction Treaty
JCS	Joint Chiefs of Staff
MAP	Military Assistance Program
MBFR	Mutual and Balanced Force Reduction Program
MDAP	Mutual Defense Assistance Program
MLF	Multilateral Force
NACC	North Atlantic Coordination Council
NPG	Nuclear Planning Group

NSAM	National Security Action Memorandum
OSCE	Organization on Security and Cooperation in Europe
OSD	Office of Secretary of Defense
PFP	Partnership for Peace
SACEUR	Supreme Allied Commander, Europe
SALT	Strategic Arms Limitation Talks
SDI	Strategic Defense Initiative
SEATO	Southeast Asia Treaty Organization
SFOR	Stabilization Force
START	Strategic Arms Reduction Talks
WEU	Western European Union

THE LONG
ENTANGLEMENT

I
Origins of the Alliance, 1948–1949

Fifty years ago the United States abandoned a tradition of political and military nonentanglement with Europe that stretched back to the termination of the entangling Franco-American alliance of 1778. While the United States had intimate ties with allies in World Wars I and II, the relationship was that of an "associate" in the former and as an informal collaborator in the latter. The Anglo-American connections under Roosevelt and Churchill held no formal obligations, unlike the North Atlantic Treaty of 1949. In this sense American membership in the Atlantic alliance in 1949 was indeed what historian Armin Rappaport has called "the American Revolution of 1949."

For him and other supporters of NATO the ending of isolationism marked America's acceptance of responsibility as a superpower, giving legitimacy to the massive economic aid to Western Europe under the Marshall Plan. In the effort to bring political stability to a continent threatened by Soviet expansion, the United States also committed itself to the political and military integration of the West. In another sense the creation of NATO, with the United States as a partner of Europe, may be considered an extension of Thomas Jefferson's conception of an "empire of liberty."

Marxist critics predictably labeled the alliance as an instrument of imperialist exploitation, if not the last stage of capitalism as Hobson or Lenin might have pronounced it. While there was no question that America's involvement with alliances, as in the Marshall Plan, was in the nation's self-interest to repel communism by reviving and reconstructing Europe, it also tapped a vein of altruism in American history that saw a national mission in helping other peoples to achieve the happiness and prosperity that presumably characterized the United States. And Europeans responded positively.

There was a note of triumphalism at the end of World War II when the nation could relish the notion of an "American Century" as popularized by Henry Luce, the influential publisher of *Time* magazine. American acceptance of the United Nations, with its headquarters in New York, was a symbolic recognition that the abstention from the League of Nations in the 1920s was not to be repeated in the next generation. The new challenge of Soviet-led communism, arising from the war that oversaw the destruction of another evil empire, made it unlikely that the United States would withdraw into its old shell. War-devastated Europe needed the resources and determination of the United States to cope with Communist advances. Such was the message that George Kennan sent from Moscow in his Long Telegram of 1946, distorted though it was to be in the Truman Doctrine of 1947. The Marshall Plan for the reconstruction of Europe further demonstrated an American *Weltanschauung* far different from the narrow legalisms of the loans to Europe after World War I.

Yet these actions and the impulses behind them were countered by the weight of an isolationist tradition that had not been fully extinguished by the experience of World War II. The precipitate and massive demobilization of American forces in 1946, reminiscent of the aftermaths of the Civil War and World War I, suggested a reluctance to assume the burdens of global leadership. Even the acceptance of the United Nations was too often accompanied by the expectation that the UN would serve as a surrogate for American foreign policy making, a means of keeping the outside world from interfering with more important concerns at home. While the Marshall Plan reflected the importance of European markets to the business community, domestic markets played a much larger role in the American psyche. It was the Communist menace and Soviet expansionism rather than an imperial urge that induced the Truman administration to seek ways of making Europe strong enough to cope with the new threats to its security.

It remains questionable, however, whether the Washington establishment, no matter how sensitized it may have been to Europe's distress, would have made an entangling alliance without the European "invitation," including as it did promises European leaders made to attach their interests to those of the United States. Looking back from the perspective of half a century, an American historian can accept the claims of European scholars, particularly from Britain, that the alliance was the product of a European initiative to which the United States responded. The failure of the Conference of Foreign Ministers meeting in London in December 1947 to come to an agreement over the future of a divided Germany became the occasion of an epiphany for Ernest Bevin and Georges Bidault, the foreign ministers respectively of Britain and France. Their actions in the early months of 1948 were directed toward bringing the United States into an alliance with Western Europe as the only means of assuring their security against Communist challenges, internal as well as external.

They carefully calibrated an appeal to American sensibilities. Recognizing that the passage of an economic aid program in Congress depended on the promise of self-help and mutual assistance in Europe, Bevin delivered a startling speech in the House of Commons in January 1948, in which he proposed a union of European states. This initiative developed into the Brussels Pact of 17 March 1948, in which Britain, France, and the Benelux countries signed a fifty-year treaty emphasizing those principles of self-help and cooperation so prized by Americans. Ideally, the signatories hoped that this dramatic action would lure the United States into membership in the new Western Union; and the mood in America seemed to support their aspirations. In February 1948, a *coup d'etat* in Prague placed Czechoslovakia firmly under Soviet control; in the following month, Norway reported Soviet pressure for a nonaggression pact reminiscent of Nazi behavior prior to World War II; and in April, a critical election would take place in Italy that could result in a Communist victory. Given these increased fears of Soviet aggression and Truman's warm response to the treaty on the day of its signing, the expectation of American membership was not unreasonable.

But the break with tradition did not come as easily as Europeans and some of their American friends had anticipated. Secretary of State George C. Marshall and Deputy Secretary Robert A. Lovett moved cautiously toward this goal. They did permit secret meetings in the Pentagon with British and Canadian representatives in late March that set the stage for a conference that would include the Western Union in "a collective defense agreement for the defense of the North Atlantic area." But this was the most that could be done at the time. There were still too many obstacles, many of them psychological, preventing the United States from participating in a European alliance. One of them was the easing of tension when the Czech coup did not spread elsewhere and when the Italian election in April resulted in Communist defeat. More significant were the longstanding American suspicions that they would be made victims of European exploitation, which they perceived to have been the case from the Napoleonic wars to World War I.

Resistance to an entangling military alliance stemmed from three major sources in the spring of 1948. First, there were the aforementioned traditional isolationists worrying about America's freedom of action being compromised and its resources drained. No matter how imminent the Soviet threat might be, it did not obliterate visceral doubts about Europe's intentions. A second source was the reluctance of the military establishment to confront the consequences of an alliance. Military assistance could mean depleting stocks at a time when the defense budget was under tight constraints. Nor were the Joint Chiefs of Staff comfortable with the new commitments an alliance would require. They doubted that even after combining their resources Western Europe could resist a Soviet invasion. Such defense plans as the JCS had would concede the European mainland to the Soviets, with future counteroffensives to be launched from Britain and the Suez. But it was the converts to internationalism, those who had invested their hopes in the new world of the United Nations, who were the major deterrent to the Truman administration's participation in an alliance. Many of the UN enthusiasts were former isolationists, such as Senator Arthur H. Vandenberg, the powerful chairman of the Senate Foreign Relations Committee. In their judgment, a military alliance would represent a return to the discredited concept of the balance of power that had been responsible for so much misery in the first half of the twentieth century.

All three constituencies influenced the shaping of the American conception of NATO. In some respects the military were the quickest to accept the entangling connection. Concerns about Europeans raiding so-called surplus military stocks were appeased when the Joint Chiefs of Staff recognized that a military assistance program would offer an opportunity for the services to modernize their equipment. They were further mollified by the dissociation of the treaty commitments from automatic military assistance. Not until the treaty was ratified in July 1949 was the Mutual Defense Assistance Program presented to Congress, and not until the implications of the Soviet detonation of an atomic device were realized was legislation approved. The Pentagon's influence was manifest in the act's requirement that no military aid be granted until bilateral agreements had been concluded with each partner.

The concerns of the internationalists were more difficult to satisfy. Many were convinced that the Atlantic alliance was a ruse to conceal a return to the old order of international anarchy. They recognized that the Soviet Union's veto power in the UN Security Council was frustrating hopes of creating a genuine collective security for the world and agreed with the administration on the need for economic reconstruction and political unification of Europe. Yet they balked at creating an alliance that circumvented the UN and were particularly upset over European eagerness for military aid. The administration's response was to invoke the UN Charter in most of the articles of the treaty, even as the framers knew that there was a basic incompatibility between the treaty and the charter. The treaty was made to appear as if NATO was to be just another regional organization that would fit under Article 53 in Chapter VIII of the charter. But that article is not mentioned in the text of the treaty—for good reason. Regional organizations were supposed to report their activities to the Security Council where the Soviet Union sat as a permanent member. Inevitably, the UN issue arose in the Senate hearings on ratification of the treaty in April and May 1949, but the question of compatibility was successfully evaded.

The debate on the treaty was also the occasion for isolationist spokesmen to be heard. The administration's reluctance to accept a clearcut wording over the vital Article 5 reflected their influence. The European allies wanted nothing less than the language of the Brussels Treaty, which would "afford the parties so attacked all the military and other aid and assistance in their power." This was unacceptable to American negotiators even as they understood that the pledge of American involvement was the keystone of the alliance. It required the efforts of George Kennan, chairman of the State Department's Policy Planning Committee and an opponent of the military aspects of the alliance, to supply the words to appease isolationists. This accounts for the convoluted language of Article 5, whereby the allies agreed that an attack against one would be considered an attack against all, but the measures taken by each member state would be "such action as it deems necessary, including the use of armed force, to restore and maintain the security of the North Atlantic area." Unsaid but understood was the requirement that only the United States Congress could decide if armed force would be necessary.

The watering down of the American commitment was an undesirable but unavoidable price Europeans had to pay for American involvement. But it was not the only one. The admittance of Norway, Denmark, and Iceland, as well as Portugal and Italy, was not part of the Western Union countries' intentions. But they had little choice. The Scandinavian countries and Portugal were necessary for the properties they controlled in the Atlantic Ocean, vital bases for American ships and planes carrying military supplies to Europe. Nor were the Europeans pleased with the delays in granting military aid once the treaty was passed, or with the bilateral agreements in which the allies had to agree to American inspection of the use to which aid would be put.

When the Senate passed the treaty by a vote of 82 to 13, it was a signal of American acceptance of entanglement despite the apparent caveats. The language of Article 5 may have been hedged, but the allies recognized that the president, as commander-in-chief of the armed forces, exercised powers that would activate the treaty in the event of an attack. Similarly, they could accept the "Atlantic" label on the treaty in deference to the old isolationist tradition even as they identified it as a European alliance. And while the conditions accompanying military aid seemed patronizing if not humiliating, the way was open for the kind of aid Europeans needed to assure their security.

1

An Unequal Triad: The United States, the Western Union, and NATO

The three chapters examining the origins of NATO deal with issues vital to the fashioning of the alliance. Chapter 1 is a close examination of the efforts of the Western Union to entangle the United States in a European alliance on European terms. Its success was mixed. This chapter was written for an international symposium held in Oslo in August 1983, organized by the Research Centre for Defense History at Norway's National Defense College. It was published in Olav Riste, ed., Western Security: The Formative Years *(Oslo: Norwegian University Press, 1985).*

It has been customary for observers, friendly and hostile, to look for secret protocols or codicils in any major treaty. And rightly so, for they can be found, in the American experience, from the Treaty of Paris in 1783 to the Yalta agreements in 1945. They are especially likely to be found in a wartime agreement where security conditions discourage full disclosure.

This brief peroration on the obvious is a preface to the claim that the Treaty of Brussels, which established the Western Union, was different.[1] Its meaning can be comprehended best through recognizing a hidden agenda rather than a secret codicil. This requires a reconsideration of the treaty's intention to create an integrated organization over a fifty-year time span, during which each party would afford each other in the event of attack "all the military and other aid and assistance in their power." The only enemy listed in the text is a re-militarized Germany. The Soviet Union is conspicuous by its absence. Also omitted from the text are the assumptions that governed the founding fathers of the Western Union: (1) that no purely European defense against an external threat is genuinely possible, no matter how thoroughly each member shares its resources and merges its sovereignty, (2) that only the United States either through membership in the Union or unrestricted military assistance to it could make the five nations defensible.

If these assumptions were in fact held by the founders, the Western Union becomes an elaborate device to entangle the United States in European affairs, and to do so by appeasing and appealing to the dominant sentiments in post World War II America. Obeisance in the text was given to the United Nations Charter, which presumably still possessed great weight in most circles of the American foreign policy elite, as well as among the mass of Americans. Even more significant was emphasis on "community," on "uniting efforts" for "the elimination of conflict in their economic policies, the coordination of production and the development of commercial exchanges," as expressed in Article I. The message was that the five nations of a new Western Union were complying with demands from all quarters in the United States for evidence of unity as a prerequisite for aid. This was an explicit requirement for economic aid under the Marshall Plan; it was implicitly a condition for the massive military aid wanted by the Brussels Pact nations.

Did they succeed? The elaborate organization of the "High Contracting Parties" was absorbed inside NATO within three years, and the name itself disappeared altogether when it was reorganized in 1955 as the Western European Union in order to accommodate a German membership in NATO. The Western Union failed both to bring the United States into its fold and to have unlimited access to American resources or even to become a focus for a European community. But there are other measures of the organization's impact. A case may be made that the Atlantic alliance was a direct consequence of its efforts, and that from the beginnings of that alliance the Brussels nations were the core of the European side of NATO and the major beneficiary of the United States military assistance. The Western Union's success and failures as well as its relationship with NATO deserve more consideration than they have received from historians.

In the winter of 1948 British Foreign Minister Ernest Bevin and France's Georges Bidault had some reason to hope that America's responses to the crises in Prague and Berlin, along with potential trouble in the forthcoming elections in Italy as well as Soviet intimidation of Norway would induce the United States to embrace the Western Union. On the signing of the Brussels Treaty, President Truman expressed his confidence to Congress "that the United States will, by appropriate means, extend to the free nations the support which the situation requires."[2] There was some distance, however, between these measured words and the eagerness of Bevin and Bidault in their joint response to the President's speech: "We are ready, together, with a Benelux representative, to discuss with you what further steps may be desirable."[3] The Americans were not ready.

At secret meetings of the U.S. with the United Kingdom and Canada held in the Pentagon in the same month the treaty was signed, the United States ruled out membership in the Western Union. The new organization was considered too narrow to join; a larger "Atlantic" organization would have to be devised to protect other countries in danger of Communist subversion or attack. Greece, Turkey, Italy, and even Spain and Germany came under consideration, even though the latter was the nation named as a potential enemy in the text of the Brussels Treaty. Until the time when a "North Atlantic Defense Agreement" could be framed the American position appeared to be unilateral in its relations with the European allies.[4]

Practical considerations help to account for this position. The American administration realized that a too hasty mix of military and economic aid could damage the fragile fabric of European-American relations. First priority had to be the successful passage of the Foreign Assistance Act through the Congress, and those efforts could be damaged if major beneficiaries of the Marshall Plan, the Brussels Pact countries, were perceived as being more interested in military than in economic aid. Thus the administration considered and rejected the addition of a Title VI to the Foreign Assistance Act, which would have made military assistance an important part of the foreign aid package.[5] Western European leaders were frustrated, at least initially, in winning massive military aid as well as U.S. adherence to their treaty.

Obviously, the long isolationist tradition of the United States was also a factor in inhibiting American membership in the Brussels group, or in any larger European alliance for that matter. Was the American public prepared to accept an entangling alliance in defiance of the wisdom of the Founding Fathers? The polls indicated that they would be, if the language was carefully written, but the Congress hesitated.[6] The acceptance of the ECA had been a painful effort, and that had involved neither military aid nor a military alliance, but the less sensitive issue of economic aid.

A further brake on American temptation to act came from the attitude of the American military establishment toward its involvement in Europe's defense. The Joint Chiefs of Staff (JCS) had been giving serious consideration both to the issue of alliance and to the question of military assistance. Their reactions in the beginning were resolutely negative. Military assistance sounded like permission for Europe to raid America's own severely strained supplies. They were uncomfortable with the implications of the National Security Council document (NSC–7), a general report on the "Position of the United States with respect to Soviet-directed World Communism," which on March 30 recommended a counter-offensive to "strengthen the will to resist of anti-communist forces throughout the world." First priority in this recommendation was assigned to Europe, and a strong endorsement was given to the Western Union.

A formula was to be worked out for "military action by the United States in the event of unprovoked armed attack against the nations in the Western Union or against other selected non-Communist nations."[7] While the JCS endorsed the paper's stand on compulsory military service, they looked askance at the recommendation that machine tools be provided for European arms industries and were distressed by the specific point that military equipment and technical information would be included in the "counter-offensive."[8] Secretary of Defense James V. Forrestal warned the NSC about the "extreme importance to our national security of keeping our military capabilities abreast of our military commitments."[9] The mention of tools triggered a concern that their exportation might interfere with American needs or might be subject to capture by Soviet forces.

Behind the immediate impulse to protect their own stock the JCS worried about the general weakness of European forces. They assumed that none of the Western powers individually or collectively could stop the Soviets should they wish to march to the Atlantic or to the Channel in 1948. At this point they feared that an American entanglement in an alliance would place the military in a hopeless position of "biting off more than we could chew," to use Ambassador Lewis Douglas's terms.[10]

Important as the problem of military assistance was to the JCS, it was overshadowed by the implications of NSC–9, a document prepared to respond to the Western Union's request, presented on 13 April 1948. Although, like the findings of the security conversations, it would leave the United States out of the Western Union for the time being, it opened the way for an even more ambitious undertaking, a "Collective Defense Agreement for the North Atlantic Area."[11] The JCS urgently protested against such commitments as being beyond the capacity of the nation to fulfill, "unless preparatory measures were completed first."[12]

It was not the opposition of the military, however, that delayed immediate American action. Rather, the State Department recognized that it first would have to conduct negotiations with a wary Senate. Senator Arthur H. Vandenberg, the powerful chairman of the Foreign Relations Committee was also concerned about the nature of future commitments: whether or not the Rio alliance model would allow the majority an excessive role in decision-making; whether or not the absence of the United Nations would undercut its already damaged prestige in the world. Moreover, the senator wanted more assurance that the Europeans were advancing toward integration before more American assistance was provided.[13]

The result was a major modification of NSC–9 as Deputy Secretary of State Lovett cultivated and attended Vandenberg's reservations. In NSC–9/1 issued on 23 April, the Administration won its objective of sending invitations to the countries of the North Atlantic area, including Italy, Eire, Scandinavia, Canada, and Portugal as well as the Western Union regarding a collective defense arrangement for the North Atlantic area. Self-help and mutual aid were to be required of all potential signatories.[14] Part of the price for Senate approval was delay in the proceedings, ostensibly because of the short time remaining before the adjournment of the 80th Congress. A more significant factor in Congressional delay was an expectation that a new president, undoubtedly Republican, would be needed to create a new consensus for involvement with Europe. The rest of the price was the embodying of the whole concept of an Atlantic alliance within the context of the United Nations Charter. Articles 51 and 53 relating to self-defense and regional arrangements would provide a United Nations blessing upon the enterprise. All of these ideas were expressed in the Vandenberg Resolution, reported by the Foreign Relations Committee to the Senate on 19 May and adopted as Senate Resolution 239 on 11 June 1948.[15]

Belgium's premier, Paul-Henri Spaak, had recognized the reasons for American caveats. Visiting Washington in April he was able to canvass the extent of the U.S. commitment to the Western Union, and to explain a European position to American policy makers. Spaak made a point of stating his belief that war was not imminent, that the Five powers "are not at present directly threatened by the Russians," and that a treaty between the United States and Western Union might encourage Russian aggression against those nations omitted from an alliance. But even though a larger guarantee would be welcomed, "the real need was for maximum military coordination at the earliest possible date."[16] This would be the most credible affirmation of Truman's 17 March statement. At the same time Spaak spoke emphatically to Americans about Europe's concern over defending itself. The establishment of a Secretariat and a decision to hold military conversations in April was a serious earnest of the Western Union's intentions.

In underscoring Europe's activities Spaak was sensitive to American interests in European integration, and in tune with American sensibilities about self-help. While pressure from European leaders would have to be exerted regularly, it should be carefully orchestrated to the American mood. Such was the essential information that Spaak communicated to Sir George Rendel, British ambassador to Belgium, when the foreign minister returned to Brussels. The Americans, Spaak reported, were favorably disposed toward Western Europe, and "were prepared to go a long way towards committing themselves to backing the Brussels Treaty with a promise of military assistance." He cautioned Rendel, though, that the problems of an election year and the necessity to devise the precise political formula would mean some delays.[17]

Still, the willingness of the United States to send observers to the projected defense discussions in London was a happy augury of future Amer-

ican relations. It permitted the British to relax over the slow implementation of the American part in Western Union's plans. They purposely
withdrew from their earlier pressures for a treaty or aid, knowing that
such activity for the moment would only invite a negative response, and
knowing also that the seeds sown by the Brussels Treaty would grow in
time.[18]

Some of the confusion over the differences between U.S. membership in
the Western Union and U.S. military aid to its membership arose from the
differing signals that Europeans sent to Americans. When Spaak visited
Washington, Kennan and Bohlen heard what they had preferred to believe:
namely, that the Europeans valued an alliance less than they wanted immediate military help. Under Secretary of State Robert A. Lovett, a critical
figure in the making of American policy, seemed to share the view of the
two dissidents. Spaak's comments made Lovett hesitate about proceeding
with a North Atlantic security pact.[19] The consequence might have been a
unilateral declaration of the sort which Bohlen and Kennan had recommended.

John D. Hickerson, Director of the Office of European Affairs, and Theodore C. Achilles, Director for Western European affairs in the State Department, primary actors in the secret March discussion that led to the idea
of an expanded alliance, ultimately prevailed. The Vandenberg Resolution
of 11 June terminated the debate over unilateralism versus multilateralism.
The adherents of a North Atlantic community in the State Department
triumphed, although the perceptions of the moment would identify victory
with the Senate. By transferring credit and responsibility for initiating aid
to Europe as well as a security pact in the slack period between 11 April
and 11 June, Truman and Lovett permitted the Republican-led Senate to
believe that it had been a key element in a changing American foreign
policy. As Vandenberg was reputed to ask: "Why should a Democratic
President get all the kudos in an election year? Wouldn't the chances of
Senate 'consent' to ratification of such a treaty be greatly increased by
Senatorial 'advice to the President to negotiate it.' "[20] A powerful constit-
uency was won over to the cause of European unity, to European self-help,
and to American identification with these ideas.

A second revision of NSC–9—NSC–9/2—submitted a week before the
Senate Foreign Relations Committee acted on the Vandenberg Resolution,
recommended that after the introduction of the Resolution (which had been
drafted in the State Department), State would advise the Western Union
that "the President is prepared to authorize U.S. participation in the London Five Power military talks with a view to: (a) concerting military plans
for use in the event that the U.S.S.R. should resort in the short term future
to aggressive action in Germany, Austria or elsewhere in Europe, and (b)
drawing up a coordinated military supply plan." Moreover, it made clear
that the Defense Department would participate in these conversations, and

that following the ERP precedent the Europeans "must first plan their co-ordinated defense with the means presently available . . . they must then determine how their collective military potential can be increased by co-ordinated production and supply, including standardization of equipment." At this point the United States would screen estimates of supplementary assistance needed and propose legislation accordingly. An annex to NSC–9/2 contained the Vandenberg Resolution, only slightly altered by George F. Kennan, Director of the Policy Planning Staff, before its final submission.[21] NSC–9/3 of 28 June followed, with instructions that produced the North Atlantic Treaty nine months later: namely, military conversations with Americans present, a clear European acceptance of the ERP model for self-help and coordinated defense plan, and Congressional action after the Presidential election.[22]

The Vandenberg Resolution cleared away most of the obstacles to ultimate acceptance of an American military alliance with Western Europe. On 1 July NSC–14 was adopted.[23] It essentially revived the discarded Title VI of the Foreign Assistance Act that would facilitate the procurement of massive military aid for Europe. Five days later the first session of the Washington Exploratory Talks on "regional collective security" convened.[24] The Joint Chiefs of Staff had already accepted both commitments with reluctance but also with resignation, hoping that specific military obligations would be avoided "unless preceded by at least the degree of military strengthening that the Joint Chiefs of Staff have recommended" for American forces.[25]

The one vital point on which the JCS and the State Department could agree in the summer of 1948 was that the reconciliation of economic and military differences among the allies would permit the maximal utilization of economic aid and military equipment by the recipients. In July the activity was on two fronts: in London, where the Brussels Pact military conversations were witnessed by Major General Lyman L. Lemnitzer, the official American observer; and in Washington, where exploratory talks centered on military assistance to the Brussels Pact nations and a widening of its membership to other nations, including the United States.[26]

In London the Western Union had tried to identify the establishment of its new bodies—the Permanent Consultative Council and its Military Committee—as earnest of Europe's response to the mandate of the Vandenberg Resolution.[27] Its concerns were the filling of its needs by American aid, rather than implementing or even seriously formulating plans for pooling its own resources, standardizing weapons, or expanding military production. With France leading the pressure for its own rearmament the idea of a European defense appeared to be a cover for gratifying national needs. The projected Atlantic Pact seemed a diversion from the more pressing problem of direct aid to each nation. More specifically, immediate aid to France was a first priority of negotiations, as French Ambassador Henri

Bonnet insisted.[28] "The cat then came fully out of the bag," as Lovett saw it, when Bonnet complained that the talks were wasting time on long-range programs, "instead of developing a current military program and re-equipping the French army."[29] The Americans resisted these importunities, asserting that the mandate of NSC–14 could be implemented only after the Europeans had demonstrated faith in a supranational defense plan. The hope was for a military equivalent of the Committee of European Economic Cooperation, something which the Congress would approve as a rational guide to the distribution of aid. Congress, according to Under Secretary of State Robert A. Lovett, would not accept a "military lend-lease," in the manner employed in World War II.[30]

Initially, the Western Union through its Military Committee was to map out a strategic concept to which the United States could make a contribution. But even here there were serious problems. Among them was the short-range emergency plan, HALFMOON, presented by the JCS in the event of a war with the Soviet Union. It had been approved for planning on 19 May 1948 and under different names remained a guide to U.S. military thinking throughout 1948. It assumed the necessity of evacuating Western forces from most of the Continent and making defensive stands in the Cairo-Suez area and in Great Britain; the heart of Western Europe was deemed indefensible.[31] This was a burden for General Lemnitzer's seven-man team in London, since the members of the Western Union could draw no comfort from plans that would accept their conquest before liberation. The strategy of the Western Union was to fight "as far east in Germany as possible."[32]

Yet the Western Union offered no serious alternatives, even though no military aid was supposed to be offered until its defense plans had been screened. Reluctantly in the fall of 1948 the United States agreed to an interim solution whereby the Military Committee would provide the U.S. representative with an outline for the defense of Europe at the Rhine by mid-1949 in place of an overall plan of defense.[33] Unfortunately, the Western Union Chiefs of Staff could do no more than provide a summary of forces available for mobilization in 1949 if the necessary equipment could be obtained.[34] The JCS then accepted with considerable misgivings these announcements of Field Marshal Bernard Montgomery, chairman of the WU's Commander-in-chief committee, as if they were genuine accomplishments. This permitted the United States to provide aid both to the WU and to an enlarged alliance.[35]

But emergency aid to any one European country was not the major issue before the allies. More disturbing was the threat to the primacy of the Western Union in the terms the United States was asking of the Brussels Pact partners. At the same time that United States pressed for a quickening of mutual aid and increase in self-help among the European allies, it made clear the inadequacy of the Western Union as the frame for the new security arrangements. It was both too "European" for American isolationists to accept and too small to be an appropriate deterrent to Soviet aggression. Hickerson observed that "in one sense the Brussels Pact was not broad enough as to membership and in another sense was too broad as to obligation." The economic and cultural clauses would fit an American association. The United States could not simply become an overseas member of the Western Union.[36]

The official American view differed from the Western Union's. In essence it embodied the views of John Hickerson, who wanted a widening of the Brussels Pact to include Italy and other OEEC countries. Lovett was concerned with a nation, such as a hypothetical "Neuralgia," which was prepared to defend itself if properly assisted. If it felt excluded from a particularly European alliance, it could either appeal for bilateral American assistance or yield to Soviet wishes. Both alternatives were to be avoided. The way to help such a beneficiary was to bring it into the alliance, which would ensure coordination of its need with those of the other allies.[37]

The most that the Brussels powers could salvage from this outlook appeared in the Dutch Foreign Minister's image of the alliance as "a peach, the Brussels Pact would be the hard kernel in the center and a North Atlantic Pact the somewhat less hard mass around it."[38] In this context five stepping stone countries—Norway because of Spitzbergen, Denmark because of Greenland, Portugal for the Azores, Iceland, and possibly Ireland—had claims on the alliance which the core countries could not deny if they wanted the membership of the United States. As Bohlen expressed it at the 9 August meeting of the Ambassadors Committee, "without the Azores, Iceland and Greenland, help could not be got to Europe in significant quantities at all."[39] Earlier Lovett had even suggested that "Greenland and Iceland were more important than some countries in western Europe to the security of the United States and Canada." Thus the American view was that the enlargement of the alliance was as much a benefit to the allies as it was to the potential new members.[40] The Western Union's counter argument that new commitments would weaken existing arrangements was undercut by the American perception "it is clear that they do not want others to share in the United States arms pie."[41]

Reflecting the two months of labor, the Washington paper of 9 September underscored the American position by emphasizing the danger to the security of America and Western Europe if the facilities of the stepping stone countries were not available to them. If the latter were not brought into the alliance as full members by the end of 1948 it was not for lack of trying. The Washington paper agreed to the extension of invitations to selected countries before the conclusion of a pact, to see if they would accept full responsibilities for the role assigned to them.[42] On November 26 the Brussels Pact responded by recommending Denmark, Iceland, Norway, Portugal and possibly Sweden for membership.[43] A month later this was carried out, although Ireland declined the invitation to explore the question and Sweden was finally denied an invitation.[44]

Time-consuming and emotion-ridden as the questions over the scope of the alliance were, these were not the central issue before the diplomats. The real question was the immediate and future security of Europe. It restored the credibility of the American pledge to its trans-Atlantic partners. If Europeans could be certain that American power would be inextricably harnessed to their defense, other matters—the extension of membership or the shipment of specific supplies—would dwindle in significance and urgency.

The core of the obligation was when and how the United States would come to the aid of an ally under attack. The European objective was immediate and inextricable entanglement, while the United States, fearing both exploitation and isolationism, struggled to make its pledge of support consistent with the requirements of the Federal Constitution. Not until the very end of negotiations was language worked out to satisfy the needs of all parties.

The problem stemmed from the potential models that would inform the treaty's authors. Europeans preferred understandably the deceptively simple language of the Brussels Treaty's Article IV, in which the allies would "afford the party so attacked all the military and other aid and assistance in their power." The response of the State Department Working Group to this idea was negative: "The United States could not constitutionally enter into any Treaty which would provide that the United States would be automatically at war as a result of an event occurring outside its borders or by vote of other countries without its concurrence."[45]

The recent treaty of Rio de Janeiro offered a more usable example for the United States to develop. For one thing, it was a model that the Congress had already accepted as within the tradition of a modernized Monroe Doctrine. For another, it modified the commitment to declare war. While Article 3 did observe that an attack against one shall be considered as an attack against all parties . . . Article 4 provided for "individual determination by each Party, pending agreement upon collective measures, of the immediate measures which it will individually take on fulfillment of the obligation."[46]

Nonetheless, there were drawbacks in the Rio model even from the American perspective. It was just a "take-off point," as Lovett noted.[47] The Rio pact held insufficient emphasis upon self-help and cooperation and on the integration of economic and military systems. The Europeans on the other hand were discontented with its vagueness about the aid to be supplied and about the nature of the commitment undertaken. At the Working Group meetings of the Exploratory Talks Sir Frederic Hoyer-Millar and Armand Bérard recommended that more precise language than that of the Rio Pact be devised when considering the implications of an attack on any member of the alliance. They wanted to be sure that the response would indeed be as if the attack had been made against every other member, including the United States.[48]

The French were disturbed that in the absence of exact military obligations provisions for consultations like those in the Rio Pact would increase rather than decrease the sense of insecurity in Europe. Bohlen, the United States representative at these meetings, could only answer that whatever arrangement might be made involving the United States would have to recognize the separation of powers in the American government, as does the Inter-American treaty. Although the Rio strategy differed from that of Brussels, he claimed that the "obligation to afford assistance to a country under aggression is similar." In the light of a Congressional action that had to precede a state of war, the United States could not accept the Brussels article which bound each member to provide "all military and other aid in its power."[49]

Both sides labored to bridge differences. A State Department paper carefully outlined those Rio provisions which could be mutually acceptable, and Hoyer-Millar proposed incorporation of language from the Brussels Treaty that would not directly confront the United States on constitutional issues. Fastening on Article 3 of the Rio Pact, he suggested elaborating on the method of responding to an attack: "by military, economic and all other means within its power."[50]

The result of the negotiations surfaced in the broad compromise presented in the Washington paper of September, containing a blend of language from both treaties. The document listed the American preference for language close to the Rio Treaty as well as the European variations on the Brussels Pact, and then proposed a compromise that linked individual national response to "constitutional processes."[51]

Still, the Europeans were not satisfied. There remained the implication that each party could still decide for itself whether an armed attack had occurred and what should be done about it. It could mean all aid from the United States short of war. If so, this would undercut the psychological effect which the alliance was intended to create. The concern was so deep that the United States retreated from its earlier positions. In the draft treaty of 24 December the negotiators agreed to "taking forthwith military or such other action, individually and in concert with other Parties, as may be necessary to restore and secure the security of the North Atlantic area."[52] While this was not quite all military action "in their power," it did promise action "forthwith" which might have the same effect.

As the North Atlantic Treaty slowly took form in the winter of 1949, the Brussels Pact Powers should have been able to look on their labors with considerable satisfaction. The new Atlantic alliance would have achieved their primary objective, the entangling of the United States, and along with it the prospect of vital military aid. The Western Union itself was in full operation. Under the Consultative Council it had established an integrated defense organization, including a Committee of Defense Ministers, a Chief of Staffs Committee, and a Supply Board. Under the Military Committee was a Commander-in-Chiefs Committee charged with the planning of the defense of Europe. Moreover, the Consultative Council had the help of a Finance and Economic Committee to deal with military deficits, new production programs, and the means of financing them. In brief, the Western Union seemed to have created the infrastructure to assume leadership of the enlarged alliance.

This sense of strength permitted Consultative Council members to ignore Spaak's sharp criticism of the slow progress the Union was making in the fulfillment of its objectives.[53] Instead, "the slenderness" of its power was covered by its expectation of serving as the pivotal element of the North Atlantic Treaty, the conduit for all supplies and equipment and perhaps even manpower flowing across the Atlantic.[54] In a speech to the Council of the Republic a month before the signing of the pact, Schuman alluded with some exaggeration to the powerful American presence that would compensate for the inadequacies of even a pooled Brussels Pact force.[55] Did it really matter whether or not Belgium's occupation forces in Germany were reorganized, or that Britain refused to share its weaponry with France, or that the pace of economic integration within the Union was too sluggish? What counted was the character, amount and dependability of American assistance which alone could make a reality out of European military integration.

Trouble lay ahead, however, if the United States should expose the hollowness of the allies' claims to pool resources and to identify clearly deficiencies in their production capacities.[56] Western Union nations had to satisfy not only Congress but an increasing bureaucratic infrastructure which the Truman administration had established to institutionalize the connection with the Brussels Pact powers. The Foreign Assistance Correlations Committee, coordinated by Ernest Gross of the State Department, was established in January 1949 to help the various Cabinet officials in State, Defense, and ECA to assume responsibility for the management of the projected military assistance program. The committee operated on the assumption that Europe must bear an appropriate share of the costs, or else Congress would not respond to its needs.

To this end, Paul H. Nitze, deputy to the Assistant Secretary of State for Economic Affairs, visited American and Western Union diplomats in London and Paris in January to examine the effect of an extensive American military assistance program on the European economy. He discovered that the fear of the impact of increases in military production upon their still fragile economies inhibited budgetary increases from the Western Union countries. U.S. aid in the form of dollars and raw materials were seen to be as vital as military items directly.[57] Guided by these perceptions the JCS devised an interim plan in the winter of 1949 involving up to a billion dollars to Europe mostly for small arms, artillery and communication supplies needed for the maintenance of the equivalent of nine U.S. divisions. This aid was designed to bring into full combat readiness such forces as the Western Union could maintain without affecting the economies of its members.[58]

Generous as these intentions may have been they were greeted with mixed feelings by the Western Union. It wanted at one and the same time full American participation in Western Union, including responsibility for Europe's defense, and complete exclusion from the decision-making process. Ideally then, the United States should accept requirements in materiel and arms determined by the Brussels Pact powers, and then retire from the scene while the Consultative Council decided how monies, weapons, and supplies should be shared and employed. Moreover, the Western Union wanted to be certain that its core role in NATO would not be adulterated by the presence of new members. How to reconcile these contradictory objectives became a major source of agitation among the future allies in the weeks before the completion of the North Atlantic Treaty.

A prerequisite for military aid was a European initiative and formulation of a request, which would symbolize both the desire and the ability of European nations to help themselves as well as to be helped by the United States. To aid in the coordination of European efforts U.S. Ambassador to the United Kingdom Lewis W. Douglas was appointed chief of the U.S. government's European Coordinating Committee in February.[59] Difficulties arose even before requests were filled, as each member jockeyed to avoid being the first in line. Britain hesitated for fear that if it should make commitments ahead of its allies, the others would assume that it would bear the brunt of future sacrifices. France dallied, presumably because of forthcoming cantonal elections in March, which might expose friends of the alliance to excessive public criticism.[60]

Ultimately, a response to the United States was made at a meeting of the WU's Finance and Economic Committee on 11 March, at which each member identified its perceived needs. This was not what the Americans had expected, since no plans would accompany the request to show how the aid would be used. The formal requests did not take into account methods of correcting deficiencies in current programs. In fact, the Western Union submitted its request, not as individual members on a bilateral basis, but as a single unit that would distribute aid according to the needs of individual countries.[61]

The Western Union leaders knew that the manner and content of their request would be unacceptable to the Congress. They understood too that Douglas was as sensitive to their concerns as any American could be. So when the FACC predictably objected to the proposition that the United States "participate" as a member in the Western Union rather than "assist" its development, the Europeans reacted calmly. While they did not comply fully with American requirements, they did not rule out some form of bi-lateral agreement.[62] Despite some qualms in the State Department over potentially hostile reactions in the Pentagon and on Capitol Hill, the ECC views prevailed. The day after the treaty was signed the requests of the Western Union countries were announced to the public, with the United States response following on 6 April. The agreement to postpone conflicts was best expressed in the American statement that "the allocation of this materiel and financial assistance will be effected by common agreement."[63]

This compromise did not mean that the issue of reciprocity between the Brussels Treaty powers and the United States was resolved. It would arise again as an inevitable consequence of Congressional hearings and remain to complicate American attitudes toward European integration. Still, the Western Union's success in blurring the question for the moment was a test of strength, which it appeared to pass. The Brussels Pact nations were at the center of negotiations for NATO, and their American bargaining part-ner over military assistance was the ECC. Although that body was sup-posed to oversee aid to all European members of NATO, it was primarily involved with the only effective European organization in place—the West-ern Union. The result in the spring of 1949 was almost as if the making of the Atlantic Alliance was the product of a dialogue between two equal and distinct entities—America and the Western Union.[64]

That the European partners were able to hold their own in negotiations was a tribute to the vigor with which they made their stands, both sepa-rately and as members of the Brussels Pact. It was also a reflection of American concern to put the pieces of the alliance into place as quickly as possible. Failure to make agreements would risk the loss of funds author-ized by Congress and, more significantly, a setback in the secular struggle with the Communist world. In this circumstance the semantics of the allies' compliance with American laws was as important as its substance.

For all the disarray that appeared so prominent in the day-to-day-interaction among the powers of NATO, a movement toward cohesion in the alliance proceeded concurrently with the friction. The treaty after all had passed the ratifying hurdles of all twelve members, beginning with Canada on 3 May and culminating with Italy on 24 August. In the case of the United States the passage broke a tradition against entangling alliances that went back to the beginnings of the republic. A major military assis-tance program had been initiated, no matter how many caveats the Con-gress attached to its final form. And despite American suspicions about the Western Union's intentions, its experience provided a framework for the growth of the organization. Western Union served as a regional planning group, and its subsidiary bodies such as its Military Committee offered what products it did have direct to NATO. The Western Union's Military Supply Board, on which the United States had placed an observer, was absorbed into NATO's Military Production and Supply Board, while its Finance and Economic Committee became in effect NATO's Defense Financial and Economic Committee. Moreover, the imaginative infrastructure program of building headquarters, airfields, signal communications, and pipelines across the frontiers of member states had been the work of the Western Union planners before American arms and equipment could begin to fulfill the objectives of any plan—short or middle term. When the United States and Canada joined the enterprise in 1951, it was as contributors to the second "slice." Not until the Ottawa meetings of the North Atlantic Council in the fall of 1951 was this formally a NATO project.[65]

It is not surprising then that as late as 1 August 1951, in the immediate wake of the Korean War, there was hope if not expectation that the Brussels Pact could still be the agent for Europe, if only "the Five countries could translate their efforts into facts," as Bevin put it, and prevent the Americans from receiving the impression "that the Brussels Treaty Powers were not doing their utmost."[66]

But this meeting of the Consultative Committee also reflected why the WU would become irrelevant to the future of NATO: (1) it postulated no integration of German forces into the Western Union, and (2) it showed no progress in the Franco-British rivalry personified in the ongoing conflicts between Montgomery and de Lattre de Tassigny at Military Headquarters in Fontainebleau. Without integration of forces in the Western Union there would be no American acceptance, and without British membership in integration there would be no French acceptance of a German component.

Even if these disabilities had been overcome, would the United States in NATO have turned over to the Western Union a common pool of funds that would have made all the other European member nations second-class citizens? This is what the Western Union meant after the outbreak of the Korean War when it urged that a close cooperation be maintained with NATO "whilst reaffirming the special responsibilities and duties of the Brussels Treaty Signatories."[67] But the pressures of the Korean War, particularly for expansion of the alliance to include Greece, Turkey, and Germany nullified those responsibilities. The establishment of the Supreme Command only a few miles from the Western Union's counterpart in Fontainebleau in December 1950 meant that the WU would in effect disappear along with the Western European Regional Planning Group. It would only exist in a shadow world of staff committees until its reconstitution as the Western European Union in 1955 to act as the vehicle to accept a German participation in NATO.[68] Yet, even as it expired the Western Union left another legacy to NATO in the form of the SHAPE command in the winter of 1950–51 under SACEUR Dwight D. Eisenhower. Its model was the Western Union headquarters at Fontainebleau, which had been established two years before under Field-Marshal Montgomery.

What then may be said about the role of the Brussels Pact organization in the integration of Western Europe's defense efforts? On balance it facilitated the growth of NATO and the involvement of America in the policy of Europe. In that sense the hidden agenda was far more a success than a failure. Its announced intentions of creating a broad Western European community were another matter; it was replaced by other institutions, from the Schuman Plan to the EDC to the Common Market to the European Community, precisely because it succeeded in entangling the United States in its affairs. By doing so it subverted the stated goal of a self-reliant European union. As an organization it was dominated by Britain's concern for the declining "special relationship" with the United States and by France's concern about the revival of Germany. The task of moving toward a fuller European union had to be left to other organizations.

NOTES

1. Treaty of Economic Social and Cultural Collaboration and Collective Self-Defense between the Governments of the United Kingdom of Great Britain and Northern Ireland, Belgium, France, Luxembourg, and The Netherlands, signed at Brussels, 17 March 1948. From Margaret Carlyle, ed., *Documents in International Affairs, 1947–1948* (London: Oxford University Press, 1952), pp. 225–229.

2. See Truman message to Congress, 17 March 1948, *Public Papers of the Presidents*, 1948 (Washington: GPO, 1964), p. 184.

3. Joint Message by the French Minister of Foreign Affairs (Bidault) and the British Secretary of State for Foreign Affairs (Bevin) to the Secretary of State, 17 March 1948, *Foreign Relations of the United States (FRUS)*, 1948, III, 55–56; Report Prepared by the Policy Planning Staff Concerning Western Union and Related Problems, 23 March 1948, PPS 27, ibid., III, 62.

4. Minutes of the First Meeting of the United States–United Kingdom–Canada Security Conversations, held at Washington, 22 March 1948, ibid., III, 59–61. Six meetings were held between 22 March and 1 April 1959, ibid., III, 59–72.

5. See ibid., 1948, I, p. 597n; U.S. Congress, House Committee on Foreign Affairs, Mutual Defense Assistance Act of 1949, *Hearings*, 81 Cong., 1st sess., 1 August 1949, pp. 76–77.

6. S. Shepard Jones to Bohlen, American Public Opinion and Support for the Brussels Pact Allies, 13 April 1948, "points out that by a ratio of 5–3 the public believes that the United States should promise to back up England, France, and other countries of Western Europe with our Armed Forces if they are attacked by some other country." If the action were "in line with the UN Charter" the majority would be even larger. Department of State Mss, 840.00/4–1348, Decimal File, 1945–49, Lot 57, D 271, Box 71, Rg 59, NARA.

7. *FRUS*, 1948, I, 545–550.

8. Memorandum, by the Secretary of Defense (Forrestal) to the National Security Council, 17 April 1948, ibid., I, 563.

9. Ibid.

10. Minutes of the Fourth Meeting of the United States–United Kingdom–Canada Security Conversations, Washington, 29 March 1948, ibid., III, 69.

11. NSC–9, "The Position of the United States with Respect to Support for Western Union and Other Related Countries," 13 April 1948, ibid., III, 85–88.

12. Memorandum. JCS to Secretary of Defense, "The Position of the United States with Respect to Support for Western Union and Other Related Free Countries," 23 April 1948, Records of the JCS, CCS 092 W. Europe, (3–12–48) RG 218, NARA.

13. Memorandum of Conversation, by the Acting Secretary of State (Lovett), 18 April 1948, Participants: Senator Vandenberg and Acting Secretary Lovett, *FRUS*, 1948, III, 92–96.

14. Director of Policy Planning Staff (Kennan) to Executive Secretary of the National Security Council (Souers), 23 April 1948, with enclosures making up substance of NSC 9/1, ibid., 100–101; this was followed by a meeting at Blair House on 27 April 1948 with Marshall and Dulles along with Vandenberg and Lovett, in which the idea of the Senate approving a resolution specifically endorsing a North Atlantic pact was not accepted. Instead Vandenberg's single-page draft was unveiled. See Arthur H. Vandenberg, *The Private Papers of Senator Vandenberg* (Boston: Houghton Mifflin Co., 1952), p. 406.

15. *Congressional Record*, v. 94, 80 Cong. 2d sess., 11 June 1948, p. 7791.

16. Memorandum of Conversation, by the Chief of Western European Affairs (Achilles), 5 April 1948, "U.S. Support for Brussels treaty," meeting between Spaak and Lovett, Hickerson, and Achilles, *FRUS*, 1948, III, 76–78.

17. Sir G. Rendel, Brussels to Foreign Office, 23 April 1948, No. 246, FO 371, 73057, HN 08265, Public Record Office, Kew.

18. Memorandum by the Chief of the Division of Western European Affairs (Achilles) to the Director of the Office of European Affairs (Hickerson), 19 May 1948, *FRUS*, 1948, III, 127–128.

19. Memorandum of Conversation, 5 April 1948, with Spaak, *FRUS*, 1948, III, 76; Reid, *Time of Fear and Hope*, pp. 107–109; George F. Kennan, *Memoirs (1929–1950)*, (New York: Bantam Books, 1969), p. 429.

20. Theodore C. Achilles, "US Role in Negotiations That Led to Atlantic Alliance," *NATO Review*, XXVII (August, 1979), p. 13.

21. Director of Policy Planning Staff (Kennan) to the Under Secretary of State (Lovett), 7 May 1948, *FRUS*, 1948, III, 116–119.

22. NSC–9/3, 28 June 1948, ibid., III, 140–141.

23. Note by the Executive Secretary of the Position of the United States with Respect to Providing Military Assistance to Nations of the Non-Soviet World, 1 July 1948, ibid., I, 585.

24. Ibid., III, 148ff.

25. Memorandum, JCS to Secretary of Defense, "The Position of the United States with Respect to Support for Western Union and Other Related Free Countries," 19 May 1948, CCS 092 W. Europe (3–12–48), Records of the JCS, RG 218, NARS.

26. See Instructions for the U.S. Representatives attending the Western Union Talks, an enclosure with 16 July 1948, Memorandum, for the Director of the Joint Staff (Gruenther) to the Director of the Office of European Affairs (Hickerson), *FRUS*, III, 189; the First Meeting of the Washington Exploratory Talks on Security began on 6 July 1948, see Minutes in ibid., 148ff.

27. See Western Union progress report London made by Ambassador Sir Oliver

Franks, 7 July 1948, Minutes of Third Meeting of Washington Exploratory Talks on Security, ibid., 155–156.

28. Memorandum of Conversation with Armand Berard, the French chargé d'affaires, by Charles F. Bohlen, Counselor of State Department, to Secretary of State, 6 August 1948, *FRUS*, 1948, III, 207; Memorandum of Conversation, by Lovett, 20 August 1948, ibid., 218.

29. Ibid., 219.

30. Lovett's comments at Third Meeting of the Washington Exploratory Talks on Security, ibid., 155–156.

31. See JCS 1844/13, Short Range Emergency War Plan (HALFMOON), 21 July 1948, in Thomas Etzold and John L. Gaddis, *Containment: Documents in American Policy and Strategy, 1945–1950* (New York: Columbia University Press, 1978), pp. 315, 318; It is worth noting, though that at the Hague meeting of WU's Defense Ministers Committee on 7–8 April 1949 an Outline Short Term Plan was approved, which accepted the Rhine as the defense line. This was done despite the Netherlands Defense Minister's observation that three of his nation's provinces would be unprotected in the Plan. Fifth Periodic Informal Progress Report on the Accomplishments of DELWU, for the period 15 March–15 April 1949, prepared for the Secretary of Defense, Records of the JCS, RG 218, NARS.

32. Kenneth W. Condit, *The History of the Joint Chiefs of Staff: The Joint Chiefs of Staff and National Policy* (Wilmington, Del.; Michael Glazier, Inc., 1979), II, 366–368.

33. Memorandum by the JCS to S/D, 24 November 1948, NSC 9/6, "Developments with respect to Western Union," ibid., *FRUS*, 1948, III, 291.

34. Memorandum, FC (48), appendix B to Enclosure A to JCS 1868–58, 23 November 1948, "Western Union Defense Policy," CD 6–2–46, RG 330, NARS.

35. Montgomery's good faith is not in doubt. He was concerned about suspicions among British military circles that the Continent was indefensible, which gave rise in turn to European suspicions of Britain's intentions. "I became so alarmed at this attitude that I had a meeting with the British Chiefs of Staff on the 2nd of December 1948. I told them that French morale would not recover unless that nation could be convinced that Britain would contribute a fair quota of land forces to the defence of Western Europe." *The Memoirs of Field-Marshal the Viscount Montgomery* (Cleveland: World Publishing Co., 1958), pp. 458–459.

36. Minutes of the Fifth Meeting of the Washington Exploratory Talks on Security, 9 July 1948, *FRUS*, 1948, III, 178.

37. Minutes of the Fourth Meeting of the Washington Exploratory Talks on Security, 8 July 1948, ibid., 167.

38. Minutes of the Fifth Meeting of the Washington Exploratory Talks on Security, 9 July 1948, ibid., 171.

39. Bohlen's statement was made at a meeting of the Ambassador's Committee on 9 August 1948, and quoted in Reid, *Time of Fear and Hope*, p. 195.

40. Minutes of the Fourth Meeting of the Washington Exploratory Talks on Security, 8 July 1948, *FRUS*, 1948, III, 165.

41. Lovett to Caffery, 24 August 1948, quoted in Reid, *Time of Fear and Hope*, p. 196.

42. "To be fully satisfactory, a North Atlantic security system would have to provide also for that [security] of the North Atlantic territories of Denmark (es-

pecially Greenland), Norway, Iceland, Portugal (especially the Azores) and Ireland, which, should they fall into enemy hands, would jeopardize the security of both the European and North American members and seriously impede the flow of reciprocal assistance between them," in memorandum by the Participants in the Washington Security Talks, 6 July to 9 September, 9 September, *FRUS*, 1948, III, 240.

43. Its decisions developed from the "London Paper," entitled "Notes on Paper of Washington prepared in London by the Permanent Commission of the Brussels Powers," ibid., 310, 313. See also Reid, *Time of Fear and Hope*, p. 196.

44. Action Summary, International Working Group—Washington Exploratory Talks, 15 December 1948, Lot 53 D68, NATO Box 1, RG 353, NARS: Procedure for Negotiations and Approaches to Other Governments, Annex D of Draft Treaty, 24 December 1948, *FRUS*, 1948, III, 342–343.

45. State Department Paper prepared for Working Group of Washington Exploratory Talks, 10 August 1948, 840.20/8–1048, Lot 53, D68, NATO, Box 3, RG 353, NARA.

46. Article 3 of the Inter-American Treaty of Reciprocal Assistance notes that

1. The High Contracting Parties agree that an armed attack by any State against an American State shall be considered as an attack against all the American States, and consequently, each one of the said Contracting Parties undertakes to assist in meeting the attack in the exercise of the inherent right of individual or collective self-defense recognized by Article 51 of the Charter of the United Nations.
2. On the request of the State or States directly attacked and until the decision of the Organ of Consultation of the Inter-American System, each one of the Contracting Parties may determine the immediate measures which it may individually take in fulfillment of the obligation contained in the preceding paragraph and in accordance with the principle of continental solidarity. The Organ of Consultation shall meet without delay for the purpose of examining those measures and agreeing upon the measures of a collective character that should be taken.

In Charles I. Bevans, ed., *Treaties and Other International Agreements of the United States of America, 1776–1949*, Vol. 4, 1946–1949, Department of State Publication 8521 (June, 1970), pp. 560–561.

47. Minutes of the Fifth Meeting of the Washington Exploratory Talks, 9 July 1948, on Item (4) Nature of US Association under Vandenberg Resolution with European Security Arrangements, *FRUS*, 1948, III, 176.

48. Lovett made the point that "the Rio Pact left assistance to the decision of the assisting country," ibid., 180; Memorandum of the Tenth Meeting of the Working Group Participating in the Washington Exploratory Talks, 12 August 1949, ibid., 212.

49. Memorandum of the Ninth Meeting of the Working Group Participating in the Washington Exploratory Talks, 9 August 1948, ibid., 211. Article IV of the Brussels Pact states.

If any of the High Contracting Parties should be the object of an armed attack in Europe, the other High Contracting Parties will, in accordance with the provisions of Article 51 of the Charter of the United Nations, afford the party so attacked all the military and other aid and assistance in their power.

Margaret Carlyle, ed., *Documents in International Affairs 1947–1948*, p. 227.

50. State Department Paper prepared for Working Group of Washington Exploratory Talks, 10 August 1948, 840.20/8–1048, Lot 53 D68, NATO Box 353, NARS: See also Memorandum of the Tenth Meeting of the Working Group Participating in the Washington Explorary Talks, 12 August 1948, *FRUS*, 1948, III, 212.

51. U.S. preference following closely to Rio text:

An armed attack by any State against a Party shall be considered as an attack against all the Parties and consequently, each Party undertakes to assist in meeting the attack in the exercise of the inherent right of individual or collective self-defense recognized by Article 51 of the Charter.

European preference conforming closely to corresponding article in the Brussels Treaty:

If any party should be the object of an armed attack in the area covered by the Treaty, the other Parties will, in accordance with the provisions of Article 51 of the Charter, afford the Party so attacked all the military and other aid and assistance in their power.

The following represented a compromise supported specifically by the Canadian representative:

Provision that each Party should agree that any act which, in its opinion, constituted an armed attack against any other Party in the area covered by the treaty be considered an attack against itself, and should consequently, in accordance with its constitutional processes, assist in repelling the attack by all military, economic and other means in its power in the exercise of the right of individual or collective self-defense recognized by Article 51 of the Charter.

In Annex outlining provisions suitable for inclusion in a North Atlantic Security Pact, Memorandum by the Participants in the Washington Security Talks, 9 September 1948, "Washington Paper," ibid., 247.

52. Annex A—Draft Treaty, 24 December 1948, Article 5

Paragraph 1 (Mutual Assistance)
The Parties agree that an armed attack against one or more of them occurring within the area defined below shall be considered an attack against them all; and consequently that, if such an attack occurs, each of them, in exercise of the right of individual or collective self-defense recognized by Article 51 of the Charter of the United Nations, will assist the party or parties so attacked by taking forthwith such military or other action, individually and in concert with other Parties, as may be necessary to restore and assure the security of the North Atlantic area.

Ibid., 335.

53. 2 February 1949, AV Alexander to Bevin, Z1190, FO 371/79250, PRO.

54. 3 March 1949, AAD Montague Browne comments on Schuman Statement

in Council of the Republic, 1 March 1949, No 240, Z1894/1074/72, FO 371/ 79230, PRO.

55. Schuman's statement to Council of the Republic, 1 March 1949: "Nous sommes ainsi ramenés à l'objectif essentiel de la diplomatie française depuis 1918: obtenir, en faveur d'une politique d'assistance mutuelle, l'adhesion des Etats-Unis, qui disposent d'un potential industriel écrasant et dont la présence à nos côtés rendrait certaine l'issue d'une éventuelle troisième guerre mondiale et suffirait donc toute vraisemblance à prevenir cette guerre," in *Journal Officiel, Débats Parlementaries*, 16th séance du 1 mars 1949, p. 476.

56. Appendix B to Enclosure A of JCS 1868/58, 23 November 1958, CD6–2–46 RG 330, NARS; Appendix A to Enclosure A of JCS 1868/58, 13 January 1949, ibid.; (See Chapter V (2)d, fn 16). See also L. S. Kaplan, *A Community of Interests: NATO and the Military Assistance Program, 1948–1951* (Washington, D.C.: Historical Office, Department of Defense, 1980), p. 23.

57. Ibid., pp. 23–25.

58. JCS Rpt, 1868/58, 11 February 1949, "Military Assistance Program," p. 387, CD6–2–46, RG 330, NARA.

59. Kaplan, *A Community of Interests*, p. 29.

60. 2 March 1949, Douglas to S/S, No. 750, *FRUS*, 1949, III, p. 138; 10 March 1949, Caffery to S/S, No. 1004, 840.20/3–1049, RG 59, NARA.

61. Kaplan, *A Community of Interests*, pp. 30–31.

62. 22 March 1949, Douglas to S/S, No. 1105, 840.20/3–2249, RG 59, NARS: 23 Mar 1949, Douglas to S/S, No. 1124, ibid.; Minutes, First Meeting of ECC, 25 March 1949, *FRUS*, 1949, IV, 245.

63. 6 April 1949, Reply of the US Government to the "Request from the Brussels Treaty Powers to the U.S. Government for Military Assistance," *FRUS*, 1949, IV, 287–288; see also Kaplan, *A Community of Interests*, p. 32.

64. Ibid., 33; Ambassador Franks illustrated this spirit of equality when he claimed that the United States had "jumped the gun" in inviting the stepping-stone countries to be original signatories. The action "is not in accordance with the recommendation of the Permanent Commission which hoped that these countries would accede after the signature." 8 March 1949 Franks to FO, No. 1371, PRO undated brief for Foreign Minister for Consultative Council meeting of 15 March 1949, PRO.

65. Kaplan, *A Community of Interests*, p. 167.

66. Records of the 9th session of Consultative Council, The Hague, 1 August 1950, D1/1/2, Western European Union Archives, London.

67. Ibid.

68. A resolution of the Consultative Council on the future of Western Union's Defense Organization after the establishment of SHAPE noted that "the continued existence of the Western Union defense organization is no longer necessary." At the same time the Council asserted that "The reorganization of the military machinery shall not affect the right of the Western Union Defense Ministers and Chiefs of Staff to meet as they please to consider matters of mutual concern to the Brussels Treaty Powers." Records of the 10th session of Consultative Council, Brussels, 20 December 1950, DG1/1/2, Western European Union Archives, London.

2
The "Atlantic" Component of NATO

Chapter 2 looks at the Atlantic character of NATO and its importance in winning acceptance of the treaty. It was prepared for a conference in 1989 held in Ponta Delgada and sponsored by the Centro de Estudos de Relações Internacionais e Estrategia of the University of the Azores, the Centre d'étude de rélations internationales of the University of Brussels, and the Lyman L. Lemnitzer Center of Kent State University. The essay appeared in Relações Transatlânticas no Limiar do Século XXI *(Ponta Delgada: CERIE, 1989).*

As historians look back on NATO's first forty years it seems obvious that NATO has been a Western European alliance undergirded by the membership of such non-European nations as the United States and Canada. The intention of the founding fathers in 1948 and 1949 was to defend beleaguered Western European nations against the threat of communism, either from within through national Communist parties, or from without through such military actions as the Soviet Union might mount against them. A second objective was to create a united Europe which not only could stand up by itself to any challenge from the East but also to dispense with assistance from the United States. Given this European orientation it is legitimate to explore why Europe is mentioned only once by name in the text of the treaty, and to ask whether there is such an entity as an Atlantic Community, or whether any such community was intended. In brief, what is "Atlantic" about the Atlantic alliance?

Certainly, the idea of treaty under an Atlantic title was not in the minds of the men who fashioned NATO. Foreign Ministers Georges Bidault of France and Ernest Bevin of Great Britain conceived of a treaty which would be given a European name. Indeed, NATO's origins rested on the establishment of the Brussels Pact that established the Western Union in March 1948. This treaty establishing a fifty-year alliance among five nations— Britain, France, Belgium, the Netherlands and Luxembourg—emerged from the failure of the negotiations with the Soviet Union in the Foreign Ministers' conference at London in December 1947. It reflected deep concern over communist expansionism which not only left Germany divided but placed all of Eastern Europe under Stalin's control. The Brussels Pact was signed in the wake of the communist coup d'etat in Prague. Its intention was twofold: first to engage in efforts at self-help and mutual cooperation to promote the economic recovery of Europe, and second, to assure that an attack against any member nation would automatically bring the other members to its assistance. There was nothing "Atlantic" about this pact beyond the ocean shores of some of the member states. Its eye was eastward rather than westward, and its concentration was on events in Europe's heartland.

In their planning the European leaders were hopeful that the United States would join their Western Union. In fact, a case may be made that the language of the treaty itself was structured in such a way as to attract American membership. Recognizing American requirements in the Marshall Plan for self-help and for the breakdown of economic barriers that had marked Europe's history, they sought to assure the United States that they were worthy of American support. They also recognized that without an American engagement the Western Union had no meaning; neither its economic nor military resources were sufficient to cope with Soviet military aggression. It is fair to state that if the United States had accepted the invitation in 1948 there would have been no need for an Atlantic treaty.

Although it required a year, a name change, and inclusion of other nations before an alliance between America and Europe could be formed, its continuing purpose was the maintenance of European security as a more important priority than Atlantic security. In 1949 the regional planning groups were European-oriented. With the coming of the Korean War the centrality of Europe was given even greater emphasis. Fearing that the Korean War was a consequence of the temptations that a divided nation offered to aggressors, divided Germany became the focus of NATO's attention. A paper organization developed into a military organization centered in Paris and with its forces deployed along the Iron Curtain, particularly along the inner German border.

The recruitment of new members reflected this emphasis. In 1952 Greece and Turkey joined the alliance. Under no geographic circumstance can they be identified as Atlantic powers, located as they are along the eastern shores of the Mediterranean Sea. But they were important to the new command of General Eisenhower both as suppliers of troops and as guardians of the southern flank of NATO. Similarly, the allies after Korea felt it vital that West Germany be a member of the alliance, if only because its territory was the front line of the allied forces. If it required almost five years to complete this process, it was not because of a lessening of the German role in the early 1950s. Rather it was because wartime memories of Nazi Germany were too strong to permit an easy acceptance of a German partnership, no matter how significant a contribution Germans might make. Europe not the Atlantic remained the central focus of the alliance.

It is worth adding that even in 1949 Italy became a charter member of the alliance despite its geographic location in the middle of the Mediterranean. Its inclusion was a consequence of an American concern that Italy was still vulnerable to communist subversion, and that its membership would strengthen France's flank. There was no enthusiasm on the part of the Western Union members, the United States negotiating partner in the making of the treaty, for an Italian membership. It required a concession to France—the inclusion of Algerian departments—before France would agree to Italy's membership. But if the Western Union had reservations about Italy, it had much greater reservations to the inclusion of Atlantic nations, such as Iceland, Norway, and Portugal. But the United States pressed for the expansion of the partnership, and succeeded only because of the enormous leverage it had at the time.

The Brussels powers had reasons for their wish to exclude what they called the "stepping-stone" countries. Ideally, they preferred to keep the alliance confined to their group along with the Canadian-American partners on the western side of the Atlantic. It was their ambassadors who spent six months from July to December 1948 negotiating in Washington, not the Portuguese or the Norwegian representatives. If peripheral powers joined, they would both dilute the amount of military aid that would otherwise be confined to the five core members. Their addition might also strain the defense capabilities of the alliance. Despite American preferences the Western Union nations, meeting in the Hague in July, expressed their wish to postpone conclusion of any agreement with the Scandinavian countries, including Iceland and Greenland. The most they would concede was a junior position, likened by Dutch Foreign Minister Eelco Van Kleffens, to "a peach, the Brussels Pact would be the hard kernel in the center and a North Atlantic Pact the somewhat less hard mass around it."

The core nations failed to resist American pressure successfully, and in November they recommended that Denmark, Iceland, Norway, Portugal, Ireland and possibly Sweden be sounded out for membership. In all these diplomatic manuverings neither the United States nor the Europeans had anticipated opposition on the part of the putative Atlantic beneficiaries. Each of the Atlantic nations expressed some reluctance when approached. Ireland ruled out any consideration of possible membership as long as

Northern Ireland remained part of the United Kingdom. But all had some problems with membership which they raised with the U.S. State Department. And ultimately all were resolved when appropriate assurances were given.

The only ally to embrace the widening of the alliance wholeheartedly was Canada. That North American neighbor had been in a close military alliance with the United States since the onset of World War II, and it was only natural that it would continue to be a partner when the United States explored links to Europe. But Canada had special reasons for supporting a broad alliance; a close-knit American–Western Union relationship could reduce the Canadian role in the alliance. On the one hand, Canadians wanted a European connection so that it would not be left alone in a American embrace. On the other, it did not want a European partner to monopolize the American attention. By bringing in more nations NATO could become more than just a European defense organization; it could be a vehicle of an Atlantic community centering on economic and cultural rather than military concerns. Such was the source of Canada's support for Article 2 of the North Atlantic Treaty.

The other Atlantic nations had varying caveats. While Salazar's Portugal could welcome an apparently anti-Communist bloc, it balked initially because Spain was excluded, and raised objections that its Iberian Pact with Spain precluded membership. The weight of a traditional relationship with Britain, along with Spain's lack of objection, helped to mitigate initial reservations. Similarly, Norway and Denmark held off in the hope that a Nordic Pact, which included Sweden, might be a substitute for membership in the North Atlantic Treaty. The Nordic powers experienced considerable pressure from the United States which overcame their traditional neutrality. Norway's memory of Nazi occupation in particular made a difference. So did a strong American stand against the Swedish position which the United States regarded as a dangerous appeasement of the Soviet neighbor. When no American military aid would be forthcoming for a Nordic defense group, Norway and Denmark agreed to join NATO. Iceland had a special problem. It had, as Foreign Minister Bjarni Benediktsson noted, an "unbroken tradition of peace," along with an aversion both to war and to having foreign troops on its soil in peacetime. Iceland was won over when Secretary of State Acheson pointed out the peaceful objectives of the alliance and the allies' wish to respect Iceland's position on foreign forces on its territory.

It was American influence, then, that ultimately accounted for the shape of the alliance when it was finally formed in April 1949. Certainly, it was not the work of the Brussels Pact members, who articulated their opposition clearly. Nor was it the insistence of the Atlantic nations themselves. With the exception of Canada everyone required cajoling, even intimidation, before agreeing to accept the invitation. What accounts for the apparently single minded American drive for new members, even if those members include a nation without an army and a nation with a Fascist government?

There are two explanations, one overt and the other covert. The first reason was pragmatic and strategic. If the United States was to offer major assistance to its European allies, it required bases for air and sea support. Those bases would be provided by Portugal, with its Azores Islands; Denmark, with its Greenland colony; Norway, with its command of the Norwegian sea; and Iceland, with its geographic bridge between North America and Europe. Charles Bohlen at a meeting of the Ambassadors Committee asserted that "without the Azores, Iceland, and Greenland, help could not be gotten to Europe in significant quantities." And Deputy Secretary of State Robert Lovett suggested that "Greenland and Iceland were more important than some countries in western Europe to the security of the United States and Canada." It was apparent that the American diplomatists valued the Atlantic nations for the security they could bring to the western hemisphere as well as for the aid their membership could provide the European continent.

But important as the military and logistical considerations were, there was another dimension to the role of Iceland or Portugal, and this involved the emotional issue of American isolationism. A major reason for the Truman administration to evade a commitment to Europe in the spring of 1948 was its fear that the political enemies would invoke the tradition of nonentanglement to prevent an alliance and to discredit the governing party. The founders of the Brussels Pact had recognized this tradition and thought that their efforts had circumvented this issue. While they may have been correct in the assumption that Americans were prepared after World War II to discard isolationism, the Truman administration leaders were not confident enough to act on that assumption. For this reason Iceland and Canada and even Portugal assumed a special importance. Canada was an American nation; Greenland was closer to the western hemisphere than to Europe; and the Azores were far enough into the Atlantic to allow Portugal a position it would not otherwise have enjoyed.

Adherents of the prospective North Atlantic Treaty seized on the Atlantic Character of the Alliance to convince the American public that NATO was not a European institution. Under ordinary circumstances Portugal might have been condemned, as Spain was, as a reminder of the dictatorships of the 1930s. But given the importance of Portuguese-based facilities in the Azores and given the extra-European image Portugal could project, Congressmen were able to finesse the problem of dictatorship, sometimes with a touch of absurdity. When Senator Henry Cabot Lodge asked Theodore Achilles of the Western European desk of the State Department how he could fit Portugal into the "common heritage of freedom," Achilles responded that "although its government is not the same form of democracy as we have it, it is authoritarian not totalitarian. . . . If it is a dictatorship, it is because the people freely voted for it." Senators Tom Connally and Theodore Green twisted reality to an even greater degree when the former asked rhetorically, "Don't we owe a little for Vasco da Gama?" And the former capped this query with, "Didn't she [Portugal] found Massachusetts?" While both questions held misleading implications, the fact that they were asked at all suggests the length to which pro-NATO senators would go to justify Portugal's admission into the alliance.

In essence, the United States insisted on playing a semantic game to circumvent the psychological barriers against America's joining with Britain and France, the two European powers which helped to inspire the American doctrine of non-entanglement. The bipartisan leadership of the Congress collaborated with the administration to make it appear that the North Atlantic Treaty was a modern version of the Monroe Doctrine. Their worst fears seemed vindicated during the hearings on the treaty in April and May 1949 when critics from the right and the left attempted to convince the Congress and public that the treaty violated George Washington's dictates and subjected American to the machinations of French and British manipulators. While the treaty ultimately passed the Senate by a vote of 82–13, it is questionable if that would have been the congressional tally had the Atlantic character of the alliance not been emphasized.

In retrospect, the history of NATO was what the founding fathers had hoped it would be: a firm linkage of the United States with Europe. The emphasis over time has been indeed on the defense of Western Europe and the creation of a united states of Europe. What better evidence of this emphasis can be found than an evaluation of the respective roles of the Supreme Allied Commander, Europe and the Supreme Allied Commander, Atlantic. The former was usually a dominant and prominent figure, such as Dwight Eisenhower or Lauris Norstad, leading the organization from Paris or Brussels. The latter was an anonymous admiral based in Norfolk, Virginia largely unknown to Americans and Europeans alike. It may be worthy of mention that at lunch at the Naval War College a few years ago a leading naval editor could recall the name of no more than two or three SACLANTs. He had no such difficulty with the SACEURs.

What meaning than should the historian give to the Atlantic component of NATO? Certainly there is no community comparable to the European community. Its significance lay, not simply in the form of bases, but in the vehicle the Atlantic name provided for the securing of a strong American connection with Western Europe. As the alliance moves into its fifth decade, it can observe that the Soviet threat has diminished and that the integration of Europe has progressed. This suggests that the goals of the alliance have been a success. But as long as the threat has not disappeared and the progress toward unity is not complete, NATO may continue into the 1990s as a means of keeping stability in the West. The transatlantic association is not yet obsolete.

3
The Mutual Defense Assistance Act of 1949

Chapter 3 notes the hurdles to be surmounted before the Military Assistance Program could be accepted by the U.S. Senate. This study was published in a project I had undertaken for the Office of the Historian, Office of the Secretary of Defense, under the title A Community of Interests: NATO and the Military Assistance Program, 1948–1951 *(Washington, DC: OSD Historical Office, 1980).*

PREPARING THE BILL

The signing of the North Atlantic Treaty and the publication of the Western Union requests for aid along with the U.S. favorable reply, all in the first week of April 1949, brought the Military Assistance Program closer to fulfillment. There were still numerous obstacles to be overcome, however, before the program could be presented for congressional approval. One of the more troublesome was the difference in viewpoint between the State and Defense Departments which lay beneath the surface of unanimity maintained within the Foreign Assistance Correlation Committee (FACC) and the European Coordinating Committee (ECC) in negotiations with Europeans. To a degree the difference was functional: Defense tended to think of U.S. security in terms of the military capabilities of the various world powers, while the State Department usually gave more weight to the political factors.

A major source of dissent emerged from the Policy Planning Staff of the Department of State, directed by George F. Kennan. While acknowledging and even reaffirming the interlocking character of a national security that would include the defense of Europe, Kennan repeatedly deplored the increasing emphasis on the military facets of security. Fearing misinterpretation of the military role, the PPS had opposed preparing detailed statements on security for the National Security Council (NSC). Whatever it produced, Kennan believed, could be distorted in such a way as to limit flexible responses in the future.[1]

In coping with the hostility of the Soviet Union, Kennan claimed that the basic assumption underlying the NSC's containment policies, namely, that it was possible to "describe in a few pages a program designed to achieve U.S. objectives with respect to the U.S.S.R.," gave "a misleading impression of the nature of our foreign policy problems."[2] Kennan's pessimism increased as the Military Assistance Program came into being. He was particularly upset with its implicit assumption that an arms program was the best means of overcoming the military weakness of the West, as if "total security" were a genuine possibility. If so, it might mean unacceptable insecurity for the other side. Moreover, the Policy Planning Staff wondered if the Pentagon recognized that the Politburo did not want war; it wanted the fruits of war through other means.[3]

The trouble between State and Defense derived, according to Kennan, from their differing angles of observation: "The Military, because of the nature of its own planning, seems unable to realize that in a field of foreign policy specific planning cannot be undertaken as they propose." Military combat need not be the only alternative to peace. What Kennan and his colleagues suspected was that papers produced for the NSC, such as NSC–20/4 (U.S. Objectives toward the U.S.S.R.), would be influenced excessively by the military approach to Soviet–American relations, and that the NSC would become a prisoner of the Pentagon's tunnel vision.[4]

Although Kennan won his point of limiting the NSC function to the integration of policies relating to national security rather than the determination of the measures required to implement those policies,[5] he did not win Acheson over to his view of the military. The Secretary of State believed the Department of Defense to be far more responsive to the complexities of foreign military policy than did Kennan.[6] The fact that there were distinctions between the two did not necessarily mean that Defense was rasher than State in its decisions. On occasion the opposite was true. During the negotiations on the North Atlantic Treaty the Joint Chiefs of Staff had feared that State negotiators were neglecting U.S. military capabilities in their enthusiasm for committing the nation to the defense of the non-Soviet world. Urging moderation, the military had recommended a strict delimitation of the pact area so that U.S. power would not be responsible for protecting the Asian or African colonies of Europe, and had suggested a rewording of one of the treaty's articles to restrict military assistance to situations of external aggression.[7]

But military officials who had observed the danger of overextending military commitments were not so observant of equally unwise political involvements. On the other hand, the greater sensitivity of the State Department to the political background of military action could modify a Defense Department position. Because of Spain's strategic importance, Defense saw the value of bringing it into a defense alliance and supplying it with military aid, and only reluctantly conceded that such a course would antagonize America's European allies.[8] Thus it was obvious that the U.S. role as a world power required the mutual contribution of both political and military planning for the shaping of a balanced overall policy.

Cooperation between the two agencies was not always easy to achieve despite its importance to the national welfare. The Secretary of Defense's position in the NSC was somewhat anomalous until the summer of 1949, when a thorough reorganization of the National Military Establishment terminated the military departments of NSC memberships.[9] Forrestal's task was further complicated by his difficulty in speaking as Secretary of Defense on foreign military policy when the views of his three constituent departments—Army, Navy, and Air Force—were not always in harmony. He had to cope with conflicts within his own household before he could present a Defense viewpoint to State officials.

One such divisive issue was the question of "reciprocal assistance" which had so disturbed the European nations. Even the definition of the term was uncertain. Europeans offered one meaning; Americans, another. Great Britain, for example, was satisfied with the principle of "mutual" assistance, which was to be written into the new Atlantic Pact, but had suspicions about possible interpretations of "reciprocal" assistance. Ambassador Douglas had to convince Bevin that there was more than a semantic difference between the two adjectives, and that Congress required an explicit acceptance of the principle of reciprocity before the treaty was signed or a military assistance program authorized.[10] To Americans the issue was clear—reciprocity meant bilateral arrangements granting specific concessions such as a base in Greenland in exchange for aid to Denmark.[11] Bevin and the other foreign ministers of the Western Union understandably would have preferred the "mutuality" implied by their service on the "front line" in the battle against Communist aggression.[12] Recognition that reciprocal assistance in 1949 would be translated less as base rights than as transit rights in time of war helped to relax tensions on both sides. But European uneasiness over the price they would pay in bases for U.S. money and equipment remained a sore point.

Reciprocal assistance was an equally abrasive concern for U.S. officials. Should such assistance be mandatory? What forms should it take? In what way should it be transferred? These questions evoked positive and often contradictory responses. An extreme position was taken by Munitions Board spokesmen, who suggested that each recipient should set aside in its own currency the equivalent of at least 5 percent of the value of U.S. military aid for U.S. procurement of strategic materials.[13] This proposition clashed sharply with the opinion of the National Advisory Council on International Monetary and Financial Problems that any such measure would undermine economic recovery of the European nations, disturb the strained balance of payments, and fail to produce beneficial results. Europe had little to spare. In fact, only $50 million of the $193 million set aside for such purposes under ECA had actually been used for raw materials.[14] Although General Lemnitzer of the FACC considered the Munitions Board's particular proposal unrealistic, its pressure was a factor in forming the final Defense position.[15]

Reciprocal assistance included base rights and operating rights as well as strategic materials, and on the former there was no disagreement within the Department of Defense. The differences between Defense and State, however, were marked. The three Service Secretaries were not only adamant about the importance of these forms of reciprocal assistance, they were also convinced that only through bilateral agreements could the U.S. trading position be upheld. Only at the urging of General Eisenhower did the War Council restrict bilateral negotiations to the period preceding the working out of a better system by the North Atlantic Treaty Organization.[16] The Defense attitude disturbed ECC representatives.[17] The latter claimed that they did not oppose either reciprocal assistance or bilateral negotiations in principle; they opposed the emphasis which the military placed upon them. They feared that the solidarity and cooperation which the United States sought to foster would evaporate and be replaced by resentment.[18] Actually, the schism was deeper than State admitted at first, for before the argument was finished, its spokesman made it clear that they saw no need for including reciprocal assistance in the negotiations. It was unnecessary because the United States already enjoyed base rights, formally or informally, in Iceland, Greenland, the Azores, Britain, and France, and could easily secure more if necessary; it was impractical because no nation, out of pride if not out of sound business practice, would surrender bases in return for only military assistance; it was dangerous because it would open the United States to the charge of imperialism.[19] The Defense Department disputed each point. Such was the charged atmosphere behind the united front on reciprocal assistance which Ambassador Douglas displayed to Europe.

Failing to heal the breach at the ECC level[20] as well as within its own ranks, the FACC passed the problem to the Foreign Affairs Steering Committee (FASC) for solution. Ultimately Congress decided the issue, and its decision, embodied in Section 402 of the Mutual Defense Assistance Act, gave a complete victory to the view of the Defense Department. The result was never really in doubt, for much as Congress preferred multilateral to bilateral arrangements in theory, it would not sacrifice the latter as long as it was convinced that bilateralism was the only way to secure reciprocal assistance.

Recognizing congressional feelings on the subject, the State Department sought a middle ground where specific bilateral treaties would follow general master agreement. As for the military operating rights emphasized by the Defense Department, the State Department suggested that the United States obtain as much as possible from each country before implementing MAP, but that it should not place aid on a quid pro quo basis in the actual negotiations.[21] The FACC, however, agreed that military rights would be requested from the recipients simultaneously with the bilateral agreements.[22]

The Defense Department had less success in its other controversies with State, particularly on the delicate matter of who was to run the Military Assistance Program. As in the case of reciprocal assistance, outside pressure helped to solve the problem. From the beginning, State leadership in foreign aid had been recognized because negotiations had been in the arena of diplomacy. State Department officials chaired all the preliminary organizations set up to work out a program. Nevertheless, the important role which the military was to play in MAP policy and operations made the Defense representatives unwilling to subordinate their position to that of their colleagues in State. They preferred an independent administrator of Cabinet rank with a role comparable to Paul Hoffman's in the ECA, but they would have been willing to accept State superiority if Defense interests were safeguarded by an administrator appointed by the President with a status higher than that of Assistant Secretary of State.[23] The working level of the State Department would not concede even this much, and insisted on an administrator operating within the existing framework of the Department's organization.[24] The controversy ended when the President assigned primary responsibility for the program to the State Department, as expected, and gave the post of director to an officer selected by the Secretary of State.[25]

Despite a letter of protest by the newly appointed Secretary of Defense, Louis Johnson,[26] the military opposition to this solution was essentially perfunctory. Only three days after writing to the President, Secretary Johnson offered "the support of the National Military Establishment for whatever level of program the State Department has determined it intends to advocate today before the Bureau of the Budget."[27] The Bureau of the Budget was the instrument of this spirit of compromise. A sudden threat in April 1949 that the Bureau might slash military funds made Defense officials willing to sacrifice their administrative ambitions for the cooperation of the State Department. It was not that the Defense Department had been unaware of growing congressional resistance to increased taxation, and it had expected the requested total of $1.986 billion to come under the close scrutiny of the Budget examiners.[28] It had even anticipated the areas vulnerable to attack—the self-help and emergency funds and possibly funds for some of the non-Western Union countries.[29] But it did not foresee the possibility that the entire Military Assistance Program might have to be financed by funds from the Defense budget. Such a move would have been a tremendous blow to the military, for they had considered their own budget small enough without having to set aside almost $2 billion for foreign aid. No less an economist than Edwin G. Nourse, Chairman of the President's Council of Economic Advisers, had stated publicly that the cost of the Military Assistance Program should be met out of military rather than supplemental appropriations.[30] Arguments of this sort had instant repercussions in Congress.[31]

The military made immediate refutation. Heatedly its spokesmen asserted that the security requirements of the armed forces were determined more by intentions and capabilities of potential enemies than by readiness of potential allies. It would be folly, therefore, they argued, to provide foreign aid at the expense of U.S. fighting strength, especially when U.S. aid could do no more than bring Europe's forces up to a minimum condition of preparedness. As long as Europe could not withstand Soviet aggression, America's own armed power must be kept secure. Only in the future, "when the struggle of other participating nations, through our common efforts, shall have reached the point where their military effectiveness will be a substantial contribution to the common defense of the Atlantic Pact nations, then, and not until then, an adjustment of the United States military forces may be practicable."[32]

The threat of financing the entire Military Assistance Program out of the Defense budget never materialized, but it fostered interagency cooperation. State and Defense had to speak with one voice to Congress and the Bureau of the Budget, and the case for new appropriations was more effectively handled by the State Department. The Defense Department's sense of dependence helped to compose the minor irritations as much as the work of a task force set up in March for that purpose. Complaints that the State representative on this body failed to do his share in arranging for the programming, or that the Defense spokesman was overly cautious in revealing the basis for costs, appeared progressively less important as the day of reckoning with the Bureau of the Budget drew closer.[33]

The actual Bureau of the Budget cuts, while substantial, were by no means as crippling to the program as some of its framers had feared at first. The original $2 billion figure had been reduced to approximately the level suggested by the JCS in March before the FACC was willing even to submit its recommendation to Budget. This was effected by judicious cuts in Western Europe's allotment. The Budget staff then cut the program from $1.766 billion to $1.115 billion by throwing out the $200 million scheduled to cover increased military production in Europe and the cost of its indirect impact upon the civilian economy and by eliminating an emergency fund and aid for Korea, the Philippines, and Portugal. Greece, Turkey,

Austria, and even the Western Union suffered some loss of funds, while savings were counted on from the reduced cost of administration and transportation.[34] Some of the cut was restored after subsequent conferences between the FACC and the Bureau of the Budget, and a compromise figure of $1.518 billion was arrived at.[35] This, in turn, was again modified, and the total cost of the program placed before Congress amounted to $1.45 billion.[36]

These reductions were somewhat lighter than they appeared because the pricing system was revised in a way favorable to the recipient nations. The original JCS recommendations of 11 February specified that materiel above the maximum retention level established by each Service would be charged at 10 percent of the original cost. The Bureau of the Budget recommended elimination of this charge, inasmuch as those items did not require replacement and represented no loss to the Nation's fighting strength. The cost of rehabilitation would be the only expense to the MAP. Thus a saving of $45 million was anticipated for the pact countries, making the real value of the aid considerably higher than the dollar value.[37]

The military representatives found little to complain about with respect to the precise figures in the MDAP. As long as the program did not affect adversely the budgets or stocks of the Services, they could accept the leadership of the State Department. The latter's preeminence is explained partly by the personalities of the respective Secretaries, particularly the lack of both interest and understanding on the part of Louis Johnson. But the reasons went deeper than personalities. The Defense Department, as the agent most directly responsible for implementing the program, recognized the political, economic, and psychological problems of MDAP.[38]

NATO AND THE MILITARY ASSISTANCE PROGRAM

The slow and complicated process of developing MAP legislation that led to cooperation within the FACC and understanding between FACC and the Bureau of the Budget encountered unexpected delays. Congress was not ready to deal with the bill. The hearings and final decision on the North Atlantic Pact had to be completed first in order to set up the structure on which the military assistance legislation would be hung. MAP was connected with the pact through Article 3, which provided for "continuous and effective self-help and mutual aid" among all the parties to "maintain and develop their individual and collective capacity to resist armed attack." This tie with the pact would have created no problems if the original legislative schedule had been followed. The treaty was to go to the Senate on 7 April, just 3 days after it had been signed; the official requests would be announced on 8 April and the MAP would be launched on 11 April, presumably to bolster support of the treaty in Senate hearings.[39] Arrangements for such an intricate operation required the fullest understanding and cooperation of Congress. When this was not forthcoming, the entire timetable was disrupted. Acheson recorded his concern as early as 18 April when he learned that Vandenberg and Connally, among others, were not going to set a date for hearings on the treaty until they had a better idea of the implications of its implementation.[40]

The trouble arose from the lack of information on the part of Congress and insufficient consideration on the part of the Administration of the exact position of the Military Assistance Program in the scheme of the North Atlantic Treaty. Was the pact an effective instrument in itself for repelling aggression in Europe, or was it dependent upon U.S. help? The answer to both questions was essentially affirmative, but it was no simple matter to raise the issue of military aid on the vague terms sought by the FACC without making the pact appear to be a mere vehicle for the transfer of U.S. aid. The Administration's failure to show the complementary nature of the two separate programs resulted in dissatisfaction on every side. Senators who looked on the pact as the beginning of European Union and hence as a sine qua non of U.S. aid wanted full details of the program and wondered why non-pact countries were included at all in the MAP. Some of their colleagues, on the other hand, believed that the pact was merely an excuse for an unlimited European raid on the U.S. Treasury, or a re-armament movement likely to provoke war and disrupt the United Nations.[41] Until the confusion over the pact and the Military Assistance Program was resolved, both had a hard time of it in Congress.[42]

Differences in approach to military assistance surfaced in the executive session of the Senate Foreign Relations Committee on 21 April 1949. The Senators' questions disconcerted the witnesses; their direction had not been anticipated. When Secretaries Acheson and Johnson revealed their intention to request $1.45 billion in military aid, of which $1.13 billion would be earmarked for Western Europe, Senator Vandenberg, on whose good will so much rested, demanded an itemization of the entire amount. Senator Lodge added that such a breakdown should encompass a four- or five-year period, not simply the first year. At the same time Vandenberg wondered if all the information should not be reported to the United Nations under the requirement of Article 54 of the Charter, concerned with reporting on armaments. Only the assurance of the Administration that such information had never been delivered before and that such public disclosure would create intense embarrassment abroad quieted Vandenberg.[43]

Although senatorial critics ultimately settled for a promise that all aid would fit into a common strategic plan, the Administration recognized the need for more educational efforts before the MAP could be officially presented.[44] They had failed to convince Congress of a principle which Kennan had identified in his communications, namely, that only a military aid program could stimulate the changes in Europe's attitudes toward common defense which Congress had insisted on as a precondition of U.S. support.

Military aid was the lever that could tilt Europeans toward collective planning. "Our position in trying to negotiate such arrangements," Kennan asserted, "will be very seriously weakened if we find ourselves unable to promise military assistance to other governments in question. Our whole position in argument must rest largely on the predominance of our contribution and on what we are being asked to do for the others. If we have nothing to give, we can hardly expect the others to accede to our views."[45] Despite public statements to the contrary, the proposed arms program was vitally connected to the Atlantic Pact. The Administration did not transmit this message convincingly in the spring of 1949.

Of all the Administration spokesmen, the new Secretary of Defense, Louis Johnson, suffered most from the difficulties surrounding the presentation to Congress. Having taken over the post from Forrestal on 28 March, he was new to its responsibilities and unfamiliar with the Defense role in either the pact or the Military Assistance Program. Though he had consultations with his predecessor from the beginning of January, he was understandably uneasy about presenting arguments which he had not fully digested.[46] But he needed more than careful coaching; he had to reshape opinions he had held as a private citizen—just a year before he had told the Daughters of the American Revolution that the Brussels Pact was an example of the kind of military alliance alien to the traditions of the United States.[47]

Johnson regarded himself as a watchdog of the budget, the prescribed limits of which should not be disturbed by any of the alarms and crises of the times. His loyalty to the President and to fiscal conservatism was never suspect. Military assistance was not one of Johnson's priorities. During Johnson's tenure, according to Marx Leva, President Truman gave orders on the military budget.[48] The new Secretary was persuaded that foreign military assistance was among the most expendable of Defense concerns. The MAP was not, after all, part of the Defense budget.[49]

Acheson, his counterpart at State, characterized Johnson as a bitter and vindictive man, whose conduct at the time of his dismissal in the fall of 1950 "had passed beyond the peculiar to the impossible." Johnson's sentiments about Acheson were even more strongly held and more pungently expressed.[50] Even at Defense Johnson had strong critics. General Lemnitzer noted his visceral opposition to NATO and MAP. Johnson, according to Lemnitzer, had assumed responsibility for the MDAP reluctantly, and not even the Korean conflict could shake his reluctance. Lemnitzer further speculated that Johnson's opposition derived primarily from the fact that "he wasn't in on the basic decision to undertake a military aid program." But Lemnitzer also conceded the pressure on Johnson caused by the fear of the drain on his budget created by the program.[51] As the Secretary informed the Senators—in off-the-record discussions—on 21 April 1949, he saw the purpose of military assistance to be collective military security of Europe "up to a point where this nation might begin reducing its arms programs and taxes. All U.S. contributions were to these ends." No subsequent event in his tenure as Secretary of Defense appeared to have changed his mind.[52]

His difficulties, as well as those of his colleagues, were exposed under the glare of the congressional spotlight. At the open hearings which extended from late April through mid-May, the Administration was forced into accepting the pact as a bar to aggression by itself, completely independent of U.S. military help for its success.[53] Goods sent to Europe would be only those definitely not needed by the United States, and none of the aid would interfere in any way with the economic recovery program.[54] Despite these assertions and despite assurances that the right of Congress to reject a military aid program was not compromised by U.S. negotiations with the pact countries, opponents of the treaty were convinced that a secret understanding existed between the Administration and the leaders of Europe that would make U.S. aid obligatory. The inability of the pact defenders to give details of the Military Assistance Program did not help to dispel these suspicions.[55] The Administration found itself in a dilemma: It had to admit that Europe's will to resist would be seriously injured by the failure to follow up the Atlantic Treaty with an aid bill, and at the same time it could not counter the claim that the limited aid program anticipated for that year would be insufficient to stop Russian aggression and could possibly have harmful effects upon the recovery program.[56] The treaty's isolationist critics in Congress were ready to use any weapon to defeat it, and there was no doubt that they considered the military assistance issue one of the best in their armory.[57]

The vigor of the opposition to the treaty and the role the MAP played in building up opposition discouraged many MAP proponents both in Congress and in the Administration. Failure to overcome opposition to foreign aid by the end of April, as originally expected, required that MAP be kept under wraps all spring. The Senate was in no hurry to approve the North Atlantic Treaty. Although the Administration feared that delay would disturb Europeans, the scheduling of urgent labor legislation in the Senate helped explain why a month and a half elapsed between the end of the pact hearings and the beginning of legislative debate.[58] And any hope of submitting MAP legislation prior to Senate action on the Atlantic Pact was blasted by demands from both Republican and Democratic Senate leaders that House plans for holding MAP hearings in the middle of May be canceled. Vandenberg feared that introduction of the military assistance bill before ratification of the treaty would present the treaty in the wrong light to the public, as if it were "a mere prelude" to building armies in Europe.[59] So unsure of victory were the pact sponsors that they were willing to risk disrupting the existing Greek–Turkish aid program rather than focus congressional attention upon that explosive issue.[60] At the recommendation of Secretary Acheson, the Administration postponed submission of the MAP until the North Atlantic Treaty was ratified.[61]

The delay had some compensations. It permitted FACC to acquaint itself more fully with the problems of Europe by sending out a special mission headed by Walter Surrey, Deputy Coordinator of the MAP in the State Department.[62] It was especially interested in learning ECC views on the type of organization required for efficient fusion of Western Union with the other pact countries under the overall MAP.[63] The delay also allowed time for strengthening the deficiency lists of the Western Union so that the Administration's case would be stronger when a bill finally went to Congress. During the months of May, June, and July, these activities appeared to reflect excessive optimism on the part of the Administration, but they derived their inspiration from the highest official source. The President was convinced of the final success of both the pact and the MAP, and his confidence was justified. Despite the vigor and sincerity of the critics in the Senate, according to Richard Stebbins, "the whole situation that had brought the pact into being pointed to one inescapable conclusion which no verbal technicalities could invalidate: namely, that the conditions of the modern world had irrevocably narrowed the limits within which Congress and the Nation could exercise the freedom of action to which they had been accustomed in the past."[64] On 21 July, the Senate approved the treaty by a majority of 82 to 13.

In all the deliberations, Soviet opposition, vocal though it was, played only a small part. The Soviet Union itself, through the Ministry of Foreign Affairs, denounced the forthcoming treaty as early as 29 January 1949, more than two months before the pact was signed and three weeks before its text had been made public. The Ministry claimed that it was an aggressive alliance against the Communist bloc, that it violated wartime treaties between Britain, France, and the Soviet Union, and that it distorted the purposes of the United Nations. In essence, it was a plan for world supremacy by the Anglo-Americans.[65] Yet, the official memorandum of the Soviet Government on 31 March was relatively mild, as it denied the claims of the treaty to be in accord with the United Nations Charter and reasserted the charge that it was directed against the Soviet Union.[66] Soviet complaints were repeated at the General Assembly meeting of 14 April by Polish and Byelorussian as well as by Soviet delegates, but they were not a central theme of debate. In fact, the issue arose as a digression during consideration of a report on voting procedures in the Security Council.[67] A widely held view at the time maintained that Soviet reaction against the pact would erupt in an arena other than Lake Success or the press offices of the Foreign Ministry, and that any overt crisis would come over the implementation of the pact through military aid. Later efforts by Communist labor unions to stop the first shipments of arms to Europe as they were delivered at the docks confirm this perception.

BEFORE THE BAR OF CONGRESS

The MAP bill was introduced in the House and referred to the Committee on Foreign Affairs on 25 July, the same day the President signed the instrument of ratification of the North Atlantic Treaty; two days later it was introduced in the Senate and referred jointly to the Committees on Foreign Relations and Armed Services. The proposed legislation envisaged three types of assistance: (1) dollar aid to increase direct military production; (2) direct transfer of essential U.S. equipment; and (3) loan of U.S. experts to train personnel of recipient countries in both maintenance of the equipment provided and in production of new equipment.[68] The total sum requested was $1.45 billion,[69] to be distributed in the following manner: Military equipment and technical training for NATO countries, $940 million; military aid to other countries (including Greece and Turkey), $250 million (An additional $50 million for military aid to Greece and Turkey was continued under an existing authorization); dollar aid for overseas production, $155 million; emergency fund, $45 million; and administration of the projects, $10 million.[70] To set the programs in motion, the bills authorized the Reconstruction Finance Corporation to advance up to $125 million until the money requested had been appropriated.

Remembering the ordeal over approval of the North Atlantic Treaty, Administration spokesmen tried now to anticipate arguments which opponents in Congress might bring against the complementary military assistance bill. With considerable skill, Acheson, Johnson, Bradley, and Harriman emphasized the defensive nature of the program and the extensive benefits which a strong Europe would give to U.S. security. Their presentation was even more persuasive than it had been a few months before, but their arguments were wasted and aimed at the wrong object. With the exception of a handful of irreconcilables, Congress had been convinced of the need of a treaty and a way of implementing it. Administration spokesmen belabored points already won, but they had neglected to prepare for other issues.[71]

The Administration, therefore, was surprised to find friends of the pact and the MAP joined with their opponents in attacking not the principle of mutual aid but the amount of money and equipment involved and the way it was to be disbursed.[72] Although Secretary Acheson and his colleagues made it clear that the bulk of the aid was definitely scheduled for pact countries, the scope of the bill itself was by no means restricted to the Western Union or even to "nations which have joined with the United States in collective defense and regional arrangements" based on mutual aid and self-help.[73] There was no apparent limit to the President's authority. He could extend aid to any countries he chose as long as their "increased ability to defend themselves against aggression is important to the national interest of the United States," and the aid could take the form of cash payments, outright grants, or "such other terms as he deems appropriate."[74] In other words, the President could even decide what kind of re-imbursement recipients could make in return for U.S. aid—"property, rights, equipment, materials, services, or other things of value"—and then allow imported items into the country duty free.[75] The extensive discretionary powers granted to the President under this bill immediately aroused the wrath of Congress. Why, legislators wanted to know, was such loose terminology employed when earlier briefings had specifically outlined the areas to receive aid and had broken down the amounts each would receive.[76]

Unprepared to deal with a situation that had suddenly shifted from an isolationist-internationalist conflict to a quarrel between the legislative and the executive branches, the Secretaries of State and Defense were glad to meet their congressional critics more than halfway by modifying the original bill. To secure acceptance of the amount requested, they agreed in the first week of August to make revisions limiting the President's power to send arms to any nation of the world.[77] The result of their conference with Senate leaders was the introduction of a new bill—H.R. 5895 and S.2388—on 5 August. The new bill, in unambiguous terms, limited aid recipients to three groups: Title I, the NATO countries; Title II, Greece and Turkey; and Title III, Iran, Korea, and the Philippines. Title IV laid down the conditions of aid. The total amount remained the same—$1.4 billion—but the allocations were somewhat changed: $1.161 billion to NATO countries, $211.4 million to Greece and Turkey, and $27.6 million to the remaining nations. The controversial $45 million set aside as an emergency fund to be expended at the President's discretion was eliminated, and in its place the revised bill permitted the transfer of up to 5 percent of the total sum from one group of beneficiaries to another.

The redrafting of the foreign military assistance bill left many questions still unanswered and a number of Congressmen dissatisfied. Where was the unified organization, they asked, that would distribute the aid to avoid the conflicts and waste which had allegedly plagued the European Recovery Program? And if this organization was not even in operation, why not delay military aid to Europe until the Atlantic Pact's Defense Committee had been established?[78]

Administration officials had answers to these queries, but they were not consistent. Initially, they argued that the aid program was an interim arrangement designed to tide over the existing forces of Europe with U.S. equipment so that NATO would have a working base for its integrated defense plans.[79] Under pressure, they claimed that a unified organization for the defense of Western Europe already existed in the form of the Western Union. "It is a working reality," said Secretary Johnson, "and not a mere paper organization. Its common defense policy has been agreed upon. It has been studied by the Joint Chiefs of Staff, who consider it to be basically sound and in consonance with their strategic thinking."[80]

Therefore, he concluded, congressional prerequisites for effective use of military assistance were met. Unfortunately, this line of reasoning discredited the concept of "interim" aid put forth by Secretary Acheson, and it received little support from other witnesses. General Bradley, reporting on the results of a recent JCS tour of Europe, gave no indication that the Western Union's plans were in anything but the preparatory stage.[81] Furthermore, Secretary Johnson himself admitted that U.S. equipment could not be transferred directly to the Western Union because "it is not a sovereign entity which has the means of receiving and employing such equipment."[82]

Johnson's testimony reflected American annoyance with the persistent claims of the Western Union to serve as the exclusive unit for distributing funds to Europe. Delay in sending aid would cause irreparable damage to the program of European defense by playing into the hands of the Communist parties of France and Italy.[83] But in accepting the principle of interim aid, Congress seized the arguments of the MAP's sponsors to whittle down the amount of aid authorized. In explaining the need for the immediate shipment of materiel, the Secretary of Defense had mentioned incidentally that delivery of equipment intended for foreign consumption would require from six to nine months, by which time the North Atlantic Pact organization would probably be in operation. Although this admission was intended to disarm critics who wanted only token assistance until a unified military plan was set up, those same critics regarded it as their key to the discovery of flaws in the structure of the program. Further probing revealed that only 56 percent of the goods authorized for shipment could be delivered by June 1950, and even that figure might be optimistic.[84] Undoubtedly, the life of this "interim" arrangement would continue for at least two fiscal years. Elaboration of these facts, accompanied by unsatisfactory rebuttals by the Administration, suggested to many legislators that if the bill could not be postponed, it should at least be reduced to an amount that could be obligated in one fiscal year.[85]

Just as congressional pressure had earlier imposed exact limitations upon the President's authority to grant aid at his discretion, so it now forced a reassessment of the amount of aid to be given. Changes in the bill were immediately proposed. A 50 percent cut was sought for funds in fiscal year 1950 for the NATO countries, with the suggestion that the excised half billion dollars be placed under contract authority chargeable to fiscal year 1951.[86] With even more enthusiasm, House and Senate agreed to set a dollar ceiling of $450 million for the value of materials and equipment sent to Europe.[87] On both of these issues, the Administration accepted congressional advice with good grace; the substitution of contract authorization indicated a change in form rather than substance, and the restrictions on shipment of excess equipment appeared to be a harmless precaution against excessive hidden benefits to the recipients.[88] Changes of this sort would have no appreciable effect upon FACC plans.

The FACC's relative calm over cuts in the amount to be authorized was a consequence of the limitations in the MAP itself in its early stages. While its long-range purpose was the defense of the West against external as well as internal attack, the framers recognized that the short-range objectives could be no more than a modest improvement in the Allies' capability to defend themselves. In fact, their best estimates were that the MAP, as then conceived, could delay, but not defeat, a massive Soviet assault. For fiscal year 1950, they envisaged an increase in the efficiency of ground troops already in being, along with limited training equipment of units to be mobilized by M+3, and little more.[89] If the prospect of military assistance encouraged the NATO allies in 1949, it was not because they expected new armies able to challenge any invasion from the East; it stemmed from the psychological comfort of U.S. assistance as a further earnest of participation by the United States in the alliance.[90]

But Congress did not stop with the revisions described above. The House Committee on Foreign Affairs, reporting the bill on 15 August, added a new wrinkle to the withholding of MAP funds: The full amount requested under H.R. 5895 was recommended in theory, but in practice only the sum of $655.84 million was approved for obligation during fiscal year 1950, and of this figure, $157.71 million was not to be available until after 31 March 1950. The Senate version presented on 12 September was little more encouraging to the Administration. The Senate committees wanted the total authorization trimmed to $1.314 billion, of which $1 billion was reserved for the NATO countries. Half of the latter sum, however, was in the form of contract authority, and four-fifths of the remainder was to be withheld until an approved defense plan had been formulated by the North Atlantic Defense Committee. Hence, only $100 million would be immediately available for the NATO nations, although the other areas would hold their own, and China would receive an unexpected $75 million.[91]

Disappointing as these revisions were, they were mild in comparison with other amendments introduced. In the Senate, two supporters of both NATO and the MAP, Vandenberg and Lodge, proposed to eliminate the sums provided to encourage arms production in Europe.[92] Representative John M. Vorys suggested that technical training and funds for administration be deleted as well as the $155 million for additional production.[93] These attacks seemingly struck at the peripheries of the bill, ostensibly to safeguard American interests while accepting the need for the program.

Yet the U.S. planners, particularly the ECC in Europe, understood fully the future and indirect implications of the MAP. The principle had to be established. Arms production in Europe was vital if Europeans were expected to develop an integrated defense system. But this development could take place only if the expanding arms industries did not destroy the economies of the countries involved. Congress failed to appreciate this line of reasoning in the summer of 1949 and imposed severe restrictions on the additional military production program.[94] None of the funds could be used to offset losses in export trade or to pay subsidies for increased production. The funds were primarily for materials and machine tools needed by European factories for arms manufacture. But at least the principle survived, however grudging its approval.[95]

There was no doubt of Senator Vandenberg's object, but in other quarters sniping of this sort represented a rearguard battle against both the pact and the assistance program. Some of the opponents labeled the MAP a British plot against the U.S. Treasury or a scheme for the enrichment of the Rockefeller banking interests.[96] The arguments of others were more generalized. According to Senator Robert A. Taft, "this program is completely wasteful, completely illogical, completely vain in respect to what it proposes to accomplish; not only does it seem to me that it is contrary to every principle we have formerly pursued in connection with the United Nations; but I also believe it to be a policy which is dangerous to the peace of the United States and the peace of the world."[97] In the light of such expressions, it was not surprising that complete defeat and not mere modification was the expectation of critics like Representative William Lemke, who intended "to vote for all crippling amendments and then against the cripple."[98]

The strength of the opposition forces did not suffice in the end to achieve complete defeat, just as it had not sufficed to reject the North Atlantic Treaty. But opposition efforts did succeed in withholding nine-tenths of the $1 billion originally proposed for the NATO countries. The Senate plan of assigning $500 million to contract authority and reserving $400 million until the President had approved the NATO Defense Committee's integrated defense plans won the acceptance of the House–Senate conference on 26 September. The Senators in turn accepted the House proposal that the bill be entitled the "Mutual Defense Assistance Act," and the bill passed by a vote of 223 to 109 in the House and by voice vote in the Senate.[99] The President signed it on 6 October and the Appropriations Bill which implemented the authorization on 28 October. Thus ended what Senator Tom Connally had called the most difficult foreign policy measure since the passage of the Lend-Lease Act of 1941.[100] Aside from the advice of the JCS, the personal pleas of the President, and the apparent logic of necessity, pressure for passage had mounted after the meeting of the North Atlantic Treaty Council on 17 September and the President's announcement a week later of an atomic explosion in the Soviet Union.[101]

The difficulties encountered by the MAP and the officials who formulated it were painful but not surprising. The program was admittedly a gamble: That Russia would not be provoked to war, that U.S. military and economic strength would not be taxed excessively, and that the aid would serve its intended purposes. None of these doubts could be resolved until they were tested. On a less speculative level, the program revealed structural faults which made it vulnerable to attack. The framers never made it clear whether their objective was mutual assistance built around integrated defense of specific areas or the stiffening of resistance to communism everywhere in the world regardless of the principles of mutual aid. They seemed to have had both ideas in mind, although not in equal measure. Understandably, the prospect of regional alliance cemented by an integrated defense program appeared a more attractive investment than the granting of military help to individual countries, and it followed that the non-NATO areas were slighted. The FACC therefore had only itself to blame for the congressional excision of aid to countries that had not joined the United States in regional arrangements and the consequent resentment of the unfavored lands; it had not stressed the importance of the role of Asia, Africa, and Latin America in maintaining world peace. Nevertheless, a beginning had been made in the work of extending U.S. help to other countries and regions, and Europe was the area that could most efficiently use it.

The long delay in obtaining congressional approval of the MDAP seemed equally inevitable. While the North Atlantic Treaty was a milestone in U.S. foreign policy, it was essentially a passive deed, requiring only organizational activity unless a particular territory was violated. The Mutual Defense Assistance Program was equally bold, but, unlike the Atlantic Pact, it required positive action. Superficially it had a precedent in the Lend-Lease Act of 1941, but that was a move made under great duress, a hope of warding off impending disaster with any means available rather than the product of carefully considered commitment to the strengthening of collective defense. Moreover, lend-lease connoted U.S. giving and European taking. The Greek and Turkish aid program of 1947, now encompassed within the Mutual Defense Assistance Act, similarly lacked the collective and mutual elements of the MDAP. While the ECA contained both, it was a program of economic recovery, with none of the fearful images raised by the idea of a military program.

It was not surprising, therefore, that the MAP became the object of searching investigation by Congress. If it accepted the program, it also tried to protect U.S. control as best it could, no matter what effect this protectiveness would have upon the sensibilities of allies. The commitment, however, did require, according to Senator Kenneth S. Wherry of Nebraska, that the United States be "morally bound to continue those appropriations; and if we cut them off next year, even though within this act we can do so theoretically, yet my opinion is that we would be worse off, as far as the morale of those forces are concerned, if we did not continue it than if we had never started."[102] Although these were the words of a bitter critic of MDAP, they represented also the feelings of those who accepted the responsibilities which its enactment would impose upon the United States.

The changes made during the course of the debate reflected many of the Defense Department's concerns—specific concessions from the Allies, assurance that aid would be tied to a strategic plan, and a statement that no equipment would be transferred out of military stocks without the approval of the Secretary of Defense in consultation with the JCS. Yet, the course of events in the critical year 1949 was not controlled by the Secretary of Defense or by the Joint Chiefs of Staff. The leadership remained in the hands of the State Department throughout this period. Part of the explanation for this situation lay in the prestige of the Secretary of State in his first year of office as compared with his counterpart in the Defense Department, who did not seem able to follow the implications of the MAP.

But the reasons for the State Department's predominance in a program dependent on the military Services for its implementation went deeper than the personal qualities of the respective Secretaries. The JCS had never regarded military assistance as an opportunity for enlarging their powers. On the contrary, they feared it initially as a drag upon preparedness at home, a drain upon their limited budgets, and a waste of resources on nations unable to withstand invasion. Indeed, their acceptance of State leadership arose partly from their need for the political support of the State Department. The threat of financing the MAP from current military appropriations had come from the Bureau of the Budget and had been turned aside with the help of the State Department. But military planners recognized that military aid could make no appreciable difference to the defense of Europe for the immediate future in the face of a major Soviet offensive. Not even the guarantee of new base facilities or the assurance of an integrated European force could change that fact.

NOTES

1. Memo, Kennan for Sec/State and USec/State, 14 Apr 49, *FRUS*, 1949, 1, 282; red of USec's mtg, Dept/State, 15 Apr 49, ibid., pp. 283–84.

2. Memo, Kennan for Dean Rusk, Dep USec/State for Policy Affairs, 7 Sep 49, ibid, p. 381.

3. Mins, 171st mtg of PPS, 16 Dec 49, ibid., pp. 414–15.

4. Rcd of USec's mtg, Dept/State, 15 Apr 49, ibid., p. 283; memcon, James E Webb, 4 May 49, sub: State Dept participation in NSC, ibid., pp. 296–97.

5. Memo, Acting Sec/State for Souers, 24 May 49, ibid., p. 313; memo, Sec/Def for Souers, 20 Jun 49, ibid., pp. 345–46.

6. Mins, 171st mtg of PPS, 16 Dec 49, ibid., pp. 415–16.

7. Memo, JCS for Sec/Def, 5 Jan 49, sub: North Atlantic Pact, 840.20/1–649, *FRUS*, 1949, 4, 13.

8. Ibid.; memo, JCS, 14 Mar 49, sub: Program for Foreign Military Assistance, RG 218.

9. PL216, 81st Cong, 1st sess, National Security Act Amendments of 1949, *US Statutes at Large*, 1949, 63 (pt 1), 578–92.

10. Telg 983, Douglas to Sec/State, 16 Mar 49, 840.00/3–1649, *FRUS*, 1949, 4, 230–3n.

11. Policy paper approved by FACC, MAP D-G/14, 20 May 49, sub: Military Rights Question, *FRUS*, 1949, 1, 311–12.

12. Telg 983, Douglas to Sec/State, 16 Mar 49, 840.00/3–1649, *FRUS*, 1949, 4, 231.

13. Memo, Maj Gen Patrick W Timberlake, Dep Dir of Staff, MB, for Sec/State, 25 Mar 49, sub: Acquisition of Strategic Materials through Foreign MAP's, reporting on mtg of 17 Mar 49, CD 6–2–46, RG 330, NARA.

14. Staff memo, NAC, 9 Mar 49, sub: Loan-Grant and Local Currency Counterpart Issues Raised by MAP, N7–1-(1)-E.9, RG 330, NARA.

15. Memo, Lemnitzer for Col Tischbein, Off of Intl Programs, MB, 27 May 49, sub: Acquisition of Strategic Materials through the Foreign MAP, N7–1-(8), RG 330. The Munitions Board succeeded to the extent that Defense had FACC urge ECA to take maximal advantage of its bargaining position in obtaining further strategic materials for the United States. Personal ltr, Sec/Def to Paul Hoffman, Dir, ECA, 9 Jun 49, ibid.

16. Mins, War Council, 23 Feb 49, Ohly Collection, OSD Historian files.

17. Telg 1212, Douglas to Sec/State, 26 Mar 49, 840.20/3–2649, *FRUS*, 1949, 4, 249.

18. Telg 1213, Douglas to Sec/State, 26 Mar 49, 840.00/3–2649, ibid., pp. 250–51.

19. Memo, FACC, 25 Mar 49, sub: Problems in Developing MAP, N7–1-(1)-F.3, RG 330, NARA.

20. Despite the unanimous decision of ECC to ask for no resubmission of the Western Union request, Defense and State representatives differed on the bilateral issue at the ECC meeting of 25 March 1949. See *FRUS*, 1949, 4, 247.

21. Mins, 2d mtg of ECC, 2 Jun 49, p. 10, 840.00/6–1449, RG 59, NARA.

22. Memo, Lemnitzer for Halaby, 28 Sep 49, sub: Negotiation of Base Rights in Relation to MAP Bilateral Agreement, FACC D-5/2 (draft 7), N7–1-(1)-G.5, RG 330.

23. Memo, Lemnitzer for Sec/Def, 24 Mar 49, CD 6–2–46, RG 330, NARA.

24. Memo, Adm Forrest P Sherman, CNO, for Cte of Four Secretaries, 21 Mar 49, N7–1-(1)-G.5, RG 330; policy paper approved by FACC, MAP D-F/1, 25 Jul 49, sub: Why MAP Should be Administered by State Department, *FRUS*, 1949, 1, 359–61.

25. US Dept/State *Bulletin* 20 (1949), 649.

26. Memo, Sec/Def for Truman, 16 Apr 49, N7–1, RG 330, NARA.

27. Memo, Sec/Def for Lemnitzer, 19 Apr 49, CD 6–2–46, RG 330, NARA.

28. Memo, Ohly for Sec/Def, 2 Apr 49, ibid.

29. Memo, Lemnitzer for Sec/Def, 13 Apr 49, ibid.

30. *Vital Speeches of the Day* 15 (1949), 429.

31. Memo, Goodrich for McNeil and Leva, 12 Apr 49, N7–1-(1)-B, RG 330, NARA.

32. Unsigned OSD doc shown to Truman, 10 Apr 49, CD 6–2–46, RG 330; memo, Goodrich for McNeil and Leva, 12 Apr 1949, N7–1-(1)-B, RG 330.

33. Memo, Theodore Tannenwald, Jr, Counselor to Sec/Def, for Leva, 8 Mar 49, CD 6–2–46, RG 330, NARA.

34. Memo, Leven G Allen, Exec Sec, OSD, for Sec/Army et al, 20 Apr 49, ibid. Attached is a chart, showing original figures, budget recommendations, and revised FACC estimates.

35. Ibid.; memo, Lemnitzer for Gruenther et al, 5 May 49, N7-1-(1)-B.1, RG 330; brief prepared by FACC on BoB comments on origins of foreign aid program, ibid.

36. US Dept/State, *Foreign Affairs Outlines: Building the Peace*, No 22 (Washington: GPO, 1949), p. 1.

37. Memo, Allen for JCS, 9 May 49, CD6–2–46, RG 330, NARA; memo, JCS for Sec/Def, 21 May 49, sub: Foreign MAP Pricing Policy, ibid.; this includes a change in JCS 1868/58.

38. Policy paper approved by FACC, MAP D-G/7, 1 Jul 49, sub: Relationship of MAP to US Strategic Interests, *FRUS*, 1949, 1, 347–49.

39. Memo, Ohly for Sec/Def, 2 Apr 49, CD 6–2–46, RG 330; memo, Leva for Sec/Def, 5 Apr 49, CD 6–4–18, RG 330, NARA.

40. Memcon, Acheson, of telephone conv with Sen Millard Tydings, 13 Apr 49, Acheson Papers, Harry S Truman Library.

41. Memo, Goodrich for McNeil and Leva, 12 Apr 49, N7-1-(1)-B, RG 330; red of discussions at mtg of Senate Cte on Foreign Relations, 21 Apr 49, 840.20/4–2249, *FRUS*, 1949, 1, 288–91.

42. Memo, Goodrich for McNeil and Leva, 12 Apr 49, N7-(1)-B, RG 330.

43. Red of discussions at mtg of Senate Cte on Foreign Relations, 21 Apr 49, 840.20/4–2249, *FRUS*, 1949, 1, 288–89.

44. Memcon, Webb, of conv with Truman, 2 Jun 49, sub: Plans for Improving Our Policy Determination, 711.00/6–249, *FRUS*, 1949, 1, 326. See David S McLellan, *Dean Acheson: The State Department Years* (New York: Dodd, Mead & Co, 1976), pp. 153–54.

45. Memo, Kennan for Acting Sec/State, 1 Jun 49, 840.20/6–149, *FRUS*, 1949, 4, 301.

46. Comments by Johnson at mtg of FASC and FACC personnel, 20 Apr 49, sub: Military Assistance Discussions, N7-1, RG 330, NARA.

47. US Congress, Senate, Cte on Foreign Relations, *North Atlantic Treaty*, hearings on Exec L, 81st Cong, 1st sess, 28 Apr 49, pt 1, p. 146.

48. Int with Leva, 12 Jun 70, Harry S Truman Library.

49. Walter Millis et al, *Arms and the State: Civil-Military Elements in National Policy* (New York: Twentieth Century Fund, 1958), p. 235.

50. Acheson, *Present at the Creation*, pp. 373–74, 441; memcon, Harry H Schwartz, Exec Sec, PPS, Dept/State, 22 Mar 50, *FRUS*, 1950, 1, 204–205.

51. Int with Lemnitzer, 21 Mar 74, pp 11, 18, OSD Historian files.

52. Red of discussions at mtg of Senate Cte on Foreign Relations, 21 Apr 49, 840.20/4–2249, *FRUS*, 1949, 1, 290.

53. Senate, Cte on Foreign Relations, *North Atlantic Treaty*, hearings, 81st Cong, 1st sess, 3 May 49, pt 1, p. 296 (Bradley testimony).

54. Ibid., 28 Apr 49, pp. 145ff (Johnson testimony).

55. Rcd of discussions at mtg of Senate Cte on Foreign Relations, 21 Apr 49, 840.20/4–2249, *FRUS*, 1949, 1, 289 (Acheson comments).

56. Senate, Cte on Foreign Relations, *North Atlantic Treaty*, 81st Cong, 1st sess, 29 Apr 49, pt 1, pp. 210–11 (Harriman testimony); ibid., 10 May 49, pt 2, pp. 674–77 (testimony of James P Warburg).

57. Richard P Stebbins ed *The United States in World Affairs, 1949* (New York: Harper & Bros, 1950), p. 77.

58. Mins, 2d mtg of ECC, 2 Jun 49, p. 1, 840.00/6–1449, RG 59, NARA; memo, Adams for Sec/State, 2 Jun 49, N7-1-(1)-B.3, RG 330, NARA.

59. Memcon, Acheson, of telephone conv with Vandenberg, 24 Jun 49, Acheson Papers, Harry S Truman Library.

60. Memo, Lemnitzer for Sec/Def, 13 May 49, sub: Congressional Presentation of the MAP, CD 6–2–46, RG 330; memo, Acheson for Truman, 12 May 49, 840.20/5–1249, *FRUS*, 1949, 4, 298–99.

61. Memcon, Acheson, of conv with Truman, 12 May 49, 840.20/5–1249, RG 59, NARA.

62. Telg 1629, FACC to ECC, 12 May 49, N7-1-(1)-B.3, RG 330, NARA.

63. Mins, 2d mtg of ECC, 2 Jun 49, p. 1, 840.00/6–1449, RG 59; telg 2188, Douglas to Sec/State, 840.20/6–549, ibid.

64. Stebbins, ed, *The United States in World Affairs, 1949*, p 77.

65. For the declaration by the Ministry of Foreign Affairs of the USSR, 29 Jan 49, see *International Organization* 3 (1949), 400–405.

66. For the Soviet memo of 31 Mar 49, see Alvin Z Rubinstein, ed, *The Foreign Policy of the Soviet Union*, 3d ed (New York: Random House, 1972), pp. 233–36.

67. United Nations, *Official Records of the Third Session of the General Assembly*, pt 2, pp. 110, 120, 128.

68. Stebbins, ed, *The United States in World Affairs, 1949*, p. 80.

69. Msg, Truman to Congress, 25 Jul 49, US Natl Archives, *Public Papers of the Presidents: Harry S. Truman, 1949*, pp. 395–400.

70. US Department of State, *The Military Assistance Program* (Washington: GPO, 1949), p. 2.

71. US Congress, House, Cte on Foreign Affairs, *Mutual Defense Assistance Act of 1949*, hearings on HR 5748 and HR 5895, 81st Cong, 1st sess, 28–29 Jul 49, pp. 9–15 (Acheson testimony), 45–47 (Johnson testimony), 71 (Bradley testimony).

72. Acheson, *Present at the Creation*, pp. 309–11.

73. HR 5748, Sec 2(a).

74. Ibid., Sec 3.

75. Ibid., Sec 4(d).

76. House, Cte on Foreign Affairs, *Mutual Defense Assistance Act of 1949*, 81st Cong, 1st sess, 2 Aug 49, pp. 126–30 (Harriman testimony). Representatives James Fulton and John Davis Lodge raised these issues most pointedly.

77. Brookings Institution, *Current Developments in United States Foreign Policy*, Jul–Aug 49, pp. 28–29; memo, Gross for Sec/State, 6 Aug 49, sub: Strategy on MAP, 840.20/8–649, *FRUS*, 1949, 1, 377–79, and fn 1 to that memo, p. 377.

78. House, Cte on Foreign Affairs, *Mutual Defense Assistance Act of 1949*, 81st Cong, 1st sess, 28–29 Jul 49, pp. 23, 49–50; US Congress, Senate, Ctes on Foreign Relations and Armed Services, *Military Assistance Program*, jt hearings on S 2388, 81st Cong, 1st sess, 8–11 Aug 49, pp. 19, 118–19.

79. House, Cte on Foreign Affairs, *Mutual Defense Assistance Act of 1949*, 81st Cong, 1st sess, 28 Jul 49, p. 18.

80. Senate Ctes on Foreign Relations and Armed Services, *Military Assistance Program*, 81st Cong, 1st sess, 9 Aug 49, p. 49.

81. Ibid., 10 Aug 49, pp. 88–91.

82. Ibid., p. 78.

83. Telg 2187, Douglas to Sec/State, 5 Jun 49, 840.20/6–549, *FRUS*, 1949, 4, 302–303.

84. Senate, Ctes on Foreign Relations and Armed Services, *Military Assistance Program*, 81st Cong, 1st sess, 8–9 Aug 49, pp. 25, 50–51.

85. Johnson made an unfavorable impression on Congress when he explained that he wanted a large sum at that time so that he could make a good impression on Congress when he next appeared asking for less money. Ibid., 9 Aug 49, pp. 52–53.

86. Ibid., pp. 51–52.

87. PL 329, 81st Cong, 1st sess, Mutual Defense Assistance Act of 1949, Title IV, *US Statutes at Large*, 1949, 63 (pt 1), 716–21.

88. Senate, Ctes on Foreign Relations and Armed Services, *Military Assistance Program*, 81st Cong, 1st sess, 8–9 Aug 49, pp. 53–56 (Johnson–Vandenberg exchange), 16 (Acheson–Connally exchange). The cost to recipients would still be only rehabilitation and shipment, and it was unlikely, considering the various estimates, that materials worth more than $450 million could be delivered in this period.

89. Policy paper approved by FACC, MAP D-D/1, 25 May 49, sub: Objectives of MAP, *FRUS*, 1949, 1, 314–15.

90. Policy paper approved by FACC, MAP D-G/7, 1 Jul 49, sub: Relationship of MAP to US Strategic Interests, ibid., pp. 347–49.

91. Brookings Institution, *Current Developments in United States Foreign Policy*, Jul–Aug 49, p. 30; ibid., Sep 49, p. 21. Both contain good summaries of the committee reports reflecting the influence of friends of Nationalist China.

92. *Cong Rec*, 15 Aug 49, 95 (pt 9), 11408–9.

93. Memo, Francis T Greene, Special Counsel to Sec/Def, for Lemnitzer, 10 Aug 49, sub: Briefing Outline for Sec/State with Respect to Amendments to MAP Legislation as Proposed by Members of the Cte, N7-1-(1)-B.3, RG 330, NARA.

94. PL 329, 81st Cong, 1st sess, Mutual Defense Assistance Act of 1949, Title I, *US Statutes at Large*, 1949, 63 (pt 1), 715–16.

95. Telg 2234, Holmes to Sec/State, 10 Jun 49, 840.00/6–1049, *FRUS*, 1949, 4, 305. See also William Adams Brown, Jr, and Redvers Opie, *American Foreign Assistance* (Washington: Brookings Institution, 1953), p. 466.

96. For comments of Reps William Lemke and George G Sadowski, see *Cong Rcd*, 17 Aug 49, 95 (pt 9), 11662–63, 11674, 11688–89.

97. *Cong Rcd*, 22 Sep 49, 95 (pt 10), 13150.

98. *Cong Rcd*, 18 Aug 49, 95 (pt 9), 11761.

99. Brookings Institution, *Current Developments in United States Foreign Policy*, Sep 49, p. 22.

100. Stebbins, ed, *The United States in World Affairs, 1949*, p. 80; *New York Times*, 29 Sep 49.

101. Stebbins, ed, *The United States in World Affairs, 1949*, p. 83; editorial in *New York Times*, 28 Sep 49; Acheson, *Present at the Creation*, p. 313.

102. US Congress, Senate, Cte on Appropriations, *Second Supplemental Appropriation Bill for 1950*, hearings on HR 6427, 81st Cong, 1st sess, 15 Oct 49, p. 223.

II
NATO in the First Generation, 1950–1967

The linking of the two continents through NATO did not guarantee satisfaction with every aspect of the alliance as far as Europeans were concerned. As noted, there was resentment over the terms of military assistance, particularly bilateral arrangements extracted from the beneficiaries at the same time that the donor was asking for multilateral obligations from Europeans. Nor were the European partners pleased with the shape of the strategic concept, which was mandated by the Mutual Defense Assistance Act as a prerequisite for release of U.S. funds. The United States would contribute strategic airpower, while the allies would serve as foot soldiers in a future war.

Arguably, the most serious division between Europe and America in the first year developed over defense plans devised earlier by the Joint Chiefs of Staff that would effectively abandon Europe in the first phase of a war. Even when this short-term plan was discarded, the allies had reservations about the medium-term defense plan, which was approved in April 1950 and scheduled for completion by 1954. The revised plan placed the defense line at the Rhine, a considerable improvement over its predecessor. But it was not good enough. The Dutch were understandably concerned about a defense plan that left the right bank of the Rhine outside NATO's protection. A stand at the Rhine would not suffice; it would have to be moved eastward to the Elbe at least, particularly when the status of West Germany was at stake.

If Germany was an issue in the formation of NATO, a conspiracy of silence obscured it. To suggest inviting Germans into an alliance only four years after the end of World War II was an impossibility; memories of Nazi bestiality were too strong among most NATO allies. Although Americans understood the visceral revulsion against potential German membership intellectually if not emotionally, they also saw a logical connection between the new organization and a solution to the German problem. From the beginning there was an implied linkage. The evolution of a West German state, advanced by trizonal financial arrangements and strengthened by the successful Berlin airlift in 1948, culminated in the creation of the Federal Republic in May 1949, only one month after the signing of the treaty.

From the summer of 1949, voices in Congress and the military were raised on behalf of a German contribution, if not membership, in the alliance. On the crassest level, it seemed unreasonable for Germans to enjoy the protection of NATO through the presence of allied forces without their contributing to the common defense. On a more elevated plane, linking Germany to NATO in one way or another would ensure a Western orientation in the Federal Republic and obviate temptations to accept unification on Soviet terms. The specter of a Rapallo-like rapprochement with the Soviet Union evoked the Weimar era, no matter how unfairly. Most importantly, it would accelerate the pace of democracy in West Germany.

Such were the arguments in favor of a German role in the alliance. Many of these discussions were held in Senate executive sessions or in the Pentagon planning rooms. Publicly, the idea was avoided. When asked if the inclusion of West Germany would improve NATO's strategic position, Secretary of State Acheson testified at the Senate hearings on the treaty that no consideration was given even to discussing the subject.

The Korean War dramatically changed the relationship between Germany and the Western allies, as indeed, it changed the structure of the organization itself. Initially Europeans feared that war in the Far East would divert America's attention from Europe and lead to the abandonment of the Atlantic alliance. However, Truman's response to the North Korean attack was reassuring to Europeans. According to the conventional wisdom of the time, North Korea was a Soviet satellite testing the resolve of the American adversary by attacking an American protectorate. If this were the case, Stalin then might be preparing the ground for aggression by another satellite, East Germany, to strike in another divided land.

The result was the energizing of the alliance rather than its abandonment. Instead of renewing the military assistance program at roughly the level of 1949, Congress added a four billion dollar supplement to help the allies deter the kind of assault South Korea had experienced. The specter of 60,000 East German paramilitary troops, backed by twenty-seven Soviet divisions in the eastern zone, demanded more than increased military aid. The crisis required the reorganization of the alliance.

But before the the the "O" in NATO could be made meaningful, the German issue had to be confronted, and this created new tensions within the alliance, particularly in France. The aid that the United States considered in the wake of the Korean War included troops as well as arms, but the prerequisite for this support was contingent on full utilization of German resources and ultimate admission of the Federal Republic into the alliance. This act took over four years to be consummated. West Germany entered NATO in 1955 following a tortuous path of negotiations. In an effort to defer this action as long as possible, France proposed the Pleven Plan in the fall of 1950, using the model pioneered by Jean Monnet, the architect of the European Coal and Steel Community, which would create a European force under a European minister of defense. When this army came into being, German troops would be incorporated on the battalion level. In this way, Europe's concerns about the militarization of West Germany would be relieved by the controls placed on the German contribution.

Such were the origins of the European Defense Community (EDC), which was an outgrowth of the original French ideas. American objections forced the scrapping of the requirement that German contingents join the force only after the European army had been formed. In place of battalions the French agreed to accept German combat teams at regimental strength. The EDC, with its terms and protocols painfully framed over the next few years, never came to fruition. The treaty creating the community was signed in May 1952, but French demands for changes defining connections between the community and the Anglo-Saxon allies delayed ratification. Then, in 1954, the French National Assembly scuttled the treaty. The ostensible reason was that France never accepted British and American abstention from the EDC. More persuasive factors were France's unwillingness to submerge its military inside a European army and fear of ultimate control of the community by a revived Germany.

Nonetheless, the fate of the European Defense Community was not simply a tale of failure and deception. The allies would not have accepted the Federal Republic as a NATO partner in 1950. After the collapse of the EDC they were prepared to do so. The imaginative London and Paris agreements in the fall of 1954 made German membership in NATO possible through the enlargement of the Western Union to include both Germany and Italy—granted that this arrangement made Germany's position subject to restrictions on the production of nuclear weapons and to committing its troops wholly to the alliance. With France's support, the Federal Republic became the fifteenth member of NATO. Although the European Defense Community never came to life, its demise helped to accelerate the rehabilitation of West Germany, no matter what the intentions of its farmers were.

Although it was the most significant change produced by the Korean War, German membership was not the only major change. The most immediate was American payment for France's putative concessions in 1950: namely, the dispatching of American troops to Europe. What guaranteed the success of the reorganization was the creation of supreme allied commands in Europe and in the Atlantic and the appointment of General Dwight D. Eisenhower as the first Supreme Allied Commander, Europe. The allies could not have chosen a more impressive leader to serve as a unifying figure. As in a similar role in World War II, Eisenhower's leadership was a critical factor in persuading a reluctant Congress in the winter of 1951 to dispatch four divisions to Europe, thereby deepening the entanglement with Europe. His presence at the military headquarters in Paris was more than symbolic. It signified an American military presence in Europe that was not anticipated when the North Atlantic Treaty was signed.

The reorganization of NATO pushed America into obligations beyond Western Europe itself. British aspirations notwithstanding, Eisenhower's naval equivalent, the Supreme Allied Commander, Atlantic, was also to be an American, in 1951 and beyond. And it was pressure from the Supreme Command in Paris that accounted for Greece and Turkey entering NATO in 1952, further extending the scope of the alliance. Just as in the case of Germany, the allies had little choice in the long run. If they wanted American leadership as well as four new American divisions, they had to accept such peripheral states as Greece and Turkey. Their importance was the protection they would give to the southeastern flank of NATO, along with the needed manpower they would supply. The decision to admit Greece and Turkey took place at the Lisbon meeting of the North Atlantic Council in February 1952 when the allies agreed to raise some fifty divisions in 1952, seventy-five in 1953, and ninety-six in 1954.

This transformation of the alliance of 1949 into the military organization of 1952 solidified American domination of Europe in the 1950s. While Europeans would hold the office of secretary-general, created at the Lisbon meeting, power seemed vested in the supreme commander, whose very title connoted an authority that was not found in his civilian counterpart. In these changes the British and French members of the Standing Group of the Military Committee fought a losing battle for equality with their American colleagues in the Pentagon. Neither ally could cope openly with American pressure in this decade. France's acceptance of German membership could not be delayed indefinitely; and Britain had to settle for a British admiral in charge of a Channel command when it failed to win the Atlantic command. The choice of Lord Ismay as the first secretary-general was meager compensation for Britain's failure to win equality with the United States.

In this first decade of NATO's history the European allies were torn between gratitude for the shelter of American power and resentment over their dependence on that power. From time to time resentment manifested itself more clearly than gratitude. France never forgave the United States for its apparent abandonment of French interests in Indochina and the apparent replacement by an America-controlled Vietnamese government; the United Kingdom brooded over America's disregard for its naval tradition in the building of NATO and its refusal to allow at least a Mediter-ranean command under British control; and the Federal Republic not only had periodic doubts about American commitment to unification of Germany but wondered about the wisdom of joining NATO in the wake of Operation Carte Blanche when the United States in 1955 appeared to accept with excessive equanimity a potential death toll of 1,700,000 Germans in a nuclear confrontation with the Soviet Union. The smaller members of the alliance had their own grievances, particularly over the failure of the larger powers to consult with them over NATO policies.

While West German reaction was inhibited by its tenuous position in the organization, Britain and France openly exhibited their distrust of the United States in their Suez intervention in 1956 when they collaborated in an assault against Nasser's Egypt without notifying their American partner. In that same year a committee of three ministers drawn from the smaller NATO nations recommended that consultation be initiated in the planning stages whenever the interests of the alliance were involved. Clearly, the United States was the target of its report.

Yet, until the Soviet launching of Sputnik, the United States provided a strategy for the defense of Europe that compensated for the diminution of European authority within the alliance and allowed the revival of confidence as well as revival of the economies of Western Europe in the 1950s. Although NATO's intentions at the Lisbon conference to achieve force levels of ninety-six divisions never materialized, the nuclear substitutes in the Eisenhower administrations offered a sense of security among the allies. They took the form of fewer combat forces—some thirty divisions—but armed with tactical nuclear weapons. But the most heartening aspect of the U.S. approach to NATO's defense in the Eisenhower years was the understanding that any Soviet attack would be met by massive retaliation. Strategic nuclear power was the key. And to defuse tensions over American troops stationed in Europe, status-of-forces agreements were made, arrangements whereby a host nation would have criminal jurisdiction over soldiers of a NATO power stationed on its territory. Had these agreements not been made, American forces in Europe would have been occupiers of client nations rather than welcome associates in a common effort.

NATO solidarity emanating from this strategic concept was not breached by periodic Soviet attempts to split the alliance either by blandishments or by threats. West Germany was the major target. The cost to Germans of joining NATO was the creation of the Warsaw Pact in which East Germany apparently would be permanently separated. The Communists also floated ideas of nuclear free zones and removal of all troops from Germany, none of which found their mark until the end of the decade.

Sputnik, as shown in the first chapter in this section, raised doubts about American reliability. In its wake came Khrushchev's challenge over Berlin, which gave rise to further questions about America's steadfastness as an ally. Would vulnerability to an intercontinental ballistic missile weaken America's commitment to the defense of Europe when American cities presumably might be the target of Soviet attack? While the Berlin issue was not directly a NATO matter, the fate of the city would have a serious impact on the morale of the allies. The issue was more acute in the second phase of the Berlin crisis when the Kennedy administration took office. The centrality of the Soviet efforts to remove the Western allies from Berlin and to force recognition of East German's legitimacy is the subject of the second chapter in this section.

Although there were some doubts about the validity of the concept of "massive retaliation" at the end of the Eisenhower era, President Kennedy, guided by Secretary of Defense Robert S. McNamara and his military adviser General Maxwell Taylor not only repudiated massive retaliation as unworkable but insisted upon revitalizing conventional defenses. Both these approaches distressed Europeans. On the one hand, they were concerned about the costs as well as the effectiveness of traditional armies, even if armed with battlefield nuclear weapons. Not only would they be expensive but they could not cope with the superior numbers of the Warsaw Pact armies.

On the other hand, they feared that by emphasizing ground forces the United States was abandoning the nuclear option—and with it the umbrella that had protected Europe for fifteen years. The nuclear debate between America and Europe involved more than arguments over whether "flexible response" should replace "massive retaliation" or whether the nuclear threshold should be high or low. Beneath the rhetoric was America's need to maintain its monopoly of nuclear power and Europe's wish for its own nuclear deterrent. France's departure from NATO was a consequence of this conflict, and the dissolution of the alliance might have followed. It did not. NATO survived the trials of the 1960s. This is the subject of the third chapter.

4
The Impact of Sputnik on NATO

"The impact of Sputnik on NATO" was written initially for a confer-ence in Paris in 1991 and published in Rélations Internationales *(Au-tumn, 1992). The English version was presented at a NASA conference at the Smithsonian Institution in Washington, DC, in October 1997.*

If ever there was a Pax Americana it should have been found in the decade of the 1950s. The vast power of America that was harnessed in World War II blossomed between 1950 and 1960. Not only was the United States truly the only superpower, it enjoyed a prosperity never before achieved in its history. Yet the Cold War with the Soviet Union and its allies cast a shadow on the 1950s that extended from the beginning to the end of the decade. Communism was not only a dangerous ideology threatening American val-ues but also a tool of Russian imperialism threatening American security. The decade opened with the Korean conflict and closed with the fallout from Sputnik.

Historians a generation later have noted that the nation misjudged both events: the invasion of North Korea was not a Soviet experiment to be repeated in a divided Germany; and the launching of an earth satellite was not a harbinger of Soviet technological or military superiority. But even the middle years of the decade appeared fraught with danger. The fall of French Indochina might have set in motion the fall of all South Asia to commu-nism, and the Suez crisis of 1956 might have opened all the Middle East to Soviet control. As it was, the decade's end marked the advent of a dangerous Communist leader off the Florida coast in the person of Fidel Castro of Cuba.

In retrospect, the 1950s seemed filled with illusions, which too frequently governed White House policies. Conceivably, the death of Stalin could have opened a more normal relationship with the Soviet bloc, with the Geneva summit of 1955 ushering in a genuine detente between East and West. But the mutual hostility between the United States and the Soviet Union was too firmly entrenched for the Cold War to be ended. Even if the specter of Sputnik had not hung over the nation, there was little likelihood of a permanent rapprochement between the two countries.

It is commonplace for American revisionists to cast much of the blame for the Cold War on the shortcomings of American statesmen, if not on the imperialist ethnocentric policies they pursued. The Vietnam War a decade later gave respectability to this school. But paranoia, self-aggrandizement, and misjudgment characterized the other side as much as, if not more than, the American. The Soviet Union was a police state, a closed society, its records unavailable to scholars. For the most part, American blemishes were all too visible. With all its faults, the United States as leader in the 1950s was responsible through its Atlantic alliance for the *Wirtschaftswunder* that characterized the rehabilitation of Western Europe. Whatever motives of self-interest lay behind its origins, it was enlightened self-interest. A free and thriving Europe served all members of the alliance. The contrast between the Warsaw Pact and the North Atlantic Treaty reflects the differences between the Eastern and Western worlds.

The launching of an earth satellite on 4 October 1957 did not of itself create schisms in the alliance. They already existed in the almost ten-year-old organization—and were growing. French bitterness over America's role in Indochina in 1954 and both France's and Britain's anger over America's stance in Suez in 1956 had fed existing centrifugal forces. As Europe revived and groped toward unity, there was understandable resentment over America's dominant role in the alliance. It was the smaller powers that most clearly expressed frustration over inadequate consultation by the senior ally in the appeal of a committee of three foreign ministers in 1956—Lester Pearson of Canada, Halvard Lange of Norway, and Gaetano Martini of Italy. The specter of a Soviet satellite circling the earth every ninety-five minutes, with two special passes made over Washington, DC, raised a question that had never needed to be asked before: Would America's apparent vulnerability to a Soviet attack by means of an intercontinental ballistic missile affect its commitment to the defense of Europe? For skeptics about the future of the Atlantic alliance, the Soviet satellite could be the coup de grâce to a failing institution.

American newspapers did little to reassure the publics at home or abroad; nor did Democratic congressmen in their denunciation of Eisenhower's defense policies. The sober and authoritative *New York Herald Tribune* saw the Soviet achievement as a grave defeat for the United States. Senators Stuart Symington of Missouri and Henry Jackson of Washington interpreted it to be a devastating blow against America and evidence of the bankruptcy of Republican foreign and defense affairs.[1] There was an ironic juxtaposition in reports on 4 October 1957, the day of the launching, of a cutback in the U.S. guided missile and jet aircraft program. Jackson, from the state of Washington, the home of Boeing, could not resist demanding not only a crash program for long-range missiles but also a special place for Boeing's B-52s. Jackson earned his reputation as "Senator from Boeing."[2]

The administration's initial posture was one of bluster and dismissal. White House press secretary James Hagerty piously asserted that "We never thought of our program as one which was in a race with the Soviets." Sputnik, he claimed, would have no effect upon U.S. plans for launching its own satellite in the spring of 1958, in accordance with well-laid plans in conjunction with the International Geophysical Year. Secretaries of State and Defense, John Foster Dulles and Charles Wilson, further sought to minimize the event by saying that the Soviet satellite was of dubious scientific value.[3]

The president was more circumspect. When asked at a press conference about the Soviet claim to have fired an intercontinental ballistic missile as well as having launched an earth satellite, Eisenhower attempted to defuse the tension it raised with his customary rambling rhetoric. "There never has been one nickel asked for accelerating the program," he noted. "Never has it been considered as a race; merely an engagement on our part to put up a vehicle of this kind during the period that I have already mentioned." As for the Soviet intercontinental ballistic missile, he relegated the issue to an unproven claim, and then went on to explain how the American satellite program was destined for peaceful scientific use. "Our satellite program has never been conducted as a race with other nations. Rather, it has been carefully scheduled as part of the scientific work of the International Geophysical Year." Eisenhower's performance, particularly as he congratulated Soviet scientists on putting Sputnik into orbit, was far more effective than the reactions of his aides. His apparent meandering fitted the image now current of the "hidden-hand" presidency.[4]

Unfortunately, Khrushchev was in no mood to cooperate with Eisenhower's conciliatory approach. For the Soviet leader, the triumph of Sputnik was more than a success for Soviet technology; it was a dramatic illustration of the superiority of communism over capitalism, and, as such, should be an inspiration for the Communist parties throughout the world. Khrushchev exulted over its implications. To Eleanor Roosevelt he claimed that the Soviets could destroy Britain and France without using a plane.[5] Sputnik was to be proof positive of the Soviet assertion of having successfully tested in August 1957 a long-distance intercontinental ballistic rocket.

American radar observations on the Turkish Black Sea coast seemingly confirmed this test. With claims of new, improved instruments for guidance, he could boast that America, no less than Britain and France, would be subject to Soviet missiles.[6] Soviet behavior was not such as to relieve the fears of the allies, least of all the Americans.

Soviet truculence combined with pressure from domestic critics forced the administration to discard its *sangfroid* and confess at least to misjudging Soviet prowess and to face up a lagging missile program. The American satellite, Vanguard, which was to be launched in the spring of 1958 was moved up to 23 October 1957, less than three weeks after Sputnik. But rather than calming American feelings, it exacerbated them: the rocket exploded over the Atlantic. The Defense Department also reacted by announcing on 22 October that the Defense budget would be increased by $100 million, with the implication that the funds would go toward missile buildup. Three months later the president asked for an immediate increase of $1.3 billion in spending authority for the Department of Defense for 1958, as well as a further increase of $2.5 billion in 1959 over 1958, "to be applied principally to accelerate missile procurement to strengthen our nuclear retaliatory power, and to spur military research and development programs."[7]

That the public was disturbed was well reflected in congressional behavior. It was not simply Democratic military specialists such as Jackson and Symington who wanted an investigation. There was a nationwide demand for action. For almost two months, from 25 November through 23 January 1958, the Senate Preparedness Investigating Subcommittee of the Committee on Armed Services produced a three-part hearings, totaling 2,476 pages. Among the more impressive witnesses was Nelson Rockefeller, who encapsulated the findings of the Rockefeller Brothers Fund's special study group on American military policy. His was a note of gloom: "Ever since World War II, the United States has suffered from a tendency to underestimate the military technology of the U.S.S.R. It appears that the United States is rapidly losing its lead over the U.S.S.R. in the military race. Unless present trends are reversed, the world balance of power will shift in favor of the Soviet bloc."[8]

These sentiments were echoed by two angry retired military chieftains, Maxwell Taylor and James Gavin, who were both to play a role in the Kennedy administration a few years later. Both generals wrote books, but from different angles of observation.

Gavin was as angry with the trivialization of the Soviet achievement by such figures as Secretary Wilson as he was by the failure of Defense officials to move ahead with America's own satellite, even though intelligence sources knew the fast pace of Soviet progress. He likened U.S. behavior in 1957 to the treatment accorded the young officer who saw incoming Japanese on his radarscope on 7 December 1961. His immediate response was to recommend a crash program to develop a satellite to intercept a Soviet satellite.[9]

Unlike Gavin, an Air Force general, former Army chief of staff Maxwell Taylor was distressed over Sputnik because it diverted the nation from proper attention to conventional forces and toward new funding for Air Force strategic delivery forces. His worries were over the inflexibility of NATO's defense posture and the danger of excessive reliance on massive retaliation. "By our ever-growing dependence on nuclear weapons and nuclear retaliation as the backbone of our military strength," he claimed, "we appeared to these allies to be reaching the position where we could react to Communist power" only through all-out nuclear war or to back away from a challenge.[10] In their different ways, these military leaders raised questions about the credibility of the U.S. pledge to its allies.

What was obvious from voices as diverse as Gavin's and Taylor's was the sense that action, both diplomatic and military, had to be taken to restore the apparently forfeited allied confidence in America and America's confidence in itself. These took a number of forms. One would be modernization of the forces of the European allies, developing new weapons, primarily surface-surface and surface-to-air missiles. The secretary of defense on 28 October encouraged the Army and Navy to look toward common production or coordinated production in Europe of a variety of short-range nuclear weapons.[11]

This point was taken up by Secretary of State Dulles in his news conference following a meeting with Prime Minister Macmillan of Britain on 29 October 1957. Dulles spoke of interdependence, a not unfamiliar subject of American colloquy with Europeans. It usually meant greater burden-sharing, particularly in expenses for the common defense. But in light of concerns over the commitment to Europe's defense, Dulles announced that if the United States had the primary function of managing nuclear weapons, it also had the responsibility of letting its allies know what America's capabilities were, instilling confidence that in an emergency nuclear weaponry would be used.[12]

That confidence-building was necessary was made clear by Deputy Secretary of State Christian Herter's appraisal of the foreign policy implications of Sputnik's launching. While he professed to be hopeful about the reaction of allies, "even the best of them require assurance that we have not been surpassed scientifically and militarily by the USSR," he concluded on a somber note, saying that the United States would have to exert itself to counteract negative reactions.[13]

How confidence could be rebuilt was another matter. Part of the answer was to communicate clearly to the allies that the United States was attentive to their concerns. One way was to take up a French proposal at the NATO meeting at Bonn in May 1957 to build a nuclear arms stockpile for NATO in Europe. At a news conference on 5 November, Dulles assured reporters that this could be done within present laws. He cited arrangements with Canada as his example. Intermediate nuclear weapons were already in Europe, but they had been designated exclusively for the use of U.S. forces. "These would become so situated," according to Dulles, "they would also be available to the forces of our allies." Frederick Nolting, deputy chief of the U.S. mission to NATO, enthusiastically endorsed the concept of a "NATO stockpile as a means of soothing Europeans."[14]

The idea of a NATO nuclear stockpile was on the agenda of U.S. planners preparing for the December meeting of the North Atlantic Council in Paris, as were mechanisms for coordinated production of advanced weapons. The difficult problem would be to determine how to make warheads and missiles available to Europeans without violating the McMahon Act, which limited distribution of nuclear technology. This was a major element in American agenda preparations. As W. Randolph Burgess, chief of the U.S. delegation, proposed, the United States would be prepared to deploy from the NATO atomic stockpile atomic warheads that would be released from U.S. custody in the event of hostilities "to the appropriate Supreme Allied Commander for employment by the nuclear-capable forces of NATO in accordance with appropriate NATO defensive plans." In return for this largess, NATO allies having available technical data involving manufacture of nuclear weapons system would be expected to "make such data available to other nations as required."[15]

But the most urgent message to send to Europe, in the view of U.S. diplomats, was the certainty that the United States was prepared to accelerate and expand the deployment of intermediate-range ballistic missiles (IRBMs). While they would not have the dramatic impact of an intercontinental ballistic missile (ICBM), they were less expensive, more numerous, and more effective in striking potential targets in the Soviet Union. Secretary of Defense Neil McElroy noted in a meeting with the secretary of state that Defense was in a position to have ready 16 squadrons of 16 missiles each, or a total of 240 missiles to be delivered in a period extending through 1963, but beginning late in the calendar year. The Defense Department was not as anxious for their use as was the State Department. When the sea-based Polaris and the ICBMs came off the assembly lines, the IRBMs would lose their current importance. However, it was a political and psychological imperative to say something now, as Supreme Allied Commander, Europe (SACEUR), General Norstad demanded. Secretary Dulles understood Defense's concerns about costs but concluded that the "need to reassure our NATO allies regarding U.S. capabilities in the missile field," should override other considerations.[16]

Accordingly, the U.S. delegation encased the issue of IRBMs in two concrete steps: (1) to make available under the United States Military Assistance Program several squadrons of IRBMs to SACEUR, with an understanding that such deployment would be agreed upon between the supreme commander and countries concerned; and (2) to make available "under appropriate safeguards" blueprints and other necessary data relating to the IRBM deliveries systems."[17]

Britain and Turkey responded quickly to the offer to place missiles on their soil. In fact, Britain had made a preliminary agreement earlier that year, in March, at Bermuda. Italy accepted on 5 February 1958, when the Italian Chamber of Deputies approved the deployment of IRBMs, although it was not until September that a formal agreement was made.[18]

If Sputnik's success energized American foreign policy in the form of nuclear sharing, even on a limited scale, it perversely created movement in arms control. Until October 1957, it was the United States that had taken the initiative. In the summer of 1957 at London, Dulles presented an American proposal for a two-year suspension with the understanding that the Soviets would agree to a future cut-off in nuclear weapons production. The Soviets rejected the plan and broke off negotiations in August. But once Sputnik had been launched, the situation was reversed. The United States now held back as it attempted to cope with the Soviet achievement, and it was the Soviets who talked of a test ban while they appeared to have a lead. Soviet shrewdness in declaring a voluntary moratorium in March 1958 forced the United States to follow suit. The road to a test ban achievement suddenly appeared more promising than it ever had in the past.[19] The United States could not allow the Soviets to walk away with a propaganda victory, no matter how cynically they behaved.

The Soviets made the most of the advantage that Sputnik gave them. First, Premier Nikolai Bulganin asked Eisenhower for a summit meeting in early 1958, proposing a pledge by the United States, the Soviet Union, and Great Britain, to refrain from all nuclear tests for two to three years, beginning on 1 January 1958. When the United States failed to accept this plan, unless it were accompanied by a ban on production of nuclear weapons, Moscow in February 1958 asked for a summit meeting with a test ban on the agenda. The Soviets hoped that the pressure of world opinion would force Americans to accept a test ban unaccompanied by any plans for verification.

A finding from a panel of American scientists, headed by Hans Bethe of Cornell University, made it possible for Eisenhower to accept the next Soviet ploy: namely, a unilateral suspension of tests. Bethe's panel claimed that overall superiority in nuclear weaponry justified a test ban and that a network of control stations, including some on Soviet soil, could detect a nuclear blast as low as two kilotons. Prodded too by his newly appointed science adviser James Killian of MIT, the president, on 28 April 1958, agreed to separate the issues of testing and production and to join the Soviets in a moratorium. As Secretary Dulles put it, "Wholly apart from the true merits of the argument, the Russians were winning world opinion, and we were losing it."[20]

Delegations of Soviet and American scientists met for six weeks at Geneva, and, by mid-August 1958, they had reached agreement on establishing 180 control posts. Although the mutual moratorium did not last beyond 1961, it did provide an infrastructure for negotiations that were to produce the limited test ban treaty of 1963.

But if Sputnik inadvertently set the superpowers on a path leading to nuclear arms limitation, it also set in motion a massive American campaign to build up an intercontinental missile armory that led to greater arms competition in the following decade. The objective was to fill the "missile gap" that Sputnik supposedly revealed. The gap was essentially a fiction promoted by Khrushchev's rhetoric to divide the alliance.

But the Eisenhower administration was pressed to recognize that with a gross national product only a third that of the United States', the Soviets were matching the nation's expenditures in heavy industry and defense. The more urgent question was how to cope with what might be overwhelming Soviet superiority in intercontinental missiles, with figures ranging from 100 to 3,000, according to leaks from Secretary of Defense Neil McElroy's testimony before the Senate Foreign Relations Committee. Although McElroy asserted at a news conference on 2 January 1959 that the figure of 3000 was an exaggeration, he was convinced that a gap did exist. President Eisenhower in effect confirmed its existence when he informed the public a week later that the gap was being closed. His assurance did little to calm critics when he explained the problem in terms of a one-year head start on the part of the Soviets.[21]

Given this background, it was hardly surprising that the missile issue was campaign fodder in 1960. In August, Senator John F. Kennedy warned about dangerous days ahead "as the missile gap looms larger and larger."[22] Over the next two months of campaigning, he repeatedly demanded "a crash program for missiles to accompany a complete reevaluation of national defense organization." President Kennedy's first State of the Union Address, in which he "instructed the Secretary of Defense to reappraise our entire defense strategy," echoed this particular campaign theme.[23]

The new secretary of defense, Robert F. McNamara, followed the president's instructions and came up with the surprising findings that there was no missile gap in the Soviet favor. The United States possessed strategic military capability twice that of the Soviet Union. It was only in the numbers of the mix, specifically in ICBMs, that the Soviets held a lead, and it was a narrow one at that. Technically, the gap was meaningless. The real issue, as McNamara put it, was the "destruction gap," the differences in the respective nations' ability to inflict greater damage on the other. In this the United States held a commanding lead in long-range bombers at a time when the Polaris intermediate-range missile and the Minuteman intercontinental ballistic missile programs had been placed on an accelerated production schedule.[24] It appeared that Khruschev's reckless boasting had sparked a new arms race that counteracted whatever gains might have been made in banning nuclear tests.

The increased flow of the administration's adrenalin that followed Sputnik inevitable produced unanticipated side effects. The assumption that hyperactivity in defense of the alliance—increased spending on ICBMs, deployment of IRBMs and nuclear stockpiles in Europe, moratorium in nuclear testing—would invigorate the alliance and revive confidence in American leadership was not warranted. From the United States itself came unmistakable signs of discontent over the sharing of defense burdens. At a meeting with General Paul-Henri Spaak in October 1957, Secretary of State Rusk explained that the U.S. proportionate share of NATO forces was increasing, and this trend had to stop.[25]

From the European side came a counterpart complaint: namely, that the United States had undercut its profession of support by reducing its troop strength in Europe. Germans expressed concern just a few days after the appearance of Sputnik that Americans intended to reduce its forces in that country under the ambiguous concept of "Streamlining." Similarly, the Dutch journal *Het Vaderland* expressed dismay over Secretary Dulles's use of "partial" disassociation from these defense rumors which sent out alarm bells even before October 4. To the French ambassador in Washington in 1957, Deputy Secretary of Defense Donald Quarles had dismissed any idea of U.S. withdrawal, but he did admit "some downward adjustment."[26] In the Kennedy administration the vague warnings of reductions in U.S. forces became reality under McNamara's cost-conscious rationalizations of his Defense budgets.

Americans were sending conflicting signals in the wake of Sputnik. On the one hand, the major thrust of policy was to show full support of Europe despite the new vulnerability of America to missile attack. The promotion of coordinated production of weapons, the willingness to build nuclear stockpiles in Europe, and the offer of Jupiter intermediate-range missiles to NATO allies were earnests of this intention. But it could not escape the notice of European members that there were significant strings to these commitments. The Joint Chiefs of Staff made it clear that in giving American know-how and hardware they would not include nuclear warheads in the package. These would remain in American hands. The JCS, among others in the administration, were concerned that IRBMs under allied control might lead to a dangerous nuclear proliferation. Although American caveats were understandable, the response of the major European allies in seeking their own national nuclear defense capability was equally understandable.

The end result of American efforts to reassure their partners led to more tension and less confidence than in the past. In the early Kennedy years, France, distressed over American obstacles to its force de frappe, Britain, upset over America's abrupt cancellation of the Skybolt in 1962—an air-to-surface missile intended to serve its bomber fleet—and Germany, anxious to win equality through some association with nuclear programs, each expressed dissatisfaction with American leadership. With varying degrees of enthusiasm, the United States turned to a potential panacea in the Multilateral Force (MLF), promoted by SACEUR Norstad as a means of making NATO into a fourth nuclear power, armed with IRBMs and enjoying an equality with the United States. The MLF never developed into this entity, but it represented for a time a solution to the troubled European-American relationship.

In retrospect, Sputnik energized the alliance and shattered American complacency. It also exacerbated fissures within NATO. But it did not lead to fundamental changes. These were not to be made until another decade had passed. If NATO survived into the Harmel era of detente, credit may be given to the crises initiated by the adversary—Berlin and Cuba, in particular—which periodically fostered a unity among the allies that would not have existed without the Soviet threat.

NOTES

1. *New York Herald Tribune*, 6 October 1957.
2. Ibid., 4 October 1957.
3. Ibid.
4. The President's News Conference of 9 October 1957, *Public Papers of the Presidents: Dwight D. Eisenhower*, pp. 720–21; statement by the president summarizing facts in the development of an earth satellite by the United States, 9 October 1957, ibid., p. 735.
5. *Washington Post and Times-Herald*, 10 October 1957.
6. See Robert E. Osgood, *NATO: The Entangling Alliance* (Chicago: University of Chicago Press), p. 174.
7. Annual Budget Message to the Congress, Fiscal Year 1959, 13 January 1958, *Public Papers of the Presidents: Dwight D. Eisenhower*, pp. 17–18.
8. Testimony of Nelson Rockefeller, at *Hearings* before Preparedness Investigating Subcommittee of Committee on Armed Services, U.S. Senate, 85 Cong., 1st and 2d sess., "Inquiry into Satellites and Missile Programs," 10 January 1958, p. 1008.
9. James M. Gavin, *War and Peace in the Space Age* (New York: Harper & Bros., 1959), pp. 15–16.
10. Maxwell Taylor, *The Uncertain Trumpet* (New York: Harper & Bros., 1960), pp. 53, 61–62.
11. Donald Quarles, Deputy Secretary of Defense, memorandum for Secretary of the Army, Secretary of the Air Force, 28 October 1957, "Production of Modern Weapons in Europe," 330–78–141, Box 2, RG 330, National Archives and Record Administration. Hereafter cited as NARA.
12. Secretary of News Conference of 29 October 1957, Department of State *Bulletin* 37 (18 November 1957): 786–87.
13. Memorandum of Discussion at the 339th Meeting of the National Security

Council, Washington, DC, 10 October 1957, *Foreign Relations of the United States*, United Nations and General International Matters, 11: 762.

14. Secretary of State's News Conference, 5 November 1957, Department of State *Bulletin* 37 (25 November 1957): 825; Secretary of State's News Conference, 19 November 1957, ibid., 37 (9 December 1957): 917. Frederick E. Nolting, Deputy Chief of U.S. Mission to NATO, memorandum to Benson Timmons, Director, Office of European Regional Affairs, 5 November 1957, RG 59, 740.5/11–557, Box 3147, NARA.

15. W. Randolph Burgess, "Preliminary United States Views and Proposals for the December NATO Meeting," 3 December 1957, 61 A1672, Box 8, RG 330, NARA.

16. Memorandum of meeting of Secretary of State and Secretary of Defense, White House, 22 November 1957, "IRBMs for NATO," 740.5/11–2257, Box 3148, NARA.

17. Burgess memorandum, 3 December 1957, op cit; text of North Atlantic Council communiqué, 19 December 1957, Department of State *Bulletin* 38 (6 January 1958): 12–15.

18. See Larry Loeb, "Jupiter Missiles in Europe: A Measure of Presidential Power," *World Affairs* 139 (Summer 1976): 28–29.

19. Robert A. Divine, *Eisenhower and the Cold War* (New York: Oxford University Press, 1981), pp. 126–28.

20. Quoted in Robert A. Divine, *Blowing in the Wind* (New York: Oxford University Press, 1978), p. 212.

21. "Chronology of a Two-Year Dispute 'Missile Gap,' " *New York Times*, 9 February 1961.

22. Ibid.

23. State of the Union Address, 30 January 1961, *Public Papers of the Presidents: John F. Kennedy, 1961*, p. 24.

24. McNamara testimony at military posture briefings, before House Armed Services Committee, 23 February 1961, 87 Cong., 1st sess., pp. 646–47.

25. Ambassador Randolph Burgess memorandum to Secretary of State, 28 October 1957, "U.S. Contribution to NATO," 740.5/10–2857, Box 3147, NARA.

26. American Embassy, Bonn, cable to Secretary of State, no. 620, 7 October 1957, 740–5/10–757, Box 3146, NARA; American Embassy, The Hague, no. 516, 13 September 1957, cable to Secretary of State, 740.5/9–2357, Box 3146; notes of conversation held by Deputy Secretary of Defense Quarles with French Ambassador to United States, 30 October 1957, 740.5/10–3057, Box 3146, NARA.

5
The Berlin Crisis, 1958–1962:
Views from the Pentagon

"The Berlin Crisis, 1958–1962: Views from the Pentagon," was delivered in Washington in March 1994 at a conference on military history and archives sponsored by the Office of the Secretary of Defense and the U.S. Army Center of Military History. It is a case study of Cold War history based primarily on records from military archives and was published as a chapter in William W. Epley, ed., International Cold War Military Records and History *(Washington, DC: Office of the Secretary of Defense, 1996), 65–86.*

Berlin served as a potential source of conflict between the United States and the Soviet Union in the first twenty-five years of the Cold War, but for almost a decade after the lifting of the Berlin blockade there was relative calm. During that brief period, the East Berlin uprising in 1953 or the admission of West Germany into NATO in 1955 might have sparked fire over the exposed Western position in West Berlin. But in none of the incipient crises did the Soviet Union specifically challenge Western rights in West Berlin or access routes to the city under the terms of the wartime agreements of 1945. In the absence of documentation, the historian can only speculate why the lull ended abruptly in 1958.

What is not speculative is the significant role the Department of Defense played in the unfolding of the crisis in the last years of the Eisenhower administration and the first years of the Kennedy administration. While the State Department had primary responsibility for negotiations over Soviet efforts to erode the Allied status in Berlin, it was the military on the scene and in the Pentagon who had to cope with military implications of Soviet initiatives. Although petty harassment in the form of delays and "administrative" difficulties had been periodically imposed on individual passengers traveling in Allied military convoys,[1] there had been no direct challenge until 10 November 1958 when Premier Nikita Khrushchev asserted that the Soviet Union would "hand over to the sovereign German Democratic Republic those functions in Berlin which are still wielded by Soviet agencies."[2] Two weeks later the warnings became explicit. On 27 November the Soviet Union issued an ultimatum calling for an end to Allied rights in West Berlin and the conversion of West Berlin into a "free city." The United States was given a grace period of six months to make the change. If this were not done, "the Soviet Union will then carry out the planned measures through an agreement with the GDR."[3]

The U.S. response was essentially worked out in a series of State-Defense discussions in January 1959 in which there was consensus over meeting a Soviet or East German challenge to surface access by military action on the ground rather than resorting to another airlift. American resolve was tested in the next month when Soviet military authorities at the western end of the autobahn demanded the right to board the trucks in a military convoy and inspect their contents. The convoy commander refused. The vehicles were kept impounded for two days until the convoy was finally released after a protest by the embassy in Moscow.[4] Three months later Khrushchev backed away from his ultimatum. The funeral of Secretary of State Dulles provided an occasion for the deadline to be overlooked.[5]

Troubles over Berlin, however, were not over. Khrushchev renewed his threat to sign a separate peace treaty with East Germany even as a new summit meeting was planned for the spring of 1960. And, after a brief show of conciliation before President Kennedy took office, he dispatched a harsh note to the Federal Republic on 17 February 1961, indicating that if the West did not participate in a peace treaty, the Soviet Union's signature "will also mean ending the occupation regime in West Berlin with all the attendant consequences."[6]

Within a week of the presidential inauguration the Joint Chiefs sent suggestions to the secretary of defense for measures requiring early implementation. The JCS in turn had been reacting to a letter from former Secretary of State Christian Herter delivered to them in October 1960.[7] They recommended holding exercises linked to access routes. On the same day General Lyman L. Lemnitzer, chairman of the JCS, referred to another memorandum from the acting secretary of defense on 29 October 1960, urging action on a checklist that could be put into effect immediately or used for future tripartite discussions. A major concern at this stage was to work out ways of maintaining Allied legal rights in Berlin "without unduly alarming the public." For the benefit of the new secretary of defense, Robert S. McNamara, Lemnitzer noted the efforts of the U.S. Coordinating Committee on Contingency Planning for Germany to have its working group come to grips with such matters as economic sanctions against East Germany or the Soviet Union.[8]

The JCS responded to both the State and Defense requests, even before the provocative Soviet note of 17 February 1961 reached them. As Assistant Secretary of Defense for International Security Affairs Paul Nitze reported to Secretary of State Dean Rusk on 10 February, the JCS had come up with a variety of countermeasures which stopped short of overt military action. Those chosen from the checklist included: (1) intensification of a public relations campaign to influence Allies as well as to present a show of U.S. determination; (2) identification of specific economic measures to be applied; (3) leaking the existence of tripartite military plans to conduct an exercise that could force open a blocked autobahn if necessary.[9]

These countermeasures were purposely intended to avoid provocation. Nitze felt that in the absence of a direct Soviet challenge to the Allied position in Berlin, it was useful to combine preparedness with caution. A careful mix was all the more important at a time when the Western Allies and the Soviets were assessing "the timber of our new Administration and to measure that assessment against the will and solidarity of the Allies." At the same time Nitze made it clear that the capability to respond quickly and effectively to any aggression would have to be "a prelude to any serious negotiations."[10]

The difficulties in Defense planning for Berlin contingencies were complicated by divisions among the Allies and within the Defense establishment itself. They surfaced in LIVE OAK, a tripartite (later quadripartite) military staff for Berlin contingency planning under the Supreme Allied Commander, Europe (SACEUR) General Lauris Norstad, where differences developed over the utility as well as the size of a probe along the autobahn to test Soviet intentions. The Europeans believed that no amount of conventionally armed ground forces would be sufficient to defeat a determined enemy. The Joint Chiefs agreed with these beliefs. Defense of the West, including Berlin, remained anchored to a low nuclear threshold. In contrast, McNamara and Nitze, joined by former Secretary of State Dean Acheson as unofficial presidential adviser, were convinced that strong conventional forces not only would contain an attack but also would deter a nuclear exchange.[11]

What was critical in the winter of 1961 was the administration's judgment about the activities which had taken place under Eisenhower before it arrived on the scene. The McNamara team had doubts about Norstad's and the Joint Chiefs' attitude toward the role of conventional forces in Europe. The JCS thinking hitherto had been that whatever took place on the conventional plane would quickly escalate to the nuclear, a conclusion shared by the Allies. The administration's reservations about Norstad and the JCS extended to all aspects of the machinery which the Eisenhower administration had assembled. The Kennedy White House did not dismantle the older organizations, such as the U.S. Coordinating Committee; it simply by-passed them. Ad hoc studies and special investigations under new advisers took their place, until the Berlin Task Force, headed by Nitze from Defense and Foy Kohler from State, was established in the summer of 1961. Planning for the defense of Berlin was fitted into a large framework of NATO policy planning, with the Assistant Secretary of Defense for International Security Affairs taking responsibility for a full-scale review of the situation in the spring of 1961.[12]

Soviet pressures over West Berlin gave a special urgency to Dean Acheson's review of the Atlantic Alliance as a whole. His Berlin report, presented informally in June 1961, was a logical supplement to his comprehensive NATO report. Acheson recommended military preparations that would carry conviction, which bluster about a nuclear strike would fail to achieve. As in his fuller NATO report, Acheson found the appropriate response to Soviet aggression in the application of conventional forces to the problem. If the Soviets attempted to exclude the Western allies from physical access to the city, he wanted a division-sized probe to raise the stakes of the crisis. If it also raised risks of a general war, the risk was worth taking if it inhibited further provocations. Acheson's findings supported the substance of the JCS recommendations, if not their reasoning.[13]

Whether or not the Acheson intentions were less rigid than their rhetoric, he opened a round of intense examination of the extent of American and NATO preparedness in the event of a renewed crisis over Berlin. Both Secretary of Defense McNamara and Presidential Assistant McGeorge Bundy dispatched urgent requests to the JCS about the state of countermeasures against aggressive actions by the Soviets. The Joint Chiefs responded before the end of April with a mixed report. On the positive side they found that U.S. contingency planning was proceeding in line with the checklist that had been agreed upon in the winter. They were less satisfied, however, with the readiness of the two partners in Berlin, particularly with respect to planning for a division-sized probe. The JCS felt that considerably more troops had to be in place in Europe before they would give an enemy pause, and that no probe should be attempted until that time. In specific response to Acheson's recommendations, which they found for the most part to be "a realistic analysis of a complex politico-military problem," they recommended putting off his division-sized probe to a later stage in the crisis. Since a smaller force conceivably could open the autobahn by itself, a larger force should be launched only if the battalion probe failed.[14]

The JCS response contained contradictions. On the one hand, the Chiefs seemed confident that a smaller probe could settle the issue militarily, or at least push it up to the political level. On the other hand, their assumptions continued to rest on an early resort to nuclear weapons inasmuch as no long-term defense of Berlin was possible. If this were the case, nuclear arms, not conventional forces, were the only answer, both as a deterrent to war and as a weapon of war.

It was this assumption, a legacy of the previous administration, that distressed the Defense Department in 1961. The JCS position turned on a rapid acceleration from conventional to nuclear response. This might have been reasonable in 1958, but, according to Nitze, it was not feasible three years later. Nitze hoped that the possibilities of a West German contribution joining those of the British and French, even if only on a bilateral basis, might be integrated into JCS thinking. The Acheson study suggested as much. In any event, in keeping with the spirit of the Kennedy administration, Nitze wanted the president to have more flexibility in decision-making.[15]

McNamara listened more closely to Acheson's and Nitze's views than to those of the Joint Chiefs. The idea of moving directly to nuclear war after only token ground action was repugnant to him on logical as well as moral grounds. Nor were the Chief's pessimistic judgment that East Germany alone could stop a Western drive of one or two divisions acceptable to him. But given the Delphic nature of the JCS advice the secretary's report to the president on 5 May 1961 was able to incorporate their support for an exploratory probe without accepting their doubts about the defensibility of Berlin or their excessive reliance upon the nuclear thinking of the Eisenhower era. To Nitze and Lemnitzer he recommended the raising of a "substantial coventional military force" before resorting to nuclear war.[16]

The Joint Chiefs immediately challenged the Secretary of Defense. They found many of his opinions unworkable, and told him so; "substantial military force" was too vague. The SACEUR agreed with the Chiefs. Norstad saw no virtue in a large probe that would not be found in a smaller probe if the objective was only to smoke out Soviet intentions. Should the East Germans and Soviets block access to Allied traffic, they could frustrate a probe of any size. Hence, "the greater the force used the greater the embarrassment which would result from failure."[17]

Norstad's pessimism may have been a consequence of his close association with the British and French. The meeting of the North Atlantic Council in Oslo in early May 1961 did not hold out any promise of firm collective action.[18] Key questions of what economic countermeasures the Allies might take in the event that access routes were blocked, or what steps would be taken to increase manpower in the event of a major crisis in Berlin, went unanswered. Because of this vacuum, Deputy Secretary of Defense Roswell Gilpatric asked the Chairman of the JCS to weigh the merits of unilateral action, and to give his office advice on temporary reinforcement of U.S. forces in Europe as a way of demonstrating to the Soviets the seriousness with which the United States regarded their threats. Gilpatric wanted to know specifically the implications of an air mobility exercise of two battle groups, of the movement of two Strategic Army Corps (STRAC) divisions, and of the call-up of one reserve division for active duty for two months.[19]

Khrushchev's aide-memoire of 4 June 1961, which followed his meeting with Kennedy in Vienna, added a sense of urgency to the JCS response. The Soviet premier claimed that whatever the United States and its allies might do, the Soviet Union would sign a treaty with East Germany before the end of the year.[20] The Chiefs delivered their answers on 6 June to Gilpatric's query about the availability of reinforcements. Provisional reliance would be placed on two STRAC airborne groups which, along with 224 aircraft, could be dispatched to major training areas in Germany within two to three weeks. If necessary, an additional STRAC unit could be sent on a crash basis within nine days. Their preferred solution was to extend the service by 30 to 60 days of one of the 27 National Guard divisions scheduled for training exercises in the summer of 1961. The desired end product of this mobilization procedure would be a presidential declaration of a national emergency and the call-up of more reserve troops as well as more National Guardsmen.[21]

This was also the direction in which Dean Acheson was moving. It was Acheson to whom the president turned in the disarray that followed the Vienna summit, since the acerbic statesman's reports on Berlin represented the only sustained methodical thinking about the problem that was then available. Kennedy appointed him on 16 June to keep special watch over the situation. Acheson's voice, augmented by such like-minded officials as Paul Nitze of OSD, Foy Kohler of State, and Walt Rostow of the White House staff, articulated coherent as well as definite points of view which were all too rare at this time in the Kennedy foreign policy establishment. Acheson's advice, submitted on 28 June, followed the Joint Chiefs' with respect to a declaration of national emergency. The Soviets had to be convinced, he claimed, that the United States would go to war in defense of Western interests in any part of Europe. By reducing the issue to simple terms, Acheson played a pivotal but not conclusive role in determining American policy on Berlin.[22]

Despite the advice of Acheson and the JCS the president decided against declaring a state of national emergency. Such an act could have too many negative repercussions, from soaring prices through panic buying to a violent Soviet reaction. Acheson strongly disagreed with this prognosis at the NSC meeting of 13 July. He asserted that if the president deferred calling up the reserves or postponed declaring a national emergency, the deterrent effect would be lost. Secretary of State Dean Rusk, however, convinced McNamara that an orderly and sustained buildup would be more likely to reassure allies and impress enemies than a full but hasty national mobilization.[23] The way was now open for the president to lay down a clear American position in his public address of 25 July, in which the initiative would be his, not Khrushchev's. Even though he refused to accept Acheson's advice on full mobilization, he did order steps to be taken which were just short of full-blown mobilization—increasing the number of draftees, extending the terms of military service, and recalling selected reserve units to active duty. To pay for these increases he asked for an additional $3.25 billion for the Defense budget.[24]

But how meaningful were these measures? Throughout the month of August the DoD provided only a limited implementation of the buildup. Reinforcements for Europe were only on a contingency basis. The assumption in the Pentagon was that the Soviets would undertake no serious actions until after September, and possibly not until the end of the year. Deployment of the six divisions publicized in the president's address would not be in place until 1 January 1962.[25]

In retrospect, the message may have raised rather than lowered tensions. As the Congress proceeded to act on the proposals, McNamara underscored the uncertainties of the time by informing the House Committee on Armed Services that, "because we cannot foresee with certainty how events may develop over the coming months, we cannot say at this time whether the strength increases we now propose will necessarily be permanent."[26] These uncertainties were compounded by European uneasiness over the dispatch of troops, many or few. The Allies emphasized the debilitating vulnerability of conventional forces, whatever their numbers, in the face of the Warsaw Pact's overwhelming superiority in manpower and weaponry. Only the threat of a nuclear response could deter the enemy from denying the West access to Berlin.[27] Administration planners saw the situation differently. They believed that increased conventional forces would encourage flexibility, allowing the Soviets to return to the status quo before the conflict escalated to a degree that neither side wanted. Kohler and Nitze labored to make this point stick with the working group.[28]

Conflict between the approaches of the OSD and NATO became evident in the North Atlantic Council's reactions to the administration's initiatives. Here the issue was not just over the nature of the deterrent; it was over the lack of communication between the Berlin planners and the Council. Secretary-General Dirk Stikker complained to Norstad about the failure of the tripartite group to keep him informed of its preparations for a crisis over Berlin. He felt it to be important that the contingency measures be considered an "all-NATO exercise."[29]

The secretary-general found a sympathetic audience in Dean Rusk who suggested on 8 August that the military contingency group coordinate its plans with NATO as a whole. At the very least, the U.S. military representative to the Council should be kept "systematically informed of Berlin planning in all its aspects." General Clark Ruffner, the military representative, noted that no procedures had been established to make these connections up to that time.[30]

The explanation for this dysfunction was clear enough on the surface. While the tripartite force in Berlin was under the NATO rubric, NATO's authority did not encompass the tripartite powers' right of access to Berlin. For this reason LIVE OAK planning functioned outside the organization, even though General Norstad as LIVE OAK commander employed some of his SHAPE staff, and in an emergency would also use NATO's communications to "visualize realistically the execution of any Berlin contingency plan in isolation from NATO."[31]

It was in this environment of Western confusion that Khrushchev and his East German surrogates acted. Some 30,000 East Germans had fled to the West in July, and another 20,000 left in the first twelve days of August. Citing a Warsaw Pact declaration of 6 August, the GDR leader, Walter Ulbricht, blamed West German provocateurs for the exodus, and then set in motion new border controls. The "Wall" itself was first a string of cement blocks built into a wall on the Potsdamer Platz after pavement and street car tracks were torn up. It was not extended until 18 August. The Wall took its final form on 19 August.[32]

The Wall was a "complete tactical surprise," as John Ausland of the Berlin Task Force noted.[33] It could not have been better timed. Western leaders for the most part were away from their offices—Kennedy at his summer White House in Hyannisport, Macmillan on vacation in Scotland, and French officialdom presumably at the Riviera. It was August, after all. Although Ulbricht had talked about a "wall" prior to 13 August, its actual construction had not been anticipated. All the scenarios created by American planners centered on a crisis growing out of a Soviet peace treaty with East Germany, and the consequent interference with Western access to West Berlin. Problems of East Berlin, on the other hand, evoked either a hesitant reaction, or none at all. For over a decade the three powers in Berlin—the United States, the United Kingdom, and France—had accepted the erosion of their legal position in East Berlin largely because they had no means of effecting meaningful implementation of the original quadripartite agreement. In this context the building of the Wall was beyond the control of the West, another step in the incorporation of East Berlin into the GDR. But it did not affect the Western presence in West Berlin.

Initially, there was as much relief as apprehension in the U.S. and Allied response to the Soviet/East German action. Western observers had been increasingly worried over the impact of the refugee flow on the health of the GDR; the Wall at least staunched this flow of population from East to West. It appeared to be a preemptive effort to prevent a dangerous East German insurrection as its economy withered. There was certainly a sense of relief in Secretary Rusk's public statement on 13 August: "Available information indicates that measures taken so far are aimed at residents of East Berlin and East Germany and not at the allied position or access thereto." His additional comments to the effect that limitations on travel in Berlin violated the status quo were little more than a formality.[34]

Nevertheless, there was also apprehension over the deterioration of morale in West Berlin and in West Germany over what seemed to be a passive response on the part of the three occupying powers. The best that the Allies could come up with in the immediate aftermath was to impose restrictions on East Germans traveling to NATO countries. The Berlin Task Force was equally cautious. It recommended that military preparations be accelerated but not too dramatically. Its members feared that ostentatious reinforcement of the Berlin garrison would only underscore the Allied inability to defend the city. From his perspective as Chairman of the JCS, Lemnitzer observed that "everyone appeared to be hopeless, helpless, and harmless."[35]

OSD's position was similar to State's. McNamara had publicized his thoughts on Berlin two weeks before the Wall went up. He recognized that Khrushchev's recent stance "showed a marked change and a much firmer line than existed" in 1958. At the same time he cautioned against a panicky buildup in response to this change: "We should not rush to increase our forces and then rush to tear them down." The peaks and valleys of an adversarial relationship, he believed, should not deter the DoD from a steady course of planning.[36]

The Wall changed neither McNamara's rhetoric nor his reasoning, at least not immediately. On 14 August he told an interviewer that "we have two purposes in mind in connection with this build-up. The first is a clear demonstration—demonstration beyond misunderstanding—of the Western determination to defend freedom in Berlin and to defend the allied rights in Berlin. Our second purpose, associated with the first objective, is to build up military power, to provide a more effective deterrent, as to insure an increased capability for military action in the event the deterrent fails."[37]

While there was an admirable consistency in this reiteration of policy, it hardly seemed responsive to the crisis at hand. McNamara admitted that "the recent move to blockade East Berliners, of course, was a move by the Soviet Union and/or its East German satellite and certainly is unrelated to any action we have taken. It does, of course, violate the treaties which we are parties to and I understand that a strong protest therefore will be submitted against the action that has been taken."[38] If there was no complacency in his language, there was also little recognition that the actions of the Warsaw bloc could affect the timetable of the DoD's military preparations.

It was only after Berliners themselves, notably Mayor Willy Brandt, had demanded stronger protests that the United States was jarred from its relative calm. Brandt released an unsettling letter that he had sent to President Kennedy in which he demanded among other things immediate dispatch of troops to Berlin as a guarantee of continuing intention to remain in the city.[39] It resulted in the sending of two high-level figures to Berlin to buck up morale—Vice President Lyndon Johnson and General Lucius Clay. Johnson bestowed the blessings while Clay symbolized the spirit of 1948 when he commanded the forces that maintained the Berlin airlift. Johnson turned in a virtuoso performance invoking the Declaration of Independence to assure Berliners that Americans had pledged their "lives, fortunes, and sacred honor" to their survival.[40] But it was Clay who made the difference.

The presence of two leading Americans did calm German fears, at least for the moment. Clay turned out to be such a source of inspiration that the president considered making him the U.S. military commander in Berlin. That he did not pursue this approach was because of the strain that McNamara and Lemnitzer anticipated would be placed on relations with the command structure already on the scene. Instead, they recommended that he be called chief of mission with the rank of ambassador, thereby relieving ambassador Walter Dowling of additional duties. Major General Albert Watson, the U.S. Commandant in Berlin, was also deputy chief of mission, and so could report to Clay without disrupting command channels. On 30 August the president appointed Clay as his personal representative in Berlin.[41]

The significance of the general's role in Berlin did not go unrecognized in Moscow. Khrushchev claimed that he picked Marshal Ivan Konev to be the Soviet commander in Berlin as his direct response to the Clay appointment. He made it clear that it was a political gesture by observing that Konev spent most of his time in Moscow.[42]

The dispatch of a Seventh Army battle group of 1500 men to Berlin on 20 August was another effort to impress the Warsaw bloc and the West Berliners alike with the seriousness of American support of the integrity of the city. The column proceeded across the autobahn unchallenged. This action could be interpreted as a successful riposte, even if belated, to the construction of the Wall. Its success demonstrated, as William Kaufmann noted, that the Soviets "were not all that interested in a showdown." There was no question that the 1st Battle Group, 18th Infantry Regiment, entered Berlin in triumph. Vice President Johnson personally greeted the troops when they arrived, signaling, as Arthur Schlesinger, Jr., asserted, a turning point in West Berlin's crisis of confidence.[43]

But the convoy also conveyed a different message. Its commander unwittingly set a precedent that the Soviets were able to exploit in the future against subsequent troop movements from West Germany to West Berlin. As the convoy arrived at the Soviet checkpoint on the approach to the city shortly after dawn 20 August, a Soviet officer had some difficulty in counting the number of soldiers on the trucks. The U.S. officer in charge then ordered the troops to dismount to expedite the processing of the tired men. While counting was an established and accepted practice, the emptying of trucks for counting on the ground was not. In future challenges the Soviets were able to use this precedent to demand dismounting on a regular basis. The incident showed just how vulnerable the tripartite powers were to interference with their supplies and communications to Berlin.[44]

Despite the momentary lift of morale following the combination of highly visible troops and high-level Americans on the scene, there was no evidence that the Soviets were intimidated, or even impressed, by these actions. Rather, their behavior seemed to suggest that they were advancing rather than retreating after 13 August. The Wall had been extended and reinforced. On 23 August new regulations curtailed movements of West Berliners into the East; special authorization was hereafter required. No Western outcry followed this change.

Nor was there significant reaction to the ending of the quadripartite status of East Berlin. The Soviets hardened the symbol of the Wall by terminating the surviving occupation agencies in East Berlin. While they did not stop Western patrols from entering East Berlin, at least in principle, they progressively reduced the number of entry places to one—Checkpoint Charlie at Friedrichstrasse. And even this concession probably would not have been tolerated had the Soviets not wanted reciprocity in West Berlin, particularly their access to the Red Army war memorial. Before the year ended the U.S. commandant had denied himself entry into East Berlin after GDR officials insisted on processing documents of American diplomatic personnel entering the East. This self-denial severed formal relations among the four-power commandants. It seemed to be only a matter of time before East Germany would take control of Western access to West Berlin itself.[45]

The president was painfully aware of the situation the Wall had created. He goaded the secretaries of state and defense to accelerate their political and military preparations for countering the new challenges from the East. Nitze agreed by the end of August on the need for a "fundamental reappraisal" of the July decision for "restrained, gradual, military strengthening" of the U.S. position in Berlin.[46] Programs had been proceeding too gradually, their contents too restrained. McNamara had already acted. On 18 August he had asked the services what they could do to advance the readiness date from 1 January 1962 to 15 November 1961. The Secretary of Defense now realized, as he had not four days before, that the deployment of six additional divisions to Europe "at any time after 1 January 1962" was too leisurely a pace.[47] The Joint Chiefs recognized in their telegram to Norstad on 25 August that the "U.S. right of access to West Berlin from FRG is of such importance as to require, if necessary, the use of force entailing combat." By contrast, they were willing to consider the U.S. right of access to East Berlin to be satisfied "as long as one entry point is available for the unimpeded movement of allied personnel."[48]

It was in the context of a perceived emergency over Berlin that the OSD was to play a major role on the Berlin Task Force, with Nitze as an equal partner of Kohler. Such deference to Defense contributions was appropriate in light of the increasing significance of U.S. troops confronting the Soviets in Berlin. As much as any action, McNamara's decision on 18 September, supported by the JCS, revealed that the Berlin Task Force was in full motion.[49]

It was at McNamara's advice that the president moved to strengthen U.S. forces in Berlin on a crash basis, not with the six divisions Lemnitzer and Army Chief of Staff General George Decker would have preferred, but with the deployment of 73,000 reservists, along with one regular division. The risks were recognized. Even six divisions might not be enough to cope with a major Soviet attack, but might be more than enough to trigger a nuclear war. But risks had to be taken. "While a conventional build-up alone," McNamara advised, "would be unlikely to convince Khrushchev, the absence of a build-up would probably increase his doubts of our determination."[50]

This decision accelerated a process that had been underway since the spring: namely, a continuing search for "options," as Deputy Assistant Secretary of Defense (International Security Affairs) Henry Rowen put it, in response to a wide variety of Soviet actions.[51] The term "horse blanket" has been applied to the list of scenarios the West could conjure up, with Nitze of Defense and Seymour Weiss of State as the two principals charged with stuffing as many potential reactions to Soviet provocations as possible under the horse blanket. By the end of September the horse blanket had been reduced to a "poodle blanket" under which fewer but not lesser options were placed. There were four in all, ranging from probes of platoon strength on the ground as the first stage to embargo and troop mobilization as the second, to naval blockade and non-nuclear ground advance into GDR territory as the third. Lastly, if none of these efforts led to the cessation of Soviet provocations, nuclear weapons would be deployed, beginning with selective attacks for purposes of demonstration, and proceeding through tactical weapons to a general nuclear war. The final phase in the poodle blanket sounded an apocalyptic note.[52]

The administration was ready in mid-October to act on Defense recommendations. The president gave approval on 18 October for the U.S. commandant in Berlin to send up a few tanks to the checkpoint to demolish an illegal barrier. The plan then would have the tanks withdrawn from the border and stationed just inside the Allies' sector. This aggressive posture was the result of an agreement by State and Defense, with the JCS concurrence, on policy guidance for General Norstad wherein the president specifically endorsed the poodle blanket proposals. The president intended to place the United States "in position to undertake a series of graduated responses to Soviet/GDR actions in denial of our rights of access." In a cautionary addendum he mentioned that he wished to "avoid on the one hand delay that would damage the Western position and on the other an over-hasty reaction, before our forces are ready, which would sharply increase the probability of nuclear war." A second admonition was contained in his emphasis on developing the capacity to fight with non-nuclear forces. The poodle blanket plans received NSC approval when NSAM 109 was promulgated on 23 October 1961.[53]

As these plans were being formulated there was a general assumption that there would be British and French support for the American initiatives. This was not forthcoming.[54] Allied discomfort over American impulsiveness added to General Norstad's restiveness over policies flowing from Washington. He foresaw the Soviets playing one ally off against another as they exposed the weaknesses of each. As the man in the middle, Norstad was worried about his responsibilities not only as USCINCEUR and SACEUR but also as agent of the tripartite powers in LIVE OAK. He was unsure when he could act independently without excessive and time-consuming consultation with his superiors. To visiting representatives of State and Defense he unburdened himself in late September about the "inadequacies, almost the dangerous inadequacies, of the strategic concept employed in the LIVE OAK directive." He doubted NATO's willingness to use nuclear weapons *"under any contingency."*[55]

Norstad had reason for concern. Even in OSD, which should have been the strongest advocate for granting him maximum authority, there was hesitation. Nitze for a time in September seemed to waffle over rules of engagement that would authorize him to attack ground targets in the "Berlin air corridor without the approval of NATO's Defense Committee." Lemnitzer eventually convinced Nitze to accept this position on this issue.[56] But in general there was no consistent policy to guide the SACEUR beneath the level of full-scale conflict. On such an important matter as military planning in the event of an East German uprising the Secretary of Defense was unable to win agreement from the British on anticipating a decision to intervene. Such action, according to the British ally, should not be subject to determination prior to the event. While McNamara was sympathetic to Norstad's plight, he was forced to settle for "expeditious" Allied approval of plans for assuring access to Berlin.[57]

U.S. planners had to repress their frustrations in public, but behind the closed doors at White House and NSC meetings they were fully vented. When the president asked on 20 October what to do about the negative reactions of the Allies, Acheson responded: "We should make up our own minds and then *tell* heads of state what they should do. We have coordinated at the ambassadorial level long enough. Hang on. Ambassadors go to heads of state, and let them know what we propose to do."[58] This seemed to be one time that Acheson's hard line had the full backing of his colleagues. But this shared sentiment had to remain *in camera*.

While the hesitations of the Allies may have complicated, they did not prevent the United States from substantially increasing its forces in Europe. The addition of 37,000 personnel to the Seventh Army, combined with the announcement in September that 40,000 troops were enroute to Europe, may have been responsible for Khrushchev's backing away from his intention to sign a peace treaty with East Germany before the end of the year.[59]

This show of resolve should have made an impression on Khrushchev. It certainly impressed the White House sufficiently to take up negotiations with the Soviets from an assumed situation of strength. The president announced on 13 September, one month after the erection of the Wall, that he would agree to Secretary Rusk's talking with Soviet Foreign Minister Andrei Gromyko at the forthcoming meeting of the U.N. General Assembly. The initiative, however, appeared to be more Khrushchev's than Kennedy's. Through the medium of Cyrus L. Sulzberger of the *New York Times*, the Soviet leader opened personal communications with the president. In the event that his informal message miscarried, Khrushchev used his press representative in Washington to have Press Secretary Pierre Salinger transmit the message directly to Kennedy. And on 29 September he wrote a personal note to the president from his Black Sea villa.[60]

The Gromyko–Rusk talks afforded Khrushchev another opportunity to scrap his timetable for a separate treaty. He could claim that Gromyko's efforts in New York and Washington "left us with the impression that the Western powers were showing a certain understanding of the situation and they were disposed to seek a settlement of the German problem and the question of Berlin on a mutually acceptable basis." Consequently, he was ready to concede that "we shall not . . . absolutely insist on signing the peace treaty before 1 December 1961." Such was the Soviet decision on 17 October 1961, the first day of the 22nd Party Congress.[61]

Whatever the reason for his postponement of the deadline, the act was followed almost immediately by the most serious confrontation between the Soviets and the Americans in Berlin since the Berlin blockade of 1948. It was not as dramatic as the Wall but it was potentially more explosive. On 27 and 28 October, at Checkpoint Charlie separating East from West Berlin, American tanks faced Soviet tanks. Whether this was another episode in the Soviet campaign against Allied positions in West Berlin or an aberration from the more conciliatory line implied in the Pen Pal exchanges and in Khrushchev's pronouncement at the Communist party Congress is still open to debate. The confrontation may have been a reaction to what the Soviets interpreted as U.S. provocations, such as the behavior of General Clay, the president's special representative in Berlin.[62]

Clay arrived on 19 September and immediately—and ostentatiously—increased patrols on the autobahn. His aggressiveness was not only a personal gesture on behalf of worried West Berliners but also a rebuke to the cautiousness of the White House's management of the Berlin crisis. Clay's status made an intricate command relationship in Germany even more convoluted. Major General Albert Watson was the senior American officer, the commandant in Berlin, who reported in his political capacity to Ambassador Walter Dowling in Bonn and in his military role to USCINCEUR in Paris through General Bruce Clarke, commander of the U.S. Army, Europe, in Heidelberg. Additionally, there was a State Department mission in Berlin headed by Allan Lightner, who reported both to Dowling and Watson as well as directly to Washington.[63]

It was Lightner who unwittingly precipitated the crisis. He and his wife were en route to the opera in East Berlin on the evening of 22 October when he was stopped at the Friedrichstrasse checkpoint and asked to show identification. Up to this time civilian license tags were sufficient to permit passage. The U.S. position was that the ceremony of requiring a civilian official to identify himself to a GDR officer was an effort to erode the right of the occupying power to travel anywhere in Berlin. When East German guards stopped him a second time, a squad of U.S. military policy with loaded rifles escorted his car into East Berlin. After driving a block he returned to the West and then repeated the routing, driving a mile into East Berlin before turning back.[64]

On the following day GDR leader Walter Ulbricht issued a decree requiring Allied civilians to identify themselves before entering East Berlin. Two days later U.S. armed patrols again accompanied civilian officials across the line. To point attention to the significance he attached to the issue, Clay asked Watson to deploy tanks at Checkpoint Charlie, in accordance with Poodle Blanket recommendations. This action alarmed the British, who had never objected to showing their passports when asked. They were all the more alarmed when Marshal Ivan Konev, Clay's Soviet counterpart, sent his own tanks into the city. This challenge induced Clay to move U.S. tanks to the demarcation line. Six Soviet tanks were deployed just 100 yards away.[65]

The next stage might have been a shootout between the opposing sides. It did not take place. Khrushchev ordered his tanks to pull back sixteen hours after they had been moved up to the line. In his memoirs he claimed a victory in thwarting American tanks from bulldozing border installations.[66]

Khrushchev may have been mistaken about American objectives in the confrontation at Checkpoint Charlie, but he had some grounds for judging the outcome to be a Soviet triumph. Over the next few years the challenge to the West over GDR frontier controls as well as to the use of air corridors to Berlin continued, although on a less dramatic scale.[67] On an even larger canvas the Wall symbolized the achievement of an important objective: namely, the stabilization of East Germany by stopping the flow of manpower from East to West.

Yet there was a price that the East bloc had to pay for contesting the West's presence in Berlin. The tripartite powers did not budge from their position in West Berlin, or in their demand for access to the city. This was the critical issue that kept the crisis over Berlin from becoming a zero-sum game. Neither side was willing to go to war over the city in 1961. Both Clay and Konev were subsequently recalled. And while the end of this confrontation did not inhibit further Soviet harassment over the next two and a half years, the Soviets were unable to force the United States to accept East German control over access to Berlin before a treaty was signed.

When the treaty was finally concluded in June 1964, it implicitly accepted a "status quo ante bellum" over the Western position in Berlin. After six years of tension over Berlin the treaty was an anticlimax. What counted was left unsaid. Beneath the rhetoric of traditional statements of friendship and collaboration was the omission of any reference to Allied troops in West Berlin or to their right of access to the city. The only reference to West Berlin was a brief article which stated that "The high contracting parties will regard West Berlin as an independent entity." By their silence the Soviets gave up their demands.[68]

The secretary of defense's ability to fashion a policy during the extended crisis was always complicated by the difficulties in reaching consensus within the department. In Europe, Norstad, understandably sensitive to the concerns of the Allies, had continuing doubts about the utility of probes. In the Pentagon the Joint Chiefs were more supportive of these efforts, but they shared with Norstad and the Europeans fundamental suspicions about the doctrine of flexible response which McNamara's and Nitze's emphasis upon conventional forces underscored. Outside the department, McNamara had to cope with pressures from White House agents, Acheson and Clay, who would have used conventional forces more aggressively than the Defense establishment wanted. On balance the most effective contribution to McNamara's policies in the Berlin crisis was made by the Office of International Security Affairs under Paul Nitze.

On another level the Berlin crisis placed the Pentagon on center stage in shaping American foreign policy. While Defense was nominally a junior partner in the process, the nature of the Berlin crisis broadened McNamara's role in the Kennedy administration. This was reflected in dramatic increases in defense funding in the third amended budget of fiscal year 1961, in the enlargement of conventional forces, and in plans to reform the reserves system. Defense emerged from the Berlin crisis with new authority as a participant in the management of national security issues.

BIBLIOGRAPHICAL NOTE

The author gratefully acknowledges the assistance of Robert J. Watson, who provided information regarding the Berlin crisis, 1958–60, from his book *Into the Missile Age*—volume IV in the series *History of the Office of the Secretary of Defense.*

U.S. military records for this period are abundant, although many of them remain classified. The major source of information on the Berlin crisis derives from records of the Assistant Secretary of Defense for International

Security Affairs, Federal Records Center Accession 64A2382, in Record Group 330, Washington National Records Center (WNRC), Suitland, Maryland. The Joint Master Files of the Joint Chiefs of Staff and the records in the Office of the Chairman, JCS, located in the Pentagon, offer the important perspective of the Joint Chiefs. The third member of the Pentagon triad was General Norstad, both in his capacity as CINCEUCOM and SACEUR. The NATO records at SHAPE are closed, but the studies of the SHAPE historian on the workings of LIVE OAK and of Norstad's role in the crisis provide insights into the richness of the records, as do the volumes of Kenneth W. Condit and Walter S. Poole in the official history of the JCS, prepared by the Historical Division of the Joint Secretariat.

A large collection of Secretary McNamara's papers (formerly Federal Records Center Accession 71A4470) have recently been transferred from the Washington National Records Center to the National Archives in Washington and are now part of Record Group 200. Research for this paper was done when the collection was housed at the WNRC.

The papers of Generals Lyman L. Lemnitzer as JCS Chairman and Maxwell Taylor as military adviser to the President are in the National Defense University Library. Oral histories of McNamara, Lemnitzer, and Paul Nitze are kept in the OSD Historical Office.

John Ausland, a State Department representative on the Berlin Task Force, has written a memoir, *Kennedy, Khrushchev, and Berlin-Cuba Crisis, 1961–1964*. Special studies sponsored by the DoD have been prepared by P. H. Johnstone, "Military Policy Making During the Berlin Crisis of 1958–62," Institute for Defense Analysis Report R–138, under contract with the Weapons Systems Evaluation Group; and by Robert E. Coakley et al., "U.S. Army Expansion and Readiness, 1961–1962," Part 1, Office of the Chief of Military History, United States Army. The Historical Office, Department of State, prepared Research Project No. 614–E (February 1970), "Crisis Over Berlin: American Policy Concerning the Soviet Threats to Berlin, November 1958–December 1962."

NOTES

1. JCS Historical Office, "The Joint Chiefs of Staff and National Policy, 1957–1960," *The History of the Joint Chiefs of Staff*, vol. VII, pp. 493–95, 499–500, cited in Robert J. Watson, *Into the Missile Age, 1956–1960*, vol. IV in *History of the Office of the Secretary of Defense* (Washington, DC, 1997), p. 97.

2. Extract from Khrushchev address on Berlin, 10 November 1958, in Department of State, *Documents on Germany, 1944–1970* Department of State Publication 9446 (Washington: U.S. Government Printing Office, 1985), p. 545.

3. Note from the Soviet Union to the United States regarding the state of Berlin and Potsdam agreements, 27 November 1958, ibid., p. 559.

4. Nitze letter to John Ausland, 24 April 1974, Nitze Papers, Library of Congress, noted that an airlift could be interfered with. But the main reason for re-

moving that option was the need "to impress upon the Soviets that we had a *right* to be in Berlin and that we would go to extreme lengths to protect our rights." See also Watson, p. 18.

5. C. L. Sulzberger, "The Double Funeral at Arlington," *New York Times*, 27 May 1959.

6. Aide-Memoire from the Soviet Union to the Federal Republic of Germany, 17 February 1961, *Documents on Germany*, p. 726.

7. P. H. Johnstone, "Military Planning during the Berlin Crisis of 1961–1962," Institute for Defense Analyses, Vol. I, 1968. Report R–138, prepared under contract with Weapons Systems Evaluation Group as WSEG C. 11, Study No. 6, Parts II and III, pp. 149–50. Hereafter cited as IDA Report, II or III.

8. Lemnitzer memorandum for the Secretary of Defense, 26 January 1961, Subj: Berlin Countermeasures, Germany 381 1960, Box 20, Files of the Office of the Secretary of Defense, FRC 64B2093, RG 330, Washington National Records Center.

9. Nitze memorandum for Secretary of State, 10 February 1961, ibid.

10. Ibid.

11. Lemnitzer memorandum for the Secretary of Defense, 12 July 1961, Subj: Partial Mobilization, Germany 092 1961 July, Box 51, Files of the Office of the Assistant Secretary of Defense (International Security Affairs), FRC 64A2382, Washington national Records Center; McNamara memorandum for Chairman, JCS, 9 August 1961, Subj: Planning for NATO Military Operations, ibid.; Nitze letter to John Ausland, 24 April 1974, a commentary on Norstad's views, in Nitze Papers.

12. IDA Report, II, pp. 145–46; David A. Rosenberg, "The Impact of the Berlin Crisis of 1958–1962 on American Nuclear Strategy," DACS Seminar, Center for International Studies, MIT, 24 February 1993, identified the Office of the Assistant Secretary of Defense (International Affairs) as "the focal point of Berlin Crisis planning in the Kennedy administration."

13. Walter S. Poole, "The Joint Chiefs of Staff and National Policy, 1961–1964," *The History of the Joint Chiefs of Staff*, vol. VIII, Part II, p. 147 (hereafter cited as JCS History); Dean Acheson, "A Review of North Atlantic Problems for the Future," March 1961, Box 220, National Security File, John F. Kennedy Library; Acheson memorandum for the president, 3 April 1961, *Declassified Documents* Collection, 1985, item 2547; Marc Trachtenberg, *History and Strategy* (Princeton University Press, 1991), p. 21 7, fn. 175, cites an unpublished paper in the Acheson files by Thomas Schelling, entitled "On the Problem of NATO's Nuclear Strategy," dated 7 March 1961, which Acheson kept while working on NATO policies.

14. IDA Report, II. p. 172; JCS History, pp. 149–51; Lemnitzer memorandum for the Secretary of Defense, 3 April 1961, Subj: The Status of Berlin Contingency Planning, with Appendix on type and scope of U.S. unilateral and tripartite Berlin contingency plans, 310.1 (Project 87), 2/81–15–2–1, Box 51, FRC 64A2382; William Bundy memorandum for the Secretary of Defense, 21 April 1961, Subj: The Status of Berlin Contingency Plans, 092 Germany (Berlin), January–May 1961, Box 51, FRC 64A2382; Arleigh Burke for JCS, memorandum for the Secretary of Defense, 28 April 1961, Subj: Berlin, 092 Germany (Berlin), January–May 1961, Box 51, FRC 64A2382.

15. IDA Report, II, p. 173.

16. McNamara memorandum for the President, 5 May 1961, Subj: Military Planning for a Possible Berlin Crisis, *Foreign Relations of the United States, 1961–1963*, (Washington: U.S. Government Printing Office, 1994), XIV:61–63. Hereafter cited as *FRUS*. McNamara memorandum for Chairman, JCS, 19 May 1961, Subj: Berlin Contingency Planning, 092 Germany (Berlin), January–May 1961, Box 51, FRC 64A2382; McNamara memorandum for Assistant Secretary of Defense (International Security Affairs), 19 May 1961, Sub: Berlin: ibid.

17. LeMay (for JCS) memorandum for the Secretary of Defense, 25 May 1961, Subj: Berlin, 092 Germany (Berlin), ibid.

18. P. E. Barringer (Acting Director, European Region, ISA) memorandum for Nitze, 29 May 1961, Subj: Policy Guidance for NATO Defense Planning, 334, NATO, May 16–31, Box 17, FRC 64A2382.

19. IDA Report, II, pp. 187–88.

20. Aide Memoire from the Soviet Union to the United States on the German Question, Vienna, 4 June 1961, *Documents on Germany*, p. 732; memorandum by Akalovsky (D/P) of conversation—the President, Khrushchev, Gromyko et al, 4 June 1961, in Research Project No. 614–E (February 1970), "Crisis Over Berlin, American Policy Concerning the Soviet Threats to Berlin, November 1958–December 1962," Historical Office, Bureau of Public Affairs, Department of State, V:4.

21. IDA Report II, pp. 203–5.

22. Report by Dean Acheson, *FRUS*, pp. 138ff; memorandum of discussion at NSC meeting, 29 June 1961, ibid., pp. 160–62; IDA Report, II, p. 221.

23. Arthur Schlesinger, Jr., *A Thousand Days: John F. Kennedy in the White House* (Boston: Houghton Mifflin Co., 1965), pp. 389–90; McNamara memorandum for Chairman, JCS, 14 July 1961, Box 54, McNamara Papers, Washington National Records Center. McNamara asked for a timetable for deploying reinforcements to Berlin if a national emergency was not in effect.

24. Radio and Television Report to the American People on the Berlin Crisis, 25 July 1961, in *Public Papers of the Presidents, John F. Kennedy, 1961* (Washington: U.S. Government Printing Office, 1962), p. 534; JCS History, pp. 177–79; Robert T. Coakley et al., "U.S. Army Expansion and Readiness 1961–1962," Part 1, Chapter II, p. 4.

25. Bundy, National Security Memorandum No. 62, 24 July 1961, to Secretary of State, Secretary of the Treasury, Secretary of Defense, Attorney General, Director, Bureau of the Budget, Director of Central Intelligence, Director, U.S. Information Agency, *FRUS*, pp. 225–26, noted that the six divisions and supporting air units would be in Europe "any time after January 1, 1961"; IDA Report, III, pp. 134–35.

26. Vladislav M Zubok, "Khrushchev and the Berlin Crisis (1958–1962)," Working Paper No. 6, pp. 20–22, Cold War International History Project, Woodrow Wilson International Center for Scholars, May 1993; Zubok claims that Khrushchev feared that Kennedy's speech reflected lack of control over the American military. McNamara statement before House Committee on Armed Services on Joint Resolution 505, 87 Cong, 1st sess, 28 July 1961, in *Public Statements of Secretary of Defense McNamara, 1961*, Vol. III, pp. 979–80.

27. U.S. draft, 2 August 1961, Subj: Military Planning and Preparations toward a Berlin Crisis, Meeting of Foreign Ministers, Paris, August 4–9, 1961, Germany

092 Berlin, D–3946/61, Box 51, FRC 64A2382; Lemnitzer memorandum for Secretary of Defense, 12 July 1961, Subj: Partial Mobilization, Germany 0921961 July, ibid.

28. McNamara memorandum for Chairman, JCS, 9 August 1961, Subj: Planning for NATO Military Operations, Germany 0921961 August 1–16, ibid.

29. Tel, Gavin (Paris) to Secretary of State, No. 632, 3 August 1961; Finletter (Paris) to Secretary of State, POLTO 143, 5 August 1961, OSD Historical Office.

30. Gen Clark M. Ruffner memorandum for JCS, 10 August 1961, Subj: Berlin Planning, 092 Germany (Berlin), Box 32, FRC 64A2382.

31. Ibid.

32. Ausland, *Kennedy, Khrushchev, and the Berlin-Cuba Crisis* (Oslo, 1996), pp. 20–21.

33. Ibid., p. 21.

34. Rusk statement concerning travel restrictions on Berlin, 13 August 1961, *Documents on Germany*, p. 776.

35. Minutes of Meeting of the Berlin Steering Group, 15 August 1961, *FRUS*, pp. 333–34; JCS History, pp. 190–91.

36. McNamara testimony before House Committee on Armed Services, 87 Cong, 1st Sess, on House Resolution 505, 28 July 1961, in *Public Statements of Secretary of Defense McNamara, 1961*, III, p. 1011.

37. McNamara interview with Joe Campbell on "Capitol Assignment," 14 August 1961, ibid., pp. 1103–4.

38. Ibid., p. 1104.

39. Brandt letter to President, 16 August 1961, *FRUS*, pp. 345–46.

40. Ausland, *Kennedy, Khrushchev, and the Berlin-Cuba Crisis*, p. 24.

41. McNamara memorandum for the President, 24 August 1961, Box 54, McNamara Papers. Fears about Clay's propensity to act unilaterally were not fully removed in August. They would arise again as new crises developed in subsequent months; John Newhouse, *War and Peace in the Nuclear Age* (New York: Knopf, 1989), pp. 157–58.

42. Strobe Talbott, ed., *Khrushchev Remembers* (Boston: Little Brown and Co., 1970), p. 259.

43. Record of Meeting of the Berlin Steering Group, 17 August 1961, *FRUS*, p. 347; Maurice Matloff interview with William W. Kaufmann, 23 July 1986; Frank Ninkovitch, *Germany and the United States: The Transformation of the German Question since 1945* (Boston: Twayne Publishers, 1988), p. 129; Schlesinger, *Thousand Days*, p. 397.

44. Ausland, *Kennedy, Khrushchev, and the Berlin-Cuba Crisis*, pp. 78–79. On problems for the future relating to the issue of "dismounting," note communication of Gen. Freeman (Heidelberg) to Gen. Polk, 5 November 1963, referring to a letter from Soviet General Yakubovskiy of 25 October 1963, expressing his intentions to enforce existing regulations which included dismounting for counting, Box 174, Lemnitzer Papers, NDU Library.

45. *New York Times*, 24 December 1961.

46. Nitze memorandum for the Secretary of Defense, 24 August 1961, Subj: Berlin Build-up, 092 Germany (Berlin), Box 32, FRC 64A2382.

47. McNamara memorandum to service secretaries, 18 August 1961, CCS 9172

Berlin/3100 (9 Aug 61) sec 1/JCS 1961/USNA, in Trachtenberg, *History and Strategy*, p. 222, fn. 192.

48. Telegram from the Joint Chief's of Staff to the Commander in Chief, Europe (Norstad), 25 August 1961, *FRUS*, p. 370.

49. McNamara memorandum for President, 18 September 1961, Subj: Military Building and Possible Action in Europe, Germany 1961, 092, September 15–23, Box 51, FRC 64A2382; Matloff interview with Kaufmann, 23 July 1961, OSD Historical Office; ISA estimate of situation #2, 29 September 1961, 092 Germany, September 24–30, Box 51, FRC 64A2382.

50. McNamara memorandum for President, 18 September 1961, Subj: Military Build-up and Possible Action in Europe, Germany 1961, 092, September 15–23, Box 51, FRC 64A2382; McNamara Press Conference, 19 September 1961, in *Public Statements of Secretary of Defense McNamara*, 1961, III, pp. 1426–28, 1449 cont. At a White House meeting with McNamara, Nitze, Bundy, Taylor, Robert Kennedy, and members of the Berlin Planning Group, Lemnitzer made it clear that current military strength "will not enable us to reopen access to Berlin, Lemnitzer note on White House meeting, 7 September 1961, L–214–71, Box 29, Lemnitzer Papers, National Defense University Library.

51. Alfred Goldberg interview with Henry Rowen, 22 September 1966, OSD Historical Office.

52. ISA draft of "Preferred Sequence of Military Actions in Berlin Conflict," 12 October 1961, Germany 1961, 092 October 1–14, Box 51, FRC 64A2382. This document was issued as National Security Action Memorandum (NSAM) No. 109 on 23 October 1961; see Gregory W. Pedlow draft paper, "General Lauris Norstad and the Second Berlin Crisis," pp. 26–27; see also Admiral J. M. Lee letter to Steven L. Rearden, 18 May 1984, Nitze Papers, on devolution from horse to poodle by way of pony blanket.

53. Lemnitzer memorandum for Secretary of Defense, 13 October 1961, "Preferred Sequence of Military Actions in a Berlin Conflict," Germany 1961, 092 October 1–14, Box 51, FRC 64A2382; McNamara memorandum for Bundy, 18 October 1961, Subj: Presidential letter to Gen. Norstad, ibid.; "U.S. Policy on Military Actions in a Berlin Conflict," 20 October 1961, transmitted by McGeorge Bundy to Secretaries Rusk and McNamara as NSAM No. 109, *FRUS*, pp. 521–23.

54. Gavin (Paris) tel 1885 to Department of State, 7 October 1961, *FRUS*, pp. 481–83; Finletter (Paris) tel POLTO 500 to Secretary of State, 20 October 1961, and Gavin (Paris) tel 2058 to Secretary of State, 17 October 1961, both in Secretary of Defense Cable Files, OSD Historical Office.

55. Seymour Weiss memorandum for Kohler and Nitze, 28 September 1961, Subj: Reflections on Recent Trip to Germany, Germany 1961, 092 September 24–30, Box 51, FRC 64A2382.

56. Lemnitzer memorandum for Secretary of Defense, 22 September 1961, Subj: Attacking Anti-Aircraft Installations in the Soviet Corridors, Germany 1961, 092 September 15–23, Box 51, ibid.

57. Nitze memorandum for McNamara, 28 September 1961, Subj: Response to Soviet/DDR Ground-to-Air Attack in Berlin Corridor, Germany 1961, 092 September 24–30, ibid.; McNamara memorandum for Rusk, 30 September 1961, ibid.; McNamara memorandum for Chairman, JCS, 2 October 1961, Germany 1961, 092 October 1–14, ibid.

58. Lemnitzer notes on White House meeting, 20 October 1961, L–214–71, Box 29, Lemnitzer Papers. (Italics in text.)

59. Kohler memorandum for Bundy, 7 October 1961, Subj: Military Buildup for Berlin, Germany 1961, 092, October 1–14, Box 51, FRC 64A2382; McNamara memorandum for the President, 10 October 1961. NARA, McNamara Papers.

60. Theodore C. Sorensen, *Kennedy* (New York: Harper & Row, 1965), p. 599. See editorial note on Sulzberger and Salinger, *FRUS*, pp. 401–2: letter from Chairman Khrushchev to President Kennedy, 29 September 1961, ibid., pp. 444ff, the first of what has been called the "Pen Pal Correspondence."

61. *New York Times*, 18 October 1961: Ausland, "Kennedy, Khrushchev, and Berlin," 3/9.

62. Raymond Garthoff, "Berlin 1961; The Record Corrected," *Foreign Policy* (Fall 1991), 84:142–56, notes that Khrushchev's fear that the U.S. objective in using tanks was to force entry into East Berlin: see William Burr, "New Sources on the Berlin Crisis, 1958–1962," Cold War International History Project *Bulletin* (Fall 1992), 2: 21–24; 32.

63. Ausland, *Kennedy, Khrushchev, and the Berlin-Cuba Crisis*, pp. 36–41, for Clay's role seen from the perspective of a member of the Berlin Task Force.

64. Lightner's account of the incident in Lightner (Berlin) tel no. 805 to Department of State, 23 October 1961, *FRUS*, p. 524; Norstad note on incidents in Berlin, 26 October 1961, NAC Briefing File, Norstad Papers, Dwight D. Eisenhower Library.

65. Ausland, *Kennedy, Khrushchev, and the Berlin-Cuba Crisis*, pp. 40–41.

66. *Khrushchev Remembers*, pp. 459–60, see FRUS, p. 544.

67. Lemnitzer memorandum for General McConnell, 22 January 1964, Subj: Desirability of Scheduling a Non-Dismountable Autobahn Convoy in the Near Future, L–1298071, SPCOL–S–349–89, Box 134, Lemnitzer Papers.

68. Soviet–East German Treaty on Friendship, Mutual Assistance, and Cooperation, 12 June 1964, *Documents on Germany*, pp. 869–72.

6
Les débats stratégiques

"Les débats stratégiques," an examination of the debate over nuclear strategy between Europeans and Americans, was presented at a conference in Paris in February 1996 sponsored by the Centre d'études d'histoire de la défense, Ministère de la Défense and published as a chapter in Maurice Vaïsse, et al., eds., La France et L'Otan, 1949–1996 (Paris: Editions Complexe, 1996), 307–22.

The literature of what may be termed "the great nuclear debate"[1] within NATO between the United States and the European partners in the years of the Gaullist ascendancy usually has been framed in terms of low vs. high nuclear threshold. More specifically, it applies to European, particularly French, suspicions of American pressure for "flexible response" and a build-up of conventional force as evidence of a weakening of America's concern for the defense of Europe. It was a debate between two major figures—the French president Charles de Gaulle and the American secretary of Defense Robert S. McNamara. The debate had many implications: American insistence upon centralized control of nuclear decisions, European distrust and resentment of American authority, the particular French resentment of the Anglo-Saxon nuclear monopoly, and the lessening intensity of the Soviet threat which ultimately permitted France's withdrawal from the military arm of NATO in 1966.

What has received less attention is the division within the American establishment—both diplomatic and military—over the appropriate strategy toward the Communist bloc. De Gaulle may have offended other Europeans by the manner of his presentations and he certainly deviated from the rest of his allies by his departure from SHAPE, but he spoke for much of Western Europe in resisting the logic of flexible response, especially the increase in conventional forces as both a deterrent and a method of coping with Soviet invasion. By contrast, McNamara had to cope with dissent within his Defense Department, with significant elements in the State Department, and with the Supreme Allied Commander in Paris. Powerful as McNamara was in the Kennedy and Johnson administrations, he encountered more opposition than de Gaulle did from his European colleagues.

Whatever the judgments made about strategic planning in the McNamara Pentagon, they must take into account both external and internal circumstances that would have affected any occupant in the office of the secretary of Defense. Change was in the air before the presidential election of 1960, even if the specific forms they would take were not clear. Within the Republican as well as Democratic leadership there was growing uneasiness with the principle of massive retaliation as the leitmotif of America's nuclear strategy. The strategic concepts of the early 1950s were less credible at the end of the decade. Such credibility as it had depended upon a nuclear superiority that was seemingly eroded by the end of the Eisenhower administration, as the Soviet Union developed technological skills that appeared equal if not superior to those of the United States.

The launching of Sputnik in 1957 sparked massive discontent in the West. In the United States popular pressures, reflected in congressional actions, led to a rapid acceleration of the nation's missile production as well as progress in space exploration. Astronauts soon matched cosmonauts. In Europe the Soviet military achievements led to questions about the reliability of American support when for the first time the United States would be as vulnerable as Europeans to Soviet power. If Sputnik could orbit the earth, then Soviet intercontinental ballistic missiles could strike at American targets. Would the United States in the future be willing to risk destruction of its own cities in defense of Europe's?

These questions went unanswered—at least for the moment—as the nation wrestled with means to cope with changed circumstances: manned bombers vs. ICBMs, limited warfare vs. large scale conflict, counterinsurgency vs. conventional ground forces. Above all, the United States under McNamara introduced the concept of counterforce against military targets as opposed to destruction of urban centers in a new approach to nuclear strategy. This was an initial component of the doctrine of "flexible response" that was to characterize strategic thinking in the next generation.

Flexibility of response was the key to change. It was to be the polar opposite of the rigid automatic doctrine of massive retaliation. Flexible response was intended to encompass a variety of responses to potential Soviet aggression, ranging from the most traditional conventional weapon to the most sophisticated strategic missile. The idea of graduated responses would raise the nuclear threshold to levels that would permit the enemy to back away from hostilities before the nuclear was employed. This strategy was well fitted to the civilian intellectuals in the Pentagon who were wise in the ways of quantifying techniques and skeptical of putatively simplistic solutions of the military mind.

For McNamara flexible response also involved a centralized control of nuclear operations that ruffled the sensibilities of every ally, most notably France. It meant specifically that France's nuclear initiatives should be subordinated to America's. This issue was at the heart of President de Gaulle's rejection of flexible response. There were other objections as well. First, raising the nuclear threshold would encourage rather than deter aggression; the enemy could engage in conventional operations knowing that the West would hesitate before launching a massive response. Second, it invited suspicion that agreement by the superpowers to avoid nuclear warfare would ensure that the battlefield would be in Europe subject to the kind of ravages that characterized World Wars I and II. Third, emphasis on conventional forces not only would be excessively expensive, but also would be a wasted effort in light of overwhelming Soviet superiority on the ground.

General Charles Ailleret, chief of staff of France's armed forces, made the credibility of conventional defense a central theme of an address to the NATO Defense College in 1964. Given the imbalance in the size of the contending forces the most that the West could hope for would be a stand on the Rhine. More likely, the line would be at the "Somme, the Aisne, the Vosges, the Jura and the Alps."[2] As for the virtues of tactical nuclear weapons, they would complicate rather than resolve NATO's defenses by putting civilian populations at risk. Consequently, the only reasonable alternative was the strategic nuclear weapon employed at the lowest possible threshold.

The reactions of the Joint Chiefs of Staff and of the Supreme Allied Commander, Europe, were not strikingly different from those of the French military. Massive retaliation had been an article of faith in the Air Force, particularly since that service would have a primary role in its execution. The Army was also skeptical, concerned as it was with the high costs as well as with the impracticability of coping with the Soviets on the ground. And General Norstad in Paris envisioned a SHAPE possessing its own nuclear capability as a fourth NATO power, with medium-range nuclear weapons as the key to deterrence.[3] All the military departments could share a suspicion of McNamara's objective in gathering control in his own hands over the use of strategic weapons.

To win over opponents in the Pentagon as well as skeptics in Europe the secretary of defense offered "counterforce" as a substitute for massive retaliation. Counterforce relied on a technology that could pinpoint targets and ensure their destruction without destroying the civilian population. It possessed a deterrent power deriving from a knowledge that the nation had the capability of withstanding a first strike and then being able to deliver counter blows that would destroy the war-making power of the enemy. McNamara valued its function as a "second strike" which would spare urban centers.[4]

Much of what the secretary of Defense celebrated in the application of counterforce ruffled the sensibilities of the military services as well as of Gaullist France. If it had no other defect, the emphasis on a unified command-and-control authority would have aroused opposition. When he assumed office he recognized that no clear command structure was in place in the Pentagon. Its Single Integrated Operational Plan (SIOP) was anything but integrated. SIOP did not allow for probability analysis, which meant that requirements for equipment to strike targets were much higher than necessary. There were multiple estimates available, but with no verifiable means of judging their particular merits.

These problems were not on the agenda of the Joint Chiefs. When McNamara asked them in March 1961 to draft a strategic doctrine that would take into account controlled responses and negotiating pauses, they made it clear that controlled responses conflicted with their conception of the appropriate use of nuclear weapons. They opposed all alternative arrangements. Nuclear planning in their view required the removal of all limitations until "we have more knowledge of the technological possibility of creating the essential building blocks on which safe implementation of the doctrine could be based."[5]

Of all the services only the Air Force, after initial resistance, embraced counterforce, primarily because it drew attention to its own unique qualifications to carry out counterforce missions. But there was a twist to the Air Force's endorsement that ran counter to McNamara's strategy; its leaders believed that counterforce should open the way for a preemptive strike. General Thomas Power, head of the Strategic Air Command (SAC), asserted that it would be foolhardy for SAC to believe that it could knock out the Soviet Union's entire strategic force through a retaliatory attack. Planners must consider the advantages of a first strike. General Curtis LeMay, Air Force Chief of Staff, assumed that the availability of hardened and dispersed Minuteman intercontinental ballistic missiles as well as an "immediate go-ahead on the B-70" would mean that a "full first-strike capability" was in sight.[6]

Given these unsatisfactory reactions from his military advisers McNamara turned to his youthful civilian staff, the so-called Whiz Kids, to make extensive revisions in the SIOP. By September 1961 he was confident enough in the efficacy of counterforce to inform the president that "we will be able, at all times, to deny to the Soviet Union the prospect of either a military victory or of knocking out the U.S. retaliatory force. If this most likely estimate of Soviet forces proves to be correct, the forces I am recommending should provide us a capability to achieve a substantial military superiority over the Soviets even after they have attacked us."[7] His confidence in his second-strike strategy rested on the rapid build-up of Polaris seaborne and hardened Minuteman missiles which would be invulnerable to an offensive striking force.

If the nuclear threshold consequently should be so high that strategic missiles would not be employed by either side, conventional forces would be the logical alternative defense of Western Europe. Conceivably, tactical nuclear weapons, already present in profusion since the 1950s, might solve the problem without raising the level of conventional forces. But enthusiasm for these weapons had dimmed considerably since the Eisenhower years. Critics such as Whiz Kid Alain Enthoven considered placement of tactical nuclear weapons in Europe to have been a mistake. No matter how resolute NATO's intention might be to limit these weapons to distinct military objectives, he feared that their use would escalate conflict into an unrestrained exchange of strategic weapons. In light of the vulnerabilities of forward-based nuclear systems there would be pressure to employ them before they could fall into enemy hands.[8]

McNamara could cope with the negative responses of the Joint Chiefs in 1961. He had more difficulty, however, with the European allies who resisted counterforce doctrine for many of the same reasons as the American military, even more vigorously and with more credibility. The denigration of France's force de frappe, the high political and economic costs of an enlarged ground force, along with the putative subliminal message of an America decoupling from Europe, guaranteed resistance abroad. To calm Europe's concerns McNamara asked advice from former secretary of State, Dean Acheson, an eloquent and forceful advocate of the new strategy. Acheson supported McNamara's efforts to establish a more effective deterrent than massive retaliation against subatomic war by raising the capability of NATO's conventional forces to blunt a Soviet attack long enough "to allow the Soviets to appreciate the wider risks of the course on which they are embarked." On the matter of centralized control of nuclear weapons Acheson recognized that the allies would have to be given greater voice in nuclear targeting if they were to accept the U.S. position.[9]

Acheson's reasoning was no more convincing to the Joint Chiefs or to the SACEUR than McNamara's had been; and their objections had a dampening effect on the secretary's efforts to win approval for counterforce strategy from the European allies. It is hardly surprising that these sentiments would be shared in Europe. The allies ignored the call for more ground troops, and France consciously flouted American recommendations when McNamara delivered a major address to the North Atlantic Council in Athens in May 1962. He intended to use this rostrum to clear up what he felt to be misunderstandings about the meaning of flexible response. And since counterforce seemed to have been one of its most opaque components, the Athens meeting would provide an opportunity to explain fully counterforce's role in nuclear strategy. Over the span of an hour he offered information, which his adviser, William Weed Kaufmann, said was "too heavy for a single speech to bear."[10]

Instead of calming his critics he compounded his difficulties with France by stressing that the United States would offer a nuclear umbrella over NATO much as the B-29s had done, or had intended to do, in 1949. Indivisibility of control was the key term in McNamara's lexicon; unity of planning and decision-making was vital. There must not be "competing and conflicting strategies in the conduct of nuclear war," he asserted. "We are convinced that a general nuclear war target is indivisible. . . . If nuclear war should occur, our best hope lies in conducting a centrally controlled campaign against all the enemy's vital nuclear capabilities." This would not be possible if competing nuclear forces targeted against cities would operate independently. In the event of war, he maintained, the use of force "against the cities of a major power would be tantamount to suicide. . . . In short, small nuclear capabilities operating independently are expensive, prone to obsolescence, and lacking in credibility as a deterrent."[11] It took no leap of imagination for de Gaulle to identify France with the "small nuclear capabilities" deprecated in McNamara's speech.

The secretary had some appreciation of the sensibilities he might be offending when he promised to commit eventually the entire Polaris submarine force to the alliance, and to support the Multilateral Force (MLF) which would give Europeans their own medium-range nuclear force. How serious his commitment to the MLF was has been open to question, but he was obviously making an effort to understand the European position. That the MLF was anathema to de Gaulle was outside his range of comprehension at this time. President Kennedy, however, was more sensitive to potential French reactions than his less experienced secretary of Defense. Through McGeorge Bundy, the special assistant to the president for national security affairs, McNamara was urged to de-emphasize differences with the French.[12]

The president had good reason to be concerned about the potential impact of the Athens speech. But it was not until mid-June when McNamara delivered the commencement address at the University of Michigan at Ann Arbor, repeating in public what he had said in a closed meeting that the European allies reacted. He unintentionally highlighted the more sensitive portions of the Athens address without presenting the reasoning that underlay them. The careful explanations of May were oversimplified in June. Opponents were able to seize on particular phrases, take them out of context, and twist their meanings. When the secretary claimed that "basic military strategy in a general nuclear war should be approached in the same way that most conventional military operations had been regarded in the past," he opened himself to accusations of supporting a first-strike option.[13] The special virtues of a credibly controlled use of the nuclear weapon were stigmatized as evidence of America's unwillingness to defend its European allies with strategic nuclear weapons.

The illogical aspects of counterforce as well as the perceived anti-French bias inherent in this and other forms of flexible response came under close scrutiny of French strategists. That they collectively embraced all of de Gaulle's grand design is debatable; years of working inside NATO left their mark. The withdrawal of France from the organization on the ground that the Cold War had essentially terminated was essentially a presidential decision. What they shared with de Gaulle were criticisms of an American strategy which they regarded as a threat to both Europe's security and to France's role in the world. General Pierre Gallois scorned counterforce as a recipe for a standoff between the superpowers that would make Europe once again a battlefield in the event of Soviet aggression, as it had been twice before in the twentieth century. A *force de frappe*, by contrast, would be a force of dissuasion, with enough strength to destroy a significant number of the enemy's cities. McNamara's warning, underscored by Kennedy's advice, which raised the specter of France as the first victim of a Soviet counterstroke, went unheeded. General André Beaufre approached the same issue from another angle of observation in asserting that national nuclear forces, no matter how small, would strengthen deterrence by increasing a sense of insecurity on the part of a potential aggressor.[14] The *force de frappe* could be the trigger that would bring if necessary America's nuclear power to bear, and so serve as a further deterrent to Soviet aggression.

France's rejection of America's leadership, reflected as it was in its reaction to McNamara's strategy, was never unqualified. Even the most articulate of the Gaullist critics, General Ailleret, never urged withdrawal from the alliance. His celebrated remarks about a foreign policy aimed at *tous azimuts* was more rhetorical than factual; the compass was directed to the east at the end of the Gaullist decade when the Warsaw Pact forces invaded Czechoslovakia as it had been at the beginning of de Gaulle's presidency after Sputnik intruded into French skies. Nevertheless, whatever differences French military intellectuals may have had among themselves over the value of the *force de frappe*, they were united for the most part in opposition to the American demand for centralized control of nuclear policy.[15]

French criticism of McNamara's strategy had relatively little impact on American strategic thinking. The secretary of defense, however, was vulnerable to domestic critics within the Defense establishment, particularly as his faith in counterforce as a centerpiece of flexible response waned. By 1963 the price of an acceptable counterforce strategy had proved to be too high. As the Soviets developed more sophisticated offensive weaponry it became evident that the ability of the United States to survive the full force of a massive nuclear assault was questionable. Too many lives and too much property were at stake. Even if anti-ballistic missiles (ABMs) were able to shoot down a sufficient number of enemy missiles to make possible a second strike the cost would be astronomical. It was likely that an effective defense would be impossible at any price.

If there was a particular event that marked a break with counterforce, it was the Cuban missile crisis of 1962. This incident sensitized McNamara to a deeper awareness of the implications of nuclear war, and strengthened his conviction that the nuclear weapon was not a useful tool in a superpower conflict. "One of the reasons why McNamara backed off the no-cities doctrine," according to Alain Enthoven, "is that it was erroneously interpreted as a theory whereby thermonuclear war could be made tolerable, and thereby won. Gradually he turned against it because it seemed to be getting bent out of shape."[16]

After 1962 McNamara turned to "assured destruction." This doctrine assumed that defense against nuclear attack was hopeless. Since a nuclear exchange would probably result in over 100 million fatalities in both the United States and the Soviet Union, neither active nor passive defenses would make a difference; improvements in offensive forces on both sides would defeat all defensive efforts. The key to successful deterrence then lay in the ability of the strategic force to destroy 30 percent of the Soviet population, 50 percent of its industrial capacity, and 150 cities. Since the United States possessed that capacity in 1963 total destruction would be unnecessary. The urban centers of both superpowers would be hostages ensuring deterrence. The costs would be manageable because these targets were easier to locate than military bases and arsenals.[17]

Assured destruction had other virtues. Far more than counterforce, which could not assure destruction of all the enemy's nuclear installations or know where new ones might be built, the new strategy could fit into the approaches to nuclear warfare followed by the team of system analysts advising the secretary of Defense. These civilian analysts claimed to know just how much force was enough to destroy the adversary's ability to survive.[18] With this knowledge McNamara could rebut demands from the military departments and their congressional supporters to invest more funds in strategic nuclear weaponry. The shift in strategic concept would have the effect, among other benefits, of reducing pressures for a first-strike capability which the Air Force was exerting on behalf of its version of counterforce.

Unlike his projections in 1961, McNamara was prepared by December 1963 to recommend to the president a nuclear force aimed at vulnerable cities as well as at military targets. In essence his recommendations were a confession that counterforce could not be counted on to make a second strike a sufficient deterrent if technology—American and Soviet—would make their respective military installations less vulnerable. By contrast, the offensive capability of the United States nuclear arsenal to destroy enemy cities and industries gives "us a high degree of confidence that, under all foreseeable conditions, we can deter a calculated deliberate Soviet nuclear attack."[19]

A year later McNamara had another confession to make: namely, that the doctrine of "assured destruction" offered an uncertain assurance. America appeared increasingly vulnerable to sophisticated Soviet ICBMs, which made damage limitation an important part of the new strategic concept. Unfortunately, the plans for damage limitation through anti-ballistic defenses and fallout shelter programs in urban centers were not being realized. Technical problems hampered the effectiveness of the Nike-X anti-ballistic missile system, while the number of additional survivors per billion dollars spent would not justify the marginal returns on the investment in fall-out shelters. He pointed out to the House Armed Services Committee on 18 February 1965 that "over and above the technical problems there are even greater uncertainties concerning the preferred concept of deployment, the relationship of the Nike-X system to other elements of a balanced damage-limiting effort, the timing of the attainment of an effective nationwide fall-out shelter system and the nature and effect of an opponent's possible reaction to our Nike-X deployment."[20] The strategy of assured destruction was stripped of its damage-limitation component.

These conclusions were the product of studies conducted in 1964 within the Defense Department. They determined that even a fully deployed Nike-X defense system would not offset the additional forces which the Soviets could acquire to penetrate the system. Whatever promise damage control might have had become as irrelevant for assured destruction as it was for counterforce.[21]

Nevertheless, assured destruction was at least a working substitute for counterforce despite its shortcomings. Actually, the Pentagon's shift from counterforce to assured destruction was a modest movement, more of emphasis than separation. Counterforce targeting of Soviet bases continued even as cities were declared to be the primary targets. U.S. ICBMs were aimed at new Soviet installations as soon as they were identified. As Enthoven noted in 1967: "Our targeting policy . . . has not changed. From 1961–62 on, the targeting plan has been based on the principle that we should have different options that target the strategic forces and cities."[22]

The shifting of counterforce along with questions about assured destruction suggest that neither concept was vital to McNamara's conception of American strategy. What he and his colleagues sought was not to be found in any specific doctrine. Rather, it was flexibility itself that they were seeking, and the denigration as a means of effecting a flexible response to Soviet initiatives was not equated with rejection of its concept. Having reached a point by 1963 where he perceived nuclear warfare itself to be rationally unacceptable, any particular nuclear strategy was ultimately irrelevant. McNamara wanted the nuclear component to ensure that it would not be used.

Hence the blurring of counterforce and assured destruction, and consequently the emphasis on conventional forces as the most viable way of defending Europe.

But as he left office in 1968 the secretary had come around to a conviction that assured destruction had to be the "cornerstone of our strategic policy in order to deter deliberate nuclear attack on the United States or its allies. . . . Assured destruction is the very essence of the whole deterrence concept." It has to mean the "certainty of suicide to the aggressor."[23] Only by such assurance would the weapon be neutralized. Such was the reasoning for keeping the nuclear option as the ultimate nuclear response, despite McNamara's genuine revulsion against the weapon.

There was no alternative to this position. On one level there was the military factor that prevented its removal from the American arsenal, the fear of encouraging a nuclear strike if this deterrent were abandoned. Even more compelling in the 1960s was the political factor, the recognition that the European allies would see in the abandonment of this option as an American abandonment of the alliance itself. For them to accept renunciation of massive retaliation required a substitute that retained the strategic weapon no matter how high the threshold had to be reached before it could be employed. No less daunting was the opposition removal of the option would arouse within the Defense Department and in the Congress. The result was a schizophrenic advocacy of a nuclear strategy that the secretary privately deplored.

Given his deserved reputation for analytic skills of the highest order, it seems out of character that he would lurch from one tactic to another as he tried to cope with contradictions within each of them. For examples, he touted counterforce as a second-strike strategy without apparently realizing its first-strike potential. He disparaged tactical nuclear weapons on some occasions, and justified their presence in Europe on others. Even as he stressed the importance of a credible conventional force he had no compunction about removing American troops for service in Vietnam, claiming that a smaller troop presence would be as efficient as a larger one. And when he spoke about the futility of nuclear weapons as instruments of war, his words have to be measured against the 1000 Minuteman missiles he was seeking for 1968.

The inconsistencies which French critics have leveled against McNamara's strategic policies masked a reality that no American nuclear policy would have met France's strategic concerns. In this light McNamara's inconsistencies never mattered very much. If the United States had retained massive retaliation it would have been stigmatized as too crude a strategy to be used; fearing retaliation the United States would hesitate to apply it to a minor infraction on the part of the Soviets. As for flexible response, whether in the form of counterforce or assured destruction, it indicated America's willingness to abandon its European allies. And the MLF, with its own nuclear arm, was a farce as long as the nuclear warhead remained under American control; de Gaulle scorned it as an inept attempt to undermine the *force de frappe*. In essence de Gaulle's statement in 1959 to the École Militaire made it clear that the defense of the nation could not be subject to the rule of an alliance: "The defense of the country is the first duty. It is even its raison d'être' "[24] France's nuclear strategy was the guarantor of its independence.

If French criticism of his nuclear strategy did not make a serious dent on his course of action, domestic criticism within the Defense establishment and in the Congress forced him to proclaim its virtues. But his professions were frequently suspect. Wherever he turned he struck some nerve or other among the military services, the State Department, and their congressional allies.

Within the Defense Department the Air Force nourished a grievance against his preference for missiles over manned aircraft. And when the generals accepted defeat in their campaign for the B-70, they asked for more missiles than the secretary felt was necessary. Always more comfortable with massive retaliation in which the Air Force was the major player, they were reluctant converts to counterforce, and then only when they envisioned it as a first-strike instrument. They did not join McNamara in minimizing counterforce.

In Europe the commanding general of U.S. forces held strong reservations about both counterforce and assured destruction. General Norstad's eye was on NATO as "a fourth atomic power" under the authority of the Supreme Allied Commander Europe.[25] His discomfort with flexible response was one of the factors that hastened his departure from Paris. General Lyman L. Lemnitzer, his successor, was less inclined to argue with the Pentagon, and in general was less politically attuned than Norstad. But even the equitable Lemnitzer had his doubts about McNamara's strategy, less about assured destruction than about the conventional posture of NATO, particularly after the escalation of the war in Vietnam drained his troop strength in Europe.

Nor was he as sanguine as McNamara had been about the impact of France's withdrawal from SHAPE upon the alliance's military posture. French territory was not necessary for the defense of NATO. According to the secretary, "neither the United States nor its allies ever contemplated a way in which falling back upon French soil through the battlefield of Germany was an acceptable strategy for the alliance." McNamara's alternative was a forward defense at the West German frontier. As for the reduction of U.S. manpower in Europe, the secretary saw in de Gaulle's actions an opportunity to make the American contribution more efficient, which led the SACEUR to comment that "one more benefit of this sort and we will be out of business." By emphasizing the greater efficiency that would result from the reduction of American forces Lemnitzer feared that McNamara would provide a rationale for the European allies to cut back on their own conventional forces.[26]

The secretary found even less support for his strategic concepts in the State Department. What disturbed many in that department (excepting Dean Rusk, the secretary of state) was McNamara's insistence on a unified command-and-control of nuclear strategy. This approach conflicted with the views of the so-called "theologians" of the State Department who were true believers in the virtues of an integrated Europe and who supported a European nuclear force, though without control of the nuclear warhead.[27] While such formidable figures as Under Secretary George Ball and directors of the Policy Planning Staff Robert Bowie and Walt Rostow, in the Eisenhower and Kennedy administrations respectively, were acolytes of the Multilateral Force (MLF), they identified the program as a means of undercutting national nuclear forces such as France was developing. In this respect they shared McNamara's position. But only in this respect. The adherents of the MLF would downplay the ICBM in favor of a medium-range missile owned by a consortium of European allies. This sharing of the nuclear weapon presumably would take the curse off America's command of the warhead. But from McNamara's perspective not only was there an element of sham in the MLF but there was the danger that its development would divert attention from the building of conventional forces as well as elevate the importance of nuclear weaponry in general at a time when he was trying to move it to the periphery.

The most severe problem in his relations within the administration and with the NATO allies was his ambivalence toward any kind of nuclear strategy. At the heart of his seeming inconsistencies was a conflict between his demands for expanded European ground forces and his apparent support for the nuclear weapon throughout his tenure of office—from his acceptance of tactical nuclear weapons to repeated guarantees of a strategic nuclear response and—after France's departure from SHAPE—to the creation of a Nuclear Planning Group where the voices of allies would carry weight. Yet there is sufficient evidence on the record to cast doubt on his frequent assertions that the nuclear option would be used as a last resort. His more credible belief was that it was a useless instrument of warfare which could never be used under any circumstance. In this context "flexible response" was a misnomer; its limits were reached when mutual suicide was the last step. The Cuban missile crisis led him to observe in 1962 that "our Allies all too often act as though they were living in a period of nuclear monopoly. This condition no longer exists."[28]

In 1994 he admitted that he had reached these conclusions in the early 1960s. In private conversations with Presidents Kennedy and Johnson he "had recommended without qualification that they never, under any circumstances, initiate the use of nuclear weapons. I believe they accepted my recommendations. But neither they nor I could discuss our position publicly because it was contrary to established NATO policy."²⁹ He might have added that such an admission would have raised a storm of protest within the Defense and State establishments as well as with the European allies. He might also have added that "flexible response" was an elliptical way of expressing these convictions. Its ambiguity may have been a liability to military planners, but it was its ambiguity that permitted the NATO (absent France) in 1967 to adopt at its Brussels meeting in December 1967 a strategic concept "based upon a flexible and balanced range of appropriate responses, conventional and nuclear, to all levels of aggression or threats of aggression."³⁰ Flexible response may not have banned the bomb but it emphasized the importance of conventional defense and raised the nuclear threshold to stratospheric heights.

NOTES

1. Aron, Raymond, *Le Grand Débat* (Paris: Calmann-Lévy, 1963); Kugler, Richard, *The Great Strategy Debate: NATO's Evolution in the 1960s*, A RAND Note, 1991, N-3252, FY/RC.
2. Ailleret, General Charles, "Flexible Response: A French View" in: *Survival*, no. 6, November–December 1964, p. 261, from *Revue de Défense nationale*.
3. Norstad, General Lauris, "NATO as the Fourth Atomic Power," address at Pasadena, California in: *Survival*, vol. 2, no. 3, May-June 1960, pp. 106-7.
4. McNamara testimony on Department of Defense Appropriations for Fiscal year 1964, *Hearings* before a subcommittee of the Committee on Appropriations, House of Representatives, 88 Congress, 1 session, 6 February 1963, p. 110; Goldberg, Alfred, "A Brief Survey of the Evolution of Ideas about Counterforce," RAND Memorandum, RM 5431-PR, October 1967, vi–vii.
5. Lemnitzer memorandum for McNamara, 21 April 1961, Subject: "Doctrine" on Thermonuclear Attack, DoD, RG 330, NARA.
6. Power, General Thomas S., *Design for Survival* (New York: Coward-McCann, 1966), pp. 83, 119–120; Le May, General Curtis E., *America is in Danger*, New York, Funk and Wagnalls, 1968, pp. 84–85.
7. Appendix I, McNamara draft memorandum for Kennedy, Subject: Recommended Long Range Nuclear Delivery Forces, 1963–1967, 23 September 1961, DoD/RG 330, NARA.
8. Enthoven, Alain, and Smith, K. Wayne, *How Much Is Enough?: Shaping the Defense Program, 1961–1969* (New York: Harper & Row, 1971), pp. 125–127; Schwartz, David N., *NATO's Nuclear Dilemma* (Washington, DC: The Brookings Institution, 1983), pp. 145–46.
9. Acheson report, A Review of North Atlantic Problems for the Future, p. 19, March 1961, National Security Files, JFK Library.
10. Quoted in Kaufmann, William W., *The McNamara Strategy* (New York: Harper & Row, 1964), pp. 96–97.
11. Remarks by Secretary McNamara, 6 May 1962. NATO Ministerial Meeting, Restricted Session, pp. 12–13. Department of State Records, Office of Atlantic Political and Military Affairs, Box 8, RG 59, NARA.

12. McGeorge Bundy memorandum for the President, 1 June 1962, National Security File, DoD, Box 274, JFK Library.

13. Remarks by Secretary McNamara at the Commencement Exercises, University of Michigan, Ann Arbor, 16 June 1962, pp. 9–11, reprinted in: *Survival*, July-August 1962, pp. 9–11.

14. See General Gallois's views in *Stratégie de l'âge mucleaire* (Paris: Calmann-Lévy, 1959); for General Beaufre, see his *Dissuasion et Stratégie* (Paris, Armand Colin, 1964).

15. Ailleret, Général Pierre, "Défense 'dirigée' ou défense 'tous azimuts' " *Revue de Défense nationale*, décembre 1967, pp. 1923–32; note Lacouture, Jean, *De Gaulle*, t. 3, *Le Souverain, 1959–1970* (Paris, Editions du Seuil, 1986), p. 483.

16. Quoted in Herken, Gregg, *Counsels of War* (New York: Knopf, 1985), p. 170.

17. McNamara draft memorandum for the president, 6 December 1963, Subject: Recommended Strategic Retaliatory Forces, DoD/RG 330, NARA.

18. Enthoven, Alain, and Smith, K. Wayne, op. cit., p. 170.

19. McNamara draft memorandum for the president, 6 December 1963.

20. *Hearings* on Military Posture before the Committee on Armed Services, House of Representatives, 89 Congress, 1st session, 18 February 1965, p. 256.

21. Weapons Systems Evaluation Report, no. 79, "A Summary Study of Strategic Offense and Defense Forces of the U.S. and U.S.S.R," 8 September 1964, cited in: Ball, Desmond et al., *Politics and Force Levels: The Strategic Missile Program of the Kennedy Administration* (Berkeley: University of California Press, 1980), p. 203.

22. *Hearings*, on Status of US Strategic Power, Preparedness Investigating Subcommittee, Senate Committee on the Armed Services, 90 Congress, 2nd session, 23 April 1968, p. 138.

23. McNamara, Robert S., *The Essence of Security: Reflections in Office*, (New York: Harper & Row 1968) pp. 52–53.

24. Gaulle, Charles de, *Discours et Messages*, t. III, *Avec le renouveau, 1958–1962*, 3 November 1959, p. 126.

25. See fn.3.

26. McNamara statement at *Hearings* on the Atlantic Alliance before the Subcommittee on National Security and International Operations of the Committee on Government Operations, U.S. Senate, 89 Cong., 2d sess., Part 6, 21 June 1966, p. 187; quoted by Sulzberger, Cyrus L., in *New York Times*, 8 June 1966.

27. Robert R. Bowie memorandum for the secretary of state, 21 August 1960, "Long-Range Planning for the Atlantic Community," enclosing "The North Atlantic Nations: Tasks for the 1960s," a report published by the Center for International Strategic Studies, University of Maryland; see also Steinbruner, John D., *The Cybernetic Theory of Decision: New Dimensions of Political Analysis* (Princeton. NJ: Princeton University Press, 1974) pp. 185, 220–23.

28. Draft for speech to the Economic Club of New York, delivered on 18 November 1963, McNamara Papers, NARS.

29. McNamara, Robert S., *Retrospect: The Tragedy and Lessons of Vietnam* (New York: Times Books, 1995), pp. 345–46; he expressed these sentiments in almost the same words in "The Military Role of Nuclear Weapons: Perceptions and Misperceptions" *Foreign Affairs*, 62, Fall 1983, p. 79.

30. Stromseth, Jane E., *The Origins of Flexible Response: Debate over Strategy in the 1960* (New York: St. Martin's Press, 1988) p. 194; Ministerial Meeting of the North Atlantic Council, Brussels, 13–14 December 1967, *Texts of Final Communiques, 1949–1974*, p. 199.

III
NATO in the Second Generation, 1968–1989

The length of a generation is often in the eye of the beholder. There is something arbitrary, though convenient, about identifying it as twenty or thirty years. In the case of the Atlantic alliance a particular milestone, the Harmel Report of 1967, ended the first generation eighteen years after the signing of the Treaty of Washington. "The Future Tasks of the Alliance," the official name of the exercise under the direction of Belgian foreign minister Pierre Harmel, was initiated by the smaller members of the alliance to examine the changing environment of Europe. The report concluded that the Soviet Union's expansion had been successfully blocked, that the Communist world was no longer monolithic, and that a policy of détente should accompany the maintenance of military security. In brief, NATO accepted the principle that defense and détente were complementary not contradictory policies. The Harmel Report marked a major change of direction in the course of NATO's internal history.

The Cold War had not ended, but the détente that followed in the 1970s made longstanding differences within the alliance seem more threatening to the future of the organization than conflicts between East and West. No event in the second generation would bring NATO and the Warsaw Pact members, or the United States and the Soviet Union, as close to a catastrophic war as the Berlin or Cuban crises had done in the first generation. While East-West problems were by no means settled, West-West difficulties were more critical to NATO's survival. Conflicts between Greece and Turkey over Cyprus, resentment in the United States over lack of European support for the Vietnam War, division between Europe and America over the Arab-Israeli Yom Kippur War defined NATO in the 1970s. American resentment over burden sharing in that decade was matched by Europe's increasing doubts about the loyalty of America's pledge, and, in the 1980s, by increasing fears of the recklessness of the Reagan administration.

But as all these issues percolated in this period they took place under the rubric of a new relationship with the Communist East. The impulse for detente, or at least for detachment from the dominant military presence of the United States had preceded Harmel and was best expressed in France's disengagement from the NATO (but not from the treaty) in 1966. De-Gaulle's action would not have occurred if the West had faced imminent Soviet attack. But France's departure from NATO military councils per-mitted the smaller nations to assume greater influence on military, espe-cially nuclear, policy through the Nuclear Planning Group than would have been possible if France had remained inside the organization. Moreover, America's preoccupation with Vietnam permitted them to achieve some of the objectives—increased consultation as well as reduction of tensions be-tween East and West—that had not been available to them in the Wise Men's recommendations a decade before. These changes are explored in the first chapter in this section on NATO in the Johnson years.

Détente as a goal seemed to flourish on both sides of the Atlantic through the Nixon and Ford presidential years. Europeans took the initiative from a more wary United States as the Federal Republic normalized relations with the Soviets in 1971, and the European allies responded with more enthusiasm than their American counterparts. The Mutual and Balanced Forces Reductions Program (MBFR) and the Conference on Security and Cooperation in Europe (CSCE) in 1971 and 1972, respectively, were es-sentially by-products of the Harmel initiative; and all three reflected a de-cline in American influence in the alliance commensurate with an equality Europeans were ready to accord to the Warsaw bloc.

For its part, the United States was not opposed to détente. In fact, the administration welcomed it for reasons that gave rise to European suspi-cions. These centered on the Nixon Doctrine, the subject of the second chapter in this section. This doctrine seemingly modified the Truman Doc-trine of 1948 by stressing limitations in America's ability to take respon-sibility for containing the global challenge of communism. While it nominally placed Europe—and NATO—as the primary concern of Amer-ican foreign policy, it was regarded as a thinly disguised means of disen-gaging from the failing Vietnam War. Moreover, if Europe was to be the first priority, its status was undermined by growing American resentment against Europe's indifference, if not hostility, to the struggle in Southeast Asia and by the concomitant congressional demands for greater burden sharing on the part of the European allies and for reducing American troop strength in Europe. Transatlantic division over Europe's behavior during the Yom Kippur War further aggravated relations. And in the background was a European worry that the bilateral SALT I Treaty served the interests of the superpowers at their expense. Limiting intercontinental weapons brought no promise of security for countries exposed to medium-range weapons In brief, the American version of détente could be interpreted as efforts to reduce its obligations to NATO as the United States in the Kissinger years made its own arrangements with the Soviet adversary. Such were some of the unintended consequences of the Nixon Doctrine.

These centrifugal forces did not dissolve the alliance in the 1970s. The Soviet threat, no matter how diminished, remained a challenge that Europeans could not manage alone. Détente with the Warsaw bloc had distinct limits. While the Soviets welcomed the Helsinki agreement in 1975 to legitimize the Yalta boundaries, they were not interested in the force reduction negotiations underway at Vienna. While the West moved toward reducing its own defenses, the adversary was developing new weapons, such as the SS-20, a medium-range mobile missile aimed at Europe's cities. To cope with the Soviet military machine, NATO looked toward new weapons of its own and for a time found one in the neutron bomb, a battlefield nuclear weapon that could destroy soldiers with minimal damage to property. Combined with the inexpensive cruise missile, a pilotless aircraft that could strike Warsaw Pact targets at low altitudes, NATO might have been in a position to neutralize Soviet power.

The policies of the Carter administration frustrated the European partners. The SALT II negotiations begun under Secretary of State Kissinger in 1972 and concluded by Secretary of State Vance in 1978 would have considered the cruise missile a strategic weapon and this removed from the U.S. arsenal in Europe. At the same time, after considerable agonizing, President Carter ruled against deployment of the neutron bomb in large part over the morality of a weapon that seemed to value property over people. With American leadership increasingly in question, the European allies, led by German chancellor Helmut Schmidt, demanded a more positive response to Soviet military power than a belated increase in defense expenditures. The upshot was a major decision in 1979 to adopt a dual-track approach: (1) to deploy 572 cruise and Pershing II missiles in five European countries to counter the SS-20s; and (2) to enter into arms negotiations with the Soviet Union to reduce the number of all medium-range missiles.

Over the next few years the alliance received more than it had anticipated, or perhaps wanted, in an American military buildup under the aggressive Reagan presidency. The harsh rhetoric as well as the massive defense expenditures of that administration contrasted sharply with Carter's, but this did not bring comfort to Europeans worrying about the intensification of the Cold War. The second part of the dual-track decision of 1979 seemed to have been pushed aside, or at best given lip service. In a surprise initiative in 1972, the United States appeared to revive détente by offering to engage in Strategic Arms Reduction Talks, that would begin with elimination of both cruise missiles and SS-20s. The Soviet adversary—and many in the West as well—did not consider this a serious proposal, as the Soviets had their weapons in place while the American concession applied to weapons not yet deployed. Over the course of three years, while the matter of missile deployment was debated in Europe, particularly in Britain and Germany, the Soviets conducted a concerted campaign against these nuclear weapons and sealed it by efforts to influence elections in both countries. In 1973 its representatives abandoned negotiations in Geneva.

If the Soviets had hoped that division within the alliance would decouple America from Europe, they were sorely disappointed. The leadership in Germany and Britain that had supported deployment was reelected in 1983. In that same year the United States unveiled the Strategic Defense Initiative (SDI), better known as "Star Wars." When archival evidence becomes more available, historians may learn that the SDI had done more damage to the Soviet empire than the firm decision of NATO partners (including Belgium, the Netherlands, and Italy) to accept theater nuclear missiles on their territory. The SDI was to realize Reagan's dream, not of defeating the "evil empire" on the battlefield, but to remove the dangers of nuclear warfare in its entirety. "Limitation" or "reduction" would be unnecessary if bolts of electrons could destroy any intercontinental ballistic missile aimed at the United States. It would be a defensive weapon, hitting a bullet with a bullet, that would make America impregnable.

Objections to this concept were articulated in many quarters. Scientists doubted the possibility of developing such a weapon. Europeans wondered if American preoccupation with the SDI presaged a renewal of decoupling sentiment in the United States. If the transatlantic ally could become impregnable, would not isolationist voices be raised once again? There was little comfort for Europeans in this new weapon. But the most immediate challenge was the enormous cost of a Star Wars program, even to provide an infrastructure. SDI has yet to materialize, but the funds expended in its inauguration and the technology it could yield to the nation and its partners made a deep impression on the Soviet leadership. The U.S.S.R. had built a First World military machine, close to parity with that of the United States, but it was built on a Third World economic base. The cost of competing with the SDI, to create a weapon that would penetrate the future defense system, could bankrupt the Communist world.

Even without the challenge of the SDI, the Kremlin had begun to reevaluate its posture on the cold war in 1985. The old Communist leaders—Brezhnev, Andropov, and Chernenko—passed away in rapid succession in the mid-1980s, leaving the 55-year-old Mikhail Gorbachev as general secretary of the Communist Party. Under his dynamic leadership, arms negotiators returned to Geneva. At a summit meeting with Reagan, Gorbachev talked of more reductions in nuclear weaponry, including acceptance of on-site inspections as advocated in 1986 by the Stockholm Conference-and-Security-Building Measures and Disarmament in Europe (CDE).

A new spirit of *glasnost* and *perestroika*, openness and reconstruction, characterized Gorbachev's approach to his nation—and apparently to the NATO alliance as well. At a meeting between Reagan and Gorbachev in Reykjavik, Iceland, the two leaders seemed to display a wish for a deeper détente than had been in place fifteen years before as well as a personal chemistry that warmed relations between the two countries. But the SDI was a sticking point. Gorbachev protested that it violated the Anti-Ballistic Missile Treaty of 1972. His defensiveness on this issue suggested that the technology the SDI might generate could be beyond the means of the Communist system to emulate. There was an implication that the need to restructure the domestic economy of the Soviet Union outweighed the importance of confrontation with the West and of missionary work in the Third World.

The way was open for the Soviets to disengage from the Cold War and allow freedom of choice to their allies. The single most important milestone along this route was the signing of the Intermediate-Range Nuclear Forces Treaty (INF) in December 1987. It validated the dual-track decision of 1979 and gave meaning to the START initiative of 1982 by setting up the machinery to remove both the Soviet and American theater nuclear weapons from Europe. It seemed that the Harmel concept that began NATO's second generation had come to fruition in the INF agreement. While NATO leaders did not anticipate the immediate implosion of the Soviet empire, the INF treaty provided the wheels that set it in motion. What had failed in the 1960s succeeded in the 1980s. This is the subject of the third chapter in this section.

7
The U.S. and NATO in the Johnson Years

"The U.S. and NATO in the Johnson Years," was prepared for Robert A. Divine, ed., The Johnson Years, *Volume 3:* LBJ at Home and Abroad *(Lawrence: University Press of Kansas, 1994), pp. 119–49. The chapters in this volume were based on the extensive records of the Lyndon B. Johnson Library in Austin, Texas.*

Since World War II, Europe has been the focus of American foreign relations. And since 1949 the Atlantic alliance has been the front line of containment of Soviet communism. In the words of David Calleo, NATO was "the rather elaborate apparatus by which we have chosen to organize the American protectorate in Europe."[1] Until 1963 other parts of the world had been fringe areas despite intrusion of crises in Korea, Guatemala, Indochina, and the Suez Canal in the 1950s. The Soviets were considered to have created turmoil in those regions to divert America from its primary concern—the defense of Europe. In the course of fashioning an Atlantic community to whose fortunes it became attached, the nation had abandoned its tradition of nonentanglement with Europe, the hallmark of American foreign policy for the first century and a half of its history.

Through its involvement in the Vietnam War the Johnson administration appeared to turn the clock back, to return the United States to its earlier concerns with the Pacific rim. It was not that the administration intended to abandon the new links to Europe; the Soviet peril there remained virulent as the status of West Berlin remained unresolved, as the Soviet buildup of nuclear weapons after the Cuban missile crisis escalated, and as the Brezhnev doctrine was imposed on Czechoslovakia at the end of the Johnson administration. But the combination of the president's unfamiliarity with Europe and the dominance of the Vietnam War in America's consciousness seemed to push NATO into the background during the Johnson years. How much attention could U.S. policymakers devote to framing a coherent NATO policy when communism's new locus of East-West confrontation was in the enclosed jungles of Southeast Asia rather than in the open plains of northern Europe?

The coincidence of rising tensions in Asia at a time of lower tensions in Europe helped to facilitate a benign neglect of Europe during the Johnson years. The removal of Berlin and Cuba as crisis points after 1962 opened the way to the Harmel initiative in 1967, with its emphasis on détente as well as on defense.[2] The relative calm in Europe permitted observers to judge that the ability of the United States during the Kennedy administration to surmount Soviet challenges in the Caribbean and in central Europe had compelled the Soviets to surrender, at least in the short run, their aspiration to dissolve the Atlantic alliance.

There is nothing unreasonable about this evaluation. Certainly there can be no caviling about the dominance of Indochina in America's consciousness in the absence of clear and present danger in Europe. The Czech crisis of 1968 was carefully identified by the Soviet Union as a problem of the Warsaw bloc and not a reason for conflict between NATO and the Warsaw countries.

Under these circumstances challenges to the survival of NATO from both Americans and Europeans were inevitable, and they stemmed in large measure from the pall cast by the Vietnam War on American foreign affairs. From the American side there was a growing public anger against a Europe that did not rally to the United States defense of South Vietnam. Congressmen were prepared to act on this discontent by withdrawing U.S. troops from Europe unless the European partners changed their behavior. From the European side there was a rising fear, stoked by Gaullists, that American anti-Communist fervor masked an essential weakness dangerous to Europeans. The issue was not simply that America would withdraw troops because of pique over its allies' behavior; Europeans were concerned that U.S. troops would be moved out of Europe to fill a need in Asia.

Another challenge to the alliance arose during the Johnson years from an apparent waning of the Cold War in Europe. Pundits in the mid-1960s speculated that the alliance had served its purposes and should disband.[3] Although Khrushchev's personality was volatile and his actions often unpredictable, his nation was not Stalin's Soviet Union. Western Europe in the mid-1960s believed that it could coexist with its eastern neighbors. Its push to détente that characterized the latter part of the Johnson administration would not have advanced as far as it did without a certain confidence that Soviet aggressiveness had abated.

Questions then may be raised: (1) In light of the nation's absorption with Vietnam, how important was the Atlantic alliance to the Johnson administration? (2) If the Soviet threat had receded, what centripetal forces were still at work to keep the alliance alive? (3) Since NATO did survive, what new relationships were fashioned between Americans and Europeans during the Johnson years? Superficial evidence points to potentially fatal divisions within NATO, divisions reflected in the failure of the multilateral force (MLF) to create a new nuclear partnership in Europe, in the expulsion of the United States and NATO from France in 1966 and the concurrent departure of France from NATO in that year, and in the recurrent Mansfield resolutions seeking American withdrawal of troops from Europe. Each of these issues created serious problems for U.S. policymakers; how they were resolved was a measure of the success or failure of Johnson's NATO policies.

The MLF, with its implications for an integrated European military entity sharing nuclear power with the United States, was a reflection of the European orientation of President Johnson's advisers. Despite the president's Texas provincialism and his discomfort with the Kennedy advisers he had inherited, Johnson's foreign policy was shaped by the same Ivy League advisers who had been associated with Kennedy—and with Eisenhower and Truman as well. Johnson may have been, as Philip Geyelin characterized him in 1966, "a caricature of an American Westerner, with an uncultivated accent and an often unintelligible turn of phrase," who resented the manners of the eastern intellectuals.[4] Still, Johnson retained most of them. McGeorge Bundy stayed on as special assistant for national security. When he left in 1966 his successor, Walt W. Rostow, was as much an Ivy League product and Kennedy administration veteran as Bundy had been. The two key figures in the cabinet, Dean Rusk and Robert McNamara, were both Kennedy appointees. For a variety of reasons the influence of these two men increased rather than decreased under Johnson; Rusk enjoyed a prominence as secretary of state he had not had under Kennedy, and McNamara's presence was increasingly felt as Johnson looked to the Pentagon for advice.

The concept of a genuinely integrated force excited and inspired a dedicated group of American diplomatists who saw in the MLF an opportunity to advance the cause of European unification. The MLF was conceived in the Eisenhower administration by former chairman of the Policy Planning Council Robert Bowie; it derived from a plan of the Supreme Allied Commander, Europe, Gen. Lauris Norstad, to fill a gap in medium-range ballistic missiles with a land-based multinational force under his authority. The concept became entangled in inter-and intradepartmental wrangling in Washington and in doubts among potential European participants during the Kennedy years. But if the MLF acolytes in the State Department, most of them followers of Jean Monnet, had failed to win the full support of the White House or the Defense Department, they did not give up their vision. For them a multilateral force represented an important step toward completing a United States of Europe; at the same time the MLF could thwart the efforts of Germany and other countries to achieve nuclear capabilities for themselves. If successful, these advocates expected even Britain and France, with their nuclear armory, to join the MLF.[5]

As of 1963 the force was to consist of twenty-five surface ships, each armed with eight Polaris A-3 missiles and having mixed-manned crews to be drawn from member nations. The ships' weapons system would be owned and controlled by the participating allies; the crews would serve as individuals rather than as members of national groups. A key element in the plan was the collective management of weapons by the MLF, not by the United States. It was clear that the use of warheads would not be freed from U.S. control, but the advocates hoped ultimately that the MLF would be independent of a U.S. veto.[6]

A new task force, headed by Gerard Smith as special adviser to the secretary of state, lobbied both in Europe and in the United States for quick implementation of the president's presumed endorsement of the MLF. Although the adherents of the concept were better posed for success in 1964 than they had been at the end of 1963, they had trouble attracting the attention of NATO governments, including their own. The Congress had more important concerns on its agenda than the vague and slightly unsettling notions about a new entity. Richard Russell, chairman of the Senate Armed Services Committee, went along with his colleagues to push aside Smith's recommendations. The forthcoming 1964 presidential election was Johnson's first priority as well as the Senate's. Before the election campaign reached a climax the momentous Civil Rights bill took center stage in summer 1964, and the amorphous MLF almost disappeared from the president's sight at this time.[7]

The European allies, except for the Germans, were equally uninterested. Both the German and the British leaders were insecure in their positions, and France was increasingly alienated from all aspects of NATO. On the other side of Europe the Soviets raised the tone of their opposition, pointing to dangers of German control of nuclear weapons.[8]

When Johnson's attention was once again focused on Europe and the MLF, it was only after his reelection and after the accession of Harold Wilson as Britain's prime minister. Whatever hopes the MLF supporters had entertained about the British Labour party maintaining its preelection position against an independent nuclear capability were quickly dashed. Wilson's Labour government had no intention of moving Britain into the MLF. The prime minister had too many negative elements to contend with, including anti-German sentiment in his own party and nationalist pride in ownership of nuclear weapons among Conservatives. Thus Wilson's need to satisfy both constituents and opponents pushed him to a search for alternatives to the MLF.[9]

Until December 1964 and Wilson's meeting with Johnson the only public supporter of the MLF in Europe was the Federal Republic. Given the fragility of the Erhard administration the MLF's friends in Washington had an incentive in Bonn to complete negotiations for an agreement by fall 1964. When Johnson met Erhard in June the Smith team tried to take advantage of Bonn's apparent support. The U.S. ambassador to NATO, Thomas Finletter, went to Bonn to follow up the Johnson-Erhard communique, which claimed that the MLF was making "a significant contribution to the military and political strength of NATO and that efforts should be continued to ready an agreement by the end of the year."[10] If this timetable could be met German Gaullists would be isolated, and Erhard's gamble in embracing the MLF would be justified. These expectations energized the MLF Working Group, established in October 1963 with permanent representatives from the United States, United Kingdom, Italy, West Germany, Greece, Turkey, and Belgium. The Working Group in turn had set up a military subgroup under the U.S. chairman, Adm. M. G. Ward, to examine and report on the military and technical aspects of the MLF.

Nothing much was to come of these preparations or of the putative German acceptance of the MLF, essentially because of the continued inattention of the Johnson administration. Partly the lack of action resulted from the wariness of the allies, who had joined the Working Group with the clear proviso, in the case of the British and the Belgians, that their attendance did not constitute any commitment. But the major obstacle in the way of the MLF's progress at this time was probably the intervention of Britain in the person of Prime Minister Harold Wilson.

To replace the MLF the British came up with the alternative of an Atlantic Nuclear Force (ANF). The idea did not originate with Wilson; British military leaders had aired it with the German defense minister Kai-Uwe von Hassel in June who in turn shared it with McNamara. But Wilson quickly seized on the ANF as a means of fulfilling the Labour pledge to renounce an independent nuclear deterrent while finding a home for the British force. And even if the ANF did not materialize, it would divert attention from the MLF. In his outline of the concept the prime minister noted that the House of Commons on December 16 would deposit the British Polaris missiles, with the British V-bombers force, and with whatever the French might wish to supply, would join these national contributions to "some kind of mixed-manned and jointly owned element in which the nuclear powers could take part." Reference to mixed-manned elements was a fig leaf to cover abandonment of an integrated force. The virtue of this broader nuclear force was that it would keep nuclear forces under national control and enlarge the British presence at the same time.[11]

President Johnson might have accepted the ANF approach during his meeting with Wilson in Washington on 7–9 December 1964. To prepare for Wilson's visit, the president finally gave the MLF his full attention, and he learned of a variety of powerful pressures inhibiting further U.S. involvement: limited congressional support, hostility of the French, uneasiness in Bonn, and opposition by Moscow, which objected to a German finger on the nuclear trigger in any form. As for the ANF, at best it could become an Anglo-American force, which would alienate the Germans and confirm de Gaulle's thesis about the Anglo-Saxon conspiracy.

In this new context Johnson's closest advisers, Bundy and McNamara, who had always entertained reservations about the MLF, worked to minimize an American role. By the end of November Bundy told his colleagues that he was "reaching the conclusion that the U.S. should let the MLF sink out of sight."[12] The critical moment occurred at a meeting between the president and his advisers two days before Wilson arrived in Washington. Undersecretary of State George Ball, the leading MLF supporter, fought a losing battle, arguing that no negative action should be taken until a major effort with Congress had been made. The president was not convinced. Though he might share with the MLF enthusiasts a concern that inaction would be potentially dangerous if it fostered an independent German nuclear effort, he sensed that he could not overcome Senate opposition. He doubted if he could sell to the Senate a proposal about which the European partners were in doubt. "I don't want to be a Woodrow Wilson," he was reported to have noted, "right on a principle, and fighting for a principle, and unable to achieve it."[13]

Nor was it clear that he truly believed in the principle. If the Europeans really wanted such a force, let them work something out and then come to Washington. The United States would not inhibit Western Europe from seeking ways to integrate the nuclear force, but it would no longer take the initiative. To make sure that the world knew the White House position, the memorandum (NSAM 322) was leaked to the press. As Harlan Cleveland, Finletter's successor as U.S. permanent representative to the North Atlantic Council, observed, Johnson had come to the same ambivalent position President Kennedy had taken, namely, to "encourage the enthusiasts to see if they could bring it off, but not get committed to it personally. When it looked as if they weren't bringing it off and there was too much flak from the Hill, and so on, the President torpedoed it on the basis of a memoir from Mac Bundy."[14]

The MLF was effectively dead in December 1964. Its vital signs had disappeared, but its acolytes continued to keep the faith, at least until an obituary had been published. They seized on vague statements and casual references as proof that their vigil ultimately would be rewarded. At his new conference in January 1965 the president fed those hopes by noting that European governments were still discussing MLF proposals and that "we will continue to follow the progress of these talks with the greatest of interest." John Leddy, who joined the administration as assistant secretary of state for European affairs in May 1965, had a vague sense that the MLF was still alive at that time, but he believed, as did George Ball, that it was finally buried in December 1965.[15]

Although many of the MLF enthusiasts in the State Department had regarded McNamara and Bundy as fellow travelers, their kinship was always questionable. McNamara's abiding conviction was that Western security rested in centralized control of nuclear weaponry in American hands and the building of conventional forces as a major deterrent. The multilateral force in contrast involved the creation of a new nuclear entity and a concomitant downplaying of conventional forces. For both McNamara and Bundy the MLF also contained too many loose ends. Their memories of the Bay of Pigs in 1961 inclined them to be skeptical of programs that were not fully thought through. Given the additional factor of widespread opposition it was not surprising that the MLF failed to materialize. The surprise in retrospect is that the concept lingered as long as it did.

A cynical interpretation of the MLF would identify it as a means of the United States fostering an illusion of sharing control of nuclear weaponry while enjoying the reality of Europeans paying for it. A more benign view would identify America's support for the concept as a genuine effort to promote European integration and an equally genuine effort to restrain the Federal Republic from developing its own nuclear capability. No matter which interpretation is the more accurate, the MLF debate served to dissolve, if not solve, some critical problems of the alliance. It did deflate excessive German pressure for more nuclear involvement. The MLF, or at least its fate, satisfied the British partner as well. The British received the POLARIS missile without having to pay the penalty of assigning their nuclear force to NATO; the ANF served as the diversion its designers had hoped it would.

The MLF did not resolve the French connection, however. Few observers in Washington seriously expected France to join the MLF or de Gaulle to lessen his opposition to U.S. leadership. But there was a possibility that if the MLF had succeeded, an isolated de Gaulle would have been compelled to join it.

This outcome was doubtful at best. The MLF's rise and fall only confirmed de Gaulle's conviction that the Anglo-Americans would never grant France equality in the alliance, and after 1964 he accelerated France's steady pace of dissociation from NATO. De Gaulle's pronouncements often had a casual air, as if they were impromptu statements, but his moves in fact were carefully prepared and brilliantly staged. Timing was always of the essence. De Gaulle would not act until all his pieces were in place: a

French nuclear capability had to be visible; the Algerian war had to be concluded; and a working relationship with both the Federal Republic and the Soviet Union had to be established.

Before Johnson entered the White House the French fleets in the Mediterranean and the Atlantic had already been removed from SHAPE and from SACLANT commands. The change was for the worse after Kennedy's death. In 1965 France ostentatiously refused to participate in FALLEX '66, a military exercise for allied general staffs, which had been proposed by Gen. Lyman L. Lemnitzer, Supreme Allied Commander (SACEUR), to test allied communications and alert systems. But because the exercise was intended to implement a new strategic concept that de Gaulle had rejected, the exercise was unacceptable to him. The only concession that Lemnitzer could achieve for the operation was an agreement with Gen. Charles Ailleret, the French chief-of-staff, to permit a few French officers to serve as token participants.[16]

It is hardly surprising, then, that Lemnitzer in letters written in spring 1965 should have characterized his relations with France as turbulent. He noted that when he took on the assignment as SACEUR he was already concerned about an "element of vindictiveness creeping into Franco-American relationships, particularly in the Political field."[17] Nevertheless, with all the problems posed by France's behavior Lemnitzer never sensed that de Gaulle's animosity was ad hominem. Conceivably, there was an element of condescension in the relationship but if so it reflected the French president's attitude toward any American.[18]

Although de Gaulle's personal treatment of Lemnitzer may have yielded some psychological balm for the wounds he inflicted, Lemnitzer's colleagues in Washington lacked even that palliative to sustain the shock caused by de Gaulle's letter to President Johnson of March 1966. In four paragraphs, the French president made it clear that France intended to withdraw from the military organization of the alliance and expected as a consequence prompt removal of NATO forces from French soil.[19] As U.S. Permanent Representative Harlan Cleveland noted, if it was a shock, it may have been because de Gaulle had spoken so often about such an outcome but had taken only piecemeal steps until then. At his previous press conference on 21 February 1966, he had implied that no definitive action would take place until 1969, when, according to Article 13 of the North Atlantic Treaty, any party may withdraw one year after it has given notice to its fellow members.[20]

De Gaulle did not say that he was withdrawing from the alliance but only from the military side of the organization. He presented similar letters to heads of states or governments of Britain, West Germany, and Italy on 9 March, yet even when those letters were delivered, ambiguities about France's position remained. In Foreign Minister Maurice Couve de Murville's explication of 9 March, it was clear that France would not denounce the North Atlantic treaty itself and that its specific objective concerned French forces in Lemnitzer's Supreme Headquarters (SHAPE) and the stationing of allied forces on French territory.[21]

The action caused consternation in the administration. Walt W. Rostow, chairman of the State Department's Policy Planning Council, tried to find compensation for "a NATO without France." Use the occasion, he suggested, to tighten the alliance and to move forward on some form of nuclear sharing or a scheme of a multilateral foreign exchange offset that would lift the morale of the allies. He also urged the president to leave "an empty chair" for France to reclaim in the future.[22]

The president did not panic. He neither granted legitimacy to de Gaulle's actions nor threatened reprisals for them. Cleveland noted that while his "private references to General de Gaulle stretched his considerable talent for colorful language," he "imposed an icy correctness on those who had reason to discuss French policy in public."[23] Johnson softened the tone of a stiff letter of protest that Secretary of State Rusk had presented on the grounds that de Gaulle was not going to change his mind regardless of the arguments Americans might take up against him. Johnson noted in his memoirs that he told the secretary of defense that "when a man asks you to leave his house, you don't argue; you get your hat and go." John L. Leddy provided Johnson's variation of that image: "Well, when that old man talks I just tip my hat to him. When he comes rushing down like a locomotive on the track, why the Germans and ourselves, we just stand aside and let him go by, then we're back together again." This remarkable composure, in Gen. Andrew Goodpaster's judgment, was maintained because Johnson did not feel he was engaged in a personal confrontation with de Gaulle; rather, it was a confrontation between two nations.[24]

Some of Johnson's advisers thought that the president's reaction was too complacent. Undersecretary of State George Ball disagreed with a soft line on the ground that de Gaulle had repudiated a "solemn agreement." France's behavior called for a rebuke far stronger than the administration's authorized response.[25]

Francis C. Bator, special assistant to the president for national security affairs, strongly supported Johnson's attitude. But Bator objected to a draft of the president's letter that would have deleted "a place of honor" from a sentence that referred to France's resuming her role in the future. Bator's logic failed to persuade Johnson, however, and the final version simply referred to "her place." Bator's point was that a gracious ending, "with an offer of a golden bridge," not only would underscore America's restraint but would also expose the fact that it was de Gaulle, not the United States, who was isolating France.[26]

Many of the allies were sympathetic to at least some of de Gaulle's charges against the United States. Europeans could agree that America was sluggish in helping the organization adjust to new circumstances and that it had exploited NATO for its own imperial purposes. Portugal, increasingly upset with the allies' lack of sympathy for its colonial problems, used de Gaulle's attack on NATO to express its own frustrations with American leadership of the alliance. Canada's conspicuous silence owed much to its concern about Quebec's reactions. West Germany and Belgium hoped that some way would be found to placate their alienated neighbor.[27]

Despite the tensions NATO succeeded in maintaining its solidarity in the face of a traumatic situation. France went ahead with its schedule, with one ultimatum following another. On March 29 de Gaulle dispatched a memorandum specifying the timetable for the transfer of American and NATO commands from French territory as well as for the termination of all French personnel in NATO commands; the target date was 1 April 1967.[28]

This deadline inevitably posed daunting challenges to General Lemnitzer both in his capacity as SACEUR and as commander of U.S. forces in Europe. The expulsion order contained special problems inasmuch as the original bilateral accords had included, as de Gaulle's note of March 10 specifically pointed out, depots at warehouses at Deols-La-Martinerie, U.S. headquarters at Saint-Germaine, and pipelines, supply lines, and air bases.[29] Lemnitzer had to meet deadlines that his political superiors had accepted, and he did so quickly and effectively.

It was a minor miracle that he was able to locate a new headquarters in Belgium and then to complete the transfer before the deadline. Finding the new headquarters in Casteau, near Mons, was itself a problem; the SACEUR would have preferred to have been as close to the capital in Brussels as he had been in Paris. Any further distance, he felt, would damage the effectiveness of his mission.[30] And though the Belgian government had welcomed NATO, it was a qualified welcome; the civilian headquarters would be allowed to move to Brussels but not the military. Claiming that it was inadvisable to place SHAPE in an urban setting, the government offered sites in the southern part of the country where there was land available belonging to the state with some of the infrastructure already established. Belgian reasoning behind the offer of Casteau was probably based less on the fear of Brussels being a magnet for an enemy attack and more on the anticipation of the economic help some 1,700 SHAPE families might give to the depressed province of Hainaut.[31]

Lemnitzer managed as well as was possible in a difficult situation. Had he pressed too hard for a better site he would have given ammunition to Gaullist charges of American domination; he had no alternative but to accept a location 50 kilometers from the capital. As it was, the Belgian press sniped at the decision. One newspaper claimed that Lemnitzer's reluctance to move to suitable quarters in Casteau was not because of the distance from the airport but because of the inconvenience it would cause families of SHAPE senior officers accustomed to the amenities of Paris.[32]

Once the question of location was settled the removal of SHAPE from Paris went quickly. As Lemnitzer recalled less than two years later, "It was an enormous undertaking and involved movement of over 100,000 U.S. personnel and over one million tons of supplies and equipment of all types. . . . We had less than six months to complete enough of the headquarters so we could shift our operations from France by 1 April 1967, thereby beating the deadline to everyone's surprise."[33]

Lemnitzer rightly took pride in his accomplishment. More than any other American leader he understood the damage that de Gaulle's actions had inflicted on the organization. McNamara seemed to regard the apparent ease with which the SACEUR effected the change as an augury of a reconstituted NATO. Yet some problems emerged from the gloss that the secretary of defense put on the meaning of the move to Belgium. The relocation, in his view, would be an opportunity to reshape the troop structure in Europe to make it more efficient and less costly.[34]

Two days after Lemnitzer opened his headquarters at Casteau, McNamara announced that the relocation would permit considerable financial savings for the United States, ranging from annual foreign exchange in excess of $100 million per year to almost 40,000 personnel and their dependents formerly stationed in France.[35] De Gaulle had accelerated the secretary's cost-cutting program, which might have required a much longer time to put into effect had France not imposed drastic changes on SHAPE.

McNamara's expectations were postulated on the assumption that the removal of France from SHAPE would be "in no way disabling" to the military posture of the alliance. French territory, he believed, was not necessary to the defense of the West: "Neither the United States nor its allies have ever contemplated a way in which falling back upon French soil through the battle field of Germany was an acceptable strategy for the alliance." Forward defense meant the West German frontier. So although French cooperation was desirable, according to the secretary of defense, it was not vital to military planning.[36]

This was not the picture of Europe seen from Lemnitzer's perspective. As he contemplated the significance of the secretary of defense's plans for streamlining America forces in Europe, he was quoted as saying that "one more benefit of this sort and we will be out of business."[37] The SACEUR was convinced that the defense of Europe, at the frontier in particular, required a commitment of manpower and equipment at a level that could not be replaced by European counterparts. Lemnitzer saw McNamara's position encouraging Senate critics to increase pressure to replace American forces with European in the central sector. McNamara had support from Secretary of the Treasury Henry Fowler, who informed the president that the financial drain in Europe "is our Achilles heel, which could destroy NATO."[38]

McNamara and his advisers failed to perceive, as did Lemnitzer, that troop levels were only part of the equation. NATO's communication system had suffered a wrenching upheaval. The east-west flow between France and Germany of the supply and communications lines had to be diverted to a north-south axis, as German ports replaced French ports for logistical materials shipped from the United States. This shift was forced on NATO only a few years after the Berlin crisis of the early 1960s had exposed the old north-south supply lines to be painfully vulnerable. Even if the dislocation were to be only a temporary problem, "the disrepair," as a Senate report observed, "of American military arrangement is apparent." This somber conclusion was reinforced by presidential adviser John J. McCloy's warnings that France's defections might be the first of many as the alliance unraveled. To restore NATO to a "strong and convincing status," he asserted, we "should be searching our minds to find a means of reestablishing the faith of our non-French allies in the NATO organization itself. It is no time to lead a procession of withdrawals."[39]

The status of NATO in 1967 was impressive not because the alliance was in a state of disarray, as Lemnitzer and McCloy saw it, but because it managed to gather new strength despite de Gaulle's action and McNamara's reaction. The alliance did not dissolve in 1967. In his own fashion de Gaulle shrewdly minimized the damage he had done without abandoning his independent stance. Even as Lemnitzer was preparing to pack up and leave France, the French leader arranged to allow continued operation of the oil pipeline from the west to Germany across French territory, and he subsequently granted permission for flights of allied aircraft from Britain to southern Europe in French airspace. Had de Gaulle continued his initial voiding of all bilateral overflight agreements, France would have joined Austria and Switzerland to form a neutral belt of nations—an Elysian Curtain, as Cyrus Sulzberger called it[40]—splitting NATO into two parts and further reducing flexibility in troop dispositions.

In exchange for this concession the French made sure that they would enjoy the benefits of the new sophisticated air alert system, NATO Air Defense Ground Environment (NADGE), which they deemed essential to France's security. Although NADGE would be an integrated as well as an improved air defense system, it was important enough to justify France's contributing a share of the costs, thus ensuring that a French company would be a member of the consortium constructing the system. A similar convergence of French national interest with the interests of the alliance permitted the French to keep a military presence in Germany, although not under NATO auspices.[41]

De Gaulle's careful concessions served to keep SHAPE alive in its new Belgian home, but other consequences of France's withdrawal energized the alliance in a more positive fashion. First, France's separation from the military organization meant separation as well from the Standing Group of the Military Committee, the Anglo-American-French inner circle at the Pentagon that excluded the other powers. The Standing Group disbanded in 1966. The North Atlantic Council then created an International Military Staff (IMS) to replace it, with headquarters in Brussels and with every nation that contributed forces to be represented in this new group.[42] Although the establishment of a broader military planning unit did not mean that each member had an equal voice in determining strategy, it responded to the long-standing demand for consultation by the smaller nations.

At the same time, by circumstance rather than by design, the enormous influence that had been exercised by the Supreme Allied Commander from Eisenhower to Norstad diminished under the new arrangements. Clearly, the loss was a product of Lemnitzer's personality, which did not lend itself to political leadership, but it was also the result of SHAPE being physically removed from the political headquarters and the International Military Staff in Brussels. The distance was psychological as well as physical; it enhanced the IMS at the expense of the SACEUR.

Arguably, the most concrete by-product of the NATO diaspora was the creation of the Nuclear Planning Group (NPG) in 1966.[43] What the MLF could not accomplish—to supply a NATO vehicle for sharing nuclear knowledge and nuclear decisions—the NPG did, up to a point. The new committee did not have the scope of the MLF, but its relatively modest aspirations offered a better chance for success. As the MLF moved away from the agendas of the Johnson administration, Secretary McNamara could claim that the "Nuclear Planning Group, which we are developing, meets the needs of our allies, especially Germany. It will more closely tie in Germany with the U.S. and U.K." How this would be done was left unsaid. McNamara's key point at the NSC meeting was that the NPG "will end talk of the Multilateral Force."[44]

The NPG's origins may be found in a formal proposal made at a meeting of NATO defense ministers in Paris on May 31, 1965, before France left the organization, to seek "ways in which consultation might be improved and participation by interested allied countries extended in the planning of nuclear forces, including strategic forces." It was McNamara who inspired the idea, according to John Leddy, and who pushed it past objections of State Department officials in May 1965 at a time when MLF adherents had not yet given up on their cause. McNamara years later noted that "if I could do things differently, I would have introduced the Nuclear Planning Group much earlier than I did as a means to draw the Europeans into nuclear affairs. The NPG only came to mind after it looked like the MLF would fail. I really didn't think of it earlier."[45]

Once the MLF was out of the way the North Atlantic Council acted with dispatch. A Special Committee of Defense Ministers collaborated in setting up three working groups that began operations in February 1966, the month that de Gaulle issued his expulsion orders. In December of that year the Defense Planning Committee agreed to establish within NATO two permanent bodies for nuclear planning—a Nuclear Defense Affairs Committee to make policy and a subordinate Nuclear Planning Group of seven members to manage the detailed work.[46] The NPG embodied McNamara's concerns for educating the allies to the realities of nuclear warfare and for sharing, at least to some degree, the nuclear planning process.

The president responded to McNamara's enthusiasm by showing a personal interest in the NPG, thereby according it a status it might not have had otherwise. Francis Bator wanted Johnson to emphasize to the allies that the establishment of the NPG was a major step forward in demonstrating "NATO's will to come to grips with the tough issues of organizing nuclear defense."[47]

As in the case of the MLF there was an element of deception in the American promotion of the NPG. The administration hoped to coax the allies into believing they were now fully involved in the planning process. Without the handicap of MLF's high visibility, where the gap between promise and fulfillment was easily exposed, the NPG meetings indulged in generalities that might become specific in the future. The administration could anticipate in April 1967 that "the main result of the meeting—apart from general education—will be agreement on a series of further joint studies . . . on such major issues as the use of tactical nuclear weapons." The ultimate acceptance of the strategy of "flexible response" (MC 14/3) had its way paved by America's openness to consultation in 1967 even though the assignment of studies for their own sake often seemed to be the main order of business.[48]

The absence of France from NATO defense councils also revived the older Defense Planning Committee (DPC). The DPC had been in existence since 1963, but as long as France remained as a member there was no consensus on advice to the SACEUR or to policymaking in any coherent form. With the French seat vacated the committee gained stature. The Council's communique of December 16, 1966, was uncharacteristically understated when it relegated to a footnote the DPC's mission to deal with all questions concerning an integrated defense system involving fourteen member nations.[49]

The new role of the DPC deserved more recognition. It was under DPC auspices that the new strategy of flexible response became NATO policy in 1967 after four years of seemingly fruitless American lobbying. Though the European allies had accepted the bankruptcy of "massive retaliation" as embodied in MC 14/2, formulated in 1957, they resisted the Kennedy and Johnson pressures to elevate conventional defense over nuclear, partly for reasons of cost, mostly for fear that raising the threshold of nuclear response could inhibit American use of the nuclear deterrent under any circumstance.

At the Athens meeting of the North Atlantic Council in 1962 McNamara had articulated his thesis about the viability of conventional warfare and the irrelevance of strategic nuclear weaponry to a cool if not hostile audience. The secretary of defense, however, did not give up his efforts to instruct the allies on the dangers of nuclear warfare. His Draft Presidential Memorandum (DPM) in 1964 spelled out the U.S. conception of the relationship between tactical nuclear weapons to nonnuclear forces; McNamara's subsequent DPMs challenged even the utility of tactical nuclear weaponry. As McNamara noted in 1967, "The danger of escalation, once the 'firebreak' between nonnuclear and nuclear war has been crossed, and the damage, if escalation occurs, cautions against our ability to limit nuclear war."[50]

The secretary of defense failed to convince the Europeans. Although they could accept a role for conventional forces, they rejected his sweeping judgment that these troops could substitute for nuclear capabilities in blocking a major Soviet nonnuclear assault. Moreover, the U.S. withdrawal of its own troops from the central sector as the demands of the Vietnam War grew increasingly damaged McNamara's credibility.

By the end of 1966 he had recognized that there would be no major increases in expenditures for conventional defense by the allies. Consequently, the United States was willing to accept a compromise in MC 14/3 that committed NATO to respond at whatever level of force—conventional or nuclear—was chosen by the aggressor. The apocalyptic level of a strategic nuclear response would be reached only in the event of a major nuclear attack. McNamara was still confident that NATO could manage with conventional means to cope with anything except a full-scale assault from the Warsaw bloc. Thus even though the nuclear option was built into NATO's new strategic concept, it was unlikely that it would be used.[51] In sum, it was apparent that a compromise, unacceptable had France kept its seat in the DPC, could be ratified after France withdrew.

NATO's acceptance of MC 14/3 signaled a renewal of faith in the American connection with Europe. If the allies were still unwilling to spend the funds needed to support one part of the flexible-response doctrine, conventional forces, at least they recognized the value of a graduated rather than an automatic response to Soviet provocation. This breakthrough in December 1967 took place at the same meeting of the North Atlantic Council in which the Harmel report on "The Future Tasks of the Alliance" was accepted.[52]

The Harmel initiative, too, was a by-product of France's departure from the organization. When Belgian Foreign Minister Pierre Harmel proposed in December 1966 a broad examination of the future tasks facing the alliance, France was too distracted by the fallout from its disengagement to raise difficulties about a political reorientation of the alliance.[53]

But the meaning of the Harmel report involved more than the diminished role of France in the alliance; it represented, as did the NPG and the re-suscitated DPC, the new authority of the smaller nations. In a sense the participants in the "Harmel exercise" were repeating the efforts that the Wise Men of 1956 had attempted in vain: namely, to find some way to tell the larger powers that their voices should be heard. In 1956 the report of the Committee of Three on Non-Military Cooperation in NATO asked and received approval from the council for wider consultation among the member states in political matters, but the larger powers largely ignored its recommendations.[54] The Suez crisis, which occurred while the Wise Men were formulating their proposals, dramatized the exclusion of their countries from the agendas of the United States, the United Kingdom, and France.

In 1967 the smaller powers were able to make the larger pay attention to their concerns, not just with a vague promise of future consultation but through a specific program that won the support of the United States. In fact, Eugene Rostow, under-secretary of state for political affairs, noted that he devoted considerable time to the Harmel exercise and took pride in generating "wholly new political impulses" in the alliance. In accepting the Harmel report in December 1967 the North Atlantic Council elevated détente to the level of defense as a major function of the alliance. Its key statement was that "military security and a policy of detente are not contradictory but complementary."[55]

American planners were under no illusion about the difficulties in moving toward a new role for the alliance. As one report prepared for the National Security Council observed, important differences remained "between nations like Denmark and Canada that placed primary emphasis on detente and Greece and Turkey whose main preoccupation is with the Communist threat." Moreover, security arrangements would have to be made to take into account German sensitivities. And even as the United States welcomed the anticipated findings of the Harmel report, Europeans had to understand that the "special responsibilities" of the superpower required American "involvement in all phases of eventual negotiations on European security." If the allies still felt that they did not have a big enough role in NATO, "the ultimate answer to the lack of balance in the Alliance can only come from the Europeans themselves—through their unification."[56]

A feeling of satisfaction was expressed in the declaration on Mutual and Balanced Force Reductions, or the "Reykjavik signal," presented at the North Atlantic Council meeting of December 1967. This declaration followed from the recommendations of the Harmel report and seemed to portend a practical means of pursuing détente without risking the destabilization of Western Europe. The ministers were now ready for further "discussions on this subject with the Soviet Union and other countries of Eastern Europe and they call on them to join in this search for progress toward peace."[57]

The optimism implicit in this communique should have been tempered by concerns about the Soviets once again hampering Western access to Berlin. Though it did contain a warning that "progress toward general détente should not be over-rated," the tone of the communique belied this mild caveat.[58] Then the sudden and brutal Soviet intervention in Czechoslovakia two months later in August 1968 shocked the allies and disrupted the momentum for détente.

But the disruption was only temporary, and the reaction of the United States and NATO was carefully measured. It was not that the president and his advisers relegated the action against Czechoslovakia to the sidelines as an internal Warsaw Pact matter. They were distressed about the overthrow of the liberal Dubcek government and would not credit Soviet Ambassador Anatoly Dobrynin's statement that the Czechs had invited Warsaw forces into the country. Rusk was particularly chagrined at the timing of this action, just when strategic-missile talks, among other aspects of détente, appeared to show promise. Gen. Earle G. Wheeler, chairman of the Joint Chiefs of Staff, claimed that the "message is an insult to the United States" but that there was no military action that the United States could take. Clark Clifford, secretary of defense since McNamara's resignation in February 1968, agreed with Wheeler. The situation appeared to be more difficult than the failed Hungarian revolution of 1956 if only because there was a better relationship with the Soviet Union in 1968.[59]

The upshot of the agonizing in the National Security Council was a vigorous protest at the United Nations but little more. The administration offered a strong affirmation of Jefferson's belief in governments based on the consent of the governed and a weak compliance with the Warsaw Pact's *coup de main* on the grounds that U.S. interests were not affected. By September it was obvious that the Soviets were not going to invade Romania, let alone West Berlin. Former U.S. ambassador to the Soviet Union Llewellyn E. Thompson underscored this passive stance when he urged that the United States should not encourage Czech refugees to come to America "but only . . . welcome them" if they managed to escape. This "welcome" was compromised by his concern that the Soviets would regard any active encouragement as evidence of the West's interfering in the internal affairs of Czechoslovakia. Secretary Rusk disagreed: the United States should open its doors to refugees "because if we do not, the refugees might return to Czechoslovakia and oppose the existing government. This would not be in our interests." Neither adviser would allow the plight of refugees to jeopardize the fragile but peaceful relationship with the Soviet Union.[60]

It is understandable that domestic tensions over the war in Vietnam have been assigned responsibility for the caution the United States displayed when the Warsaw Pact forces ousted the Dubcek regime from Prague. A presidential campaign was in progress at the time, with President Johnson a self-declared lame duck and Vietnam the preoccupation of both political parties. Yet it is doubtful if Vietnam was responsible for the mild response to the Soviet-led invasion; rather, the response reflected NATO's hope to keep détente alive and its belief in the Soviet government's assurances about the limits of its actions. If the Czech crisis had a domestic impact, according to Clifford it was to inhibit for the short run the efforts of such congressional figures as Senator Mansfield to reduce the American presence in Europe.[61]

Still, the administration was clearly diluting the caliber of American troops in Europe by transferring units to Vietnam. This action reflected the long-standing objective of the secretary of defense, beginning in the Kennedy administration, to reduce the financial burden of NATO membership by basing U.S. troops in the United States and flying them over for regularly scheduled exercises. The operation to fly the combat-ready Second Armored Division from Texas to Germany, dubbed Exercise Big Lift, was conducted in October 1963, when Vietnam posed a troublesome but not an all-absorbing problem for the Kennedy administration. McNamara found proof that an entire armored division could be flown to Europe, draw its supplies and equipment from depots there, and be ready to participate in NATO maneuvers at any time. The Vietnam War combined with France's withdrawal from the organization to facilitate reforms made in the name of efficiency and of economy. If there was no massive cut in the U.S. forces, it was due in good measure to the influence of such strong-willed presidential advisers as John J. McCloy who made a persuasive case for keeping force reductions to a minimum.[62]

Similarly, the burden of the Vietnam War accounted for the increasingly strident American cries for Europeans to assume a greater share of the costs in money and manpower. The Senate resolutions on troop reduction and burden sharing, introduced in 1966 and repeated over the next few years, reflected public resentment of Europe's indifference or hostility to America's problems in Southeast Asia.

McNamara therefore had strong popular support for his demands for the allies to pay directly for American troops on their soil or to offset the costs by purchasing weapons or bonds from the United States. One of the more enduring sources of friction in the alliance after 1960 was over the effect of the cost of financing American forces abroad upon the balance of payments, particularly in Germany. Although a dominant subject of diplomatic conversations in the Johnson administration, these matters were essentially a legacy from the Kennedy era.

From 1961 to 1964 the United States and the Federal Republic, as well as France and Italy, had worked out bilateral offset agreements, which mandated purchase of American military equipment to offset the costs of the American military presence in those countries. By mid-1966 the financial difficulties of the three major allies—the United States, the United Kingdom, and the Federal Republic—reached a point at which the Americans and the British claimed that they would keep their forces intact in Germany only if new arrangements were made. The U.S. deficit in balance of payments was blamed directly on Europe.[63]

On 31 August 1966, Mike Mansfield, Senate majority leader, gathered forty-three sponsors to introduce the first of many subsequent resolutions calling for substantial reduction of the U.S. presence in Europe unless the allies increased their support. A potential deadlock was in the making. Britain had been suffering from a sterling crisis and was in much worse financial shape than the United States. Germany enjoyed a surplus in its balance of payments, but the country was experiencing an economic recession as well as a budget deficit, brought on by its purchase of U.S. military equipment under the offset agreements.[64]

To resolve the issue, the State Department proposed a trilateral approach in August 1966. John J. McCloy was appointed the U.S. chief representative on 11 October and spent the balance of that year and part of 1967 fending off domestic critics and contending with German and British opposition. His task was made even more difficult by the fall of the Erhard government and the worsening economic crisis in Britain. Erhard's coalition government fell in late October, but it was not until 1 December that his successor Kurt Georg Kiesinger took over. Three more months passed before the Germans were ready to resume the trilateral negotiations. Wilson's government managed to survive in part because of Johnson's offer to have the Department of Defense place some $35 million worth of orders for military equipment to help Britain's foreign-exchange squeeze. At home, the secretaries of state, defense, and treasury agreed that there should be no troop reductions that would seriously reduce U.S. capacity to deter a nonnuclear attack, but they could not agree on how deep any cuts should be.[65]

State Department officials understandably were more politically attuned to European sensibilities in the internal debate over troop reductions. Although both State and Defense agreed to dual-basing in the United States and West Germany, Secretary Rusk wanted to limit the withdrawals to two of three brigades of only one army division, and McNamara asked for four of six brigades from two divisions. McCloy strongly opposed both proposals in light of the military capabilities of the Warsaw Pact countries and the volatile political situation in Europe. He did recognize some merit in the principle of dual-basing of no more than one division and three air wings if the allies agreed and if U.S. capacity to rotate and reinforce rapidly showed that no substantial impairment of the military deterrent would occur.[66]

The president essentially accepted McCloy's advice to pursue a compromise that made clear that security, not financial considerations, would be the primary factor in determining U.S. force levels. This prejudgment determined the course of the trilateral negotiations. Monetary compensation, whether in the form of European procurement of U.S. equipment or of purchases of U.S. bonds, would be a matter of diplomatic bargaining, but the negotiations would not be conducted under the threat of U.S. withdrawal from Europe.[67]

By spring 1967 the administration managed to induce the British to cut back their demands for a complete offset of their costs of their Army of the Rhine and to accept something less than a complete closing of their gap in foreign exchange. U.S. purchases of $40 million worth of British equipment helped to convince the British to scale down their claims. The Germans offered to have the Bundesbank purchase $500 million in medium-term U.S. government bonds during fiscal year 1968 and promised not to convert their dollar holdings into gold.[68] The United States in turn scaled down its redeployment plan; 96 instead of 144 aircraft would be redeployed from Germany. The "Final Report on the Trilateral Talks" was signed on 28 April 1967, at the conclusion of the last trilateral meeting.[69]

McCloy deserved Johnson's congratulations for a successful negotiation, but the president himself played a vital role in the process. He recognized the centrality of the Congress in whatever success was achieved, and he understood just how tenuous the victory might be. In 1967 there was a three-to-one majority in favor of substantial troop cuts. A few congressmen would hold out, he thought, but "the rest of them will run just like turkeys." If the administration prevails, he told McCloy after a breakfast meeting with congressional leaders, it is "not because that's the way the Congress really feels, but because it is the way I managed it; first of all they were my guests, eating my breakfast, then I laid out a very hard line, more arbitrary than I like, which made it difficult for them to disagree with the President of the United States." But tough as his stance was, Johnson understood the limits of his authority. As he pointed out, he had "dealt with those babies for thirty years."[70] Senator Mansfield's reaction to the final agreement showed the reason for his wariness; the arrangement for Germans to purchase special U.S. government securities earned his scorn. The Senate majority leader claimed that Germany would be winning new profits from their loans rather than bearing their fair share of the defense of Europe.[71]

Despite formidable opposition in the Congress and in the country Johnson managed to surmount domestic challenges to the alliance. When he left the White House in 1969, he claimed that his "greatest single fear" was that the nation would relapse into isolationism, "whether out of boredom or frustration, out of lack of money, or out of simple foolishness." In his memoirs he took issue with critics who claimed that his preoccupation with Vietnam caused neglect of Europe and of opportunities to effect a détente with the Warsaw Pact countries.[72] He had reason to protest; indeed, he might have made a stronger case than he did. Not even the Soviet intervention in Czechoslovakia stopped his efforts on behalf of a nuclear pro-liferation treaty with the Soviet Union. Although his attention was rarely focused on Europe, when it was, his reasoning on NATO affairs was usu-ally sound, particularly when he considered congressional implications. At these times he did not always follow the lead of even his most trusted advisers. Where his own experience could come into play, his expertise served him well. The Mansfield resolutions never became law.

But NATO policy was only fitfully at the head of his agenda; policy was made by the experts around him to whom he had given his trust. Logically, Secretary of State Rusk should have been *primus inter pares*, and to a degree he was. Rusk occupied a more important role than he had under Kennedy, but his personality and his focus on Vietnam stood in his way. Undersecretary of State Ball felt that it was hard to get Rusk's attention on anything except Vietnam; consequently, Ball claimed to have "sort of taken the lead on European policy."[73] Ball undoubtedly overstated his role. Al-though he did grant Bundy "some independent" views, Ball might have added that Bundy's close connections with the president in his two years as adviser on national security provided him with greater influence than the undersecretary of state ever carried: Witness their respective positions on the MLF.

Of the men around Johnson, McNamara's weight was most felt in almost every aspect of foreign military affairs, from the MLF to Vietnam. Replace-ment of the MLF with agencies that granted new authority to the smaller nations, a troop-reduction program following France's withdrawal from the organization, pressures for burden sharing and cost reduction, and movement away from nuclear defense were primarily the work of Secretary NcNamara. Not all of these efforts were positive. There was an inherent contradiction in McNamara's vigorous espousal of costly conventional-force contributions by the European partners and his emphasis on reducing the American part of the equation. If a reformed and reorganized American military establishment in Europe could be substantially smaller and still effective, Europeans had little incentive to build up their own conventional forces. McNamara never exorcised European suspicion that a high nuclear threshold in the document of flexible response masked American willing-ness to use nuclear weapons under any circumstances. While American manpower in Europe declined from 416,000 in 1962 to 291,000 at the end of the Johnson years, Soviet conventional strength in Europe increased from 475,000 to over 500,000 personnel, figures that help to explain why Europe's image of security differed from McNamara's.[74]

Diversion of resources to Vietnam did affect the Atlantic alliance as it affected other aspects of Johnson's foreign and domestic policies. Congres-sional pressures would not have been as strong as they were without the debilitating effects of an escalating war in Southeast Asia. The American military presence in Europe was a logical target for critics, particularly when Europeans appeared either to oppose or to stand aloof from the American war in Asia.

Yet the course of NATO's history probably would have been much as it was without the destructive impact of the Vietnam War. The crisis with France, the failure of the MLF, the Harmel initiative, and détente occurred independently of other facets of American foreign military policies. The issue of force withdrawals and the tensions over balance of payments with allies were still by-products of Secretary McNamara's vision even if they were exacerbated by the Vietnam conflict. NATO's departure from France was an unexpected opportunity to accelerate reforms McNamara had regarded as necessary. Whether or not the realignment of force deployments was necessary, it was not the result of the war in Asia.

The Johnson administration of the alliance was not without flaws. Its dismissal of the MLF was graceless, and in general the manipulation of allies by the superpower too often was overbearing. Even the success of the trilateral negotiations inspired rebuke for its obvious slighting of the smaller allies. And while the administration was giving its blessing to the work of the Harmel committee in 1966, it had to fend off understandable complaints by Harmel, among others, that the three larger powers were reviving the idea of a "directorate."[75] If the administration managed to calm the Harmel group, it did less well in handling a potential Turkish invasion of Cyprus in 1966. Johnson's threat to cut off all military assistance if Turkey employed weapons designed for NATO use was a crude exercise of a superpower's weight even though its intentions were reasonable.[76]

The sins of commission and omission could be expanded. But in retrospect the Johnson years found NATO accepting, no matter how reluctantly, the American position on nuclear warfare and flexible response at the same time that the United States moved, with some reservations, toward a more genuine consultation on such vital issues as nuclear technology and nuclear proliferation. The elevation of detente to equality with defense reflected the increased visibility of the smaller members of the alliance. Above all, it was on Johnson's watch that NATO successfully met de Gaulle's challenge. Given the volatile history of the alliance, John Leddy may have understated the situation when he observed shortly before the North Atlantic Council met at Reykjavik in June 1968 that "NATO is in a better state of health than the pessimists predicted a few years ago."[77]

NOTES

1. David Calleo, *The Atlantic Fantasy: The U.S., NATO, and Europe* (Baltimore: Johns Hopkins University Press, 1970), pp. 27–28.

2. See in particular Marc Trachtenberg, "The Berlin Crisis," in *History and Strategy* (Princeton, NJ: Princeton University Press, 1991), pp. 223–24.

3. John Lewis Gaddis, "The Long Peace: Elements of Stability in the Postwar

International System," in *The Long Peace: Inquiries into the History of the Cold War* (New York: Oxford University Press, 1987), pp. 215–45.

4. Philip Geyelin, *Lyndon Johnson and the World* (New York: Frederick A. Praeger, 1966), p. 7.

5. John D. Steinbruner, *The Cybernetic Theory of Decision: New Dimensions of Political Analysis* (Princeton, NJ: Princeton University Press, 1974), pp. 220–23; Arthur Schlesinger, Jr., *A Thousand Days: John F. Kennedy in the White House* (Boston: Houghton Mifflin, 1965), pp. 854–55.

6. Paul H. Nitze, *From Hiroshima to Glasnost: At the Center of Decision, A Memoir* (New York: Grove Widenfield, 1989), pp. 211–12; Steinbruner, *Cybernetic Theory*, pp. 255–56; David N. Schwartz *NATO's Nuclear Dilemmas* (Washington, DC: Brookings Institution, 1982), pp. 108–9.

7. Steinbruner, *Cybernatic Theory*, pp. 286–88.

8. Ibid., p. 287; Geyelin, *Johnson and the World*, pp. 166–67.

9. Geyelin, *Johnson and the World*, p. 166.

10. Joint communiqué issued at Washington by Johnson and the chancellor of the Federal Republic of Germany (Erhard), 12 June 1964, in *American Foreign Policy: Current Documents 1964* (Washington, DC: Government Printing Office, 1967), p. 537.

11. Andrew J. Pierre, *Nuclear Politics: The British Experience with an Independent Strategic Force, 1939–1970* (London: Oxford University Press, 1971), pp. 276–77.

12. David Klein memorandum to Bundy, October 10, 1964, White House/National Security Files (WH/NSF) MLF Gen, vol. 2, boxes 23–24, Lyndon B. Johnson Library (hereafter cited as LBJL); NATO Nuclear Policy, Bundy memorandum to Rusk, McNamara, and Ball, 25 November 1964, "The Future of NATO," National Security Archive, Washington, DC. Unless otherwise indicated, all citations to documents and oral histories refer to material in the Johnson Library.

13. Geyelin, *Johnson and the World*, pp. 169, 171; LBJ memorandum for secretary of state and secretary of defense, November 14, 1964, "The Future of the Nuclear Defense of the Atlantic Alliance," MLF Gen, vol. 2, WH/NSF, box 23.

14. White House memorandum for the president, 4 December 1964, "The Wilson visit," WH/NSF memorandum to president, vol. 7, National Security Archives, Washington, DC; Harlan Cleveland Oral History Interview, August 13, 1969, by Paige E. Mulhollan, tape 1, pp. 37–38; the memorandum mentioned by Cleveland was probably Bundy's memorandum to the president, December 6, 1964, "MLF—An Alternative View," with a copy of his memorandum of June 15, 1963, to JFK, WH/NSF memorandum to president—Bundy, vol. 7.

15. President's news conference at the LBJ Ranch, January 16, 1965, *Public Papers of the Presidents of the United States*: 1: 57–58 (hereafter cited as *Public Papers*); Oral History Interview, March 12, 1969, by Paige Mulhollan, pp. 3–4, AC 75–5; Cleveland Oral History Interview, p. 20. George W. Ball Oral History Interview, p. 20. George W. Ball Oral History Interview, July 9, 1971, by Mulhollan 2, pp. 20–21.

16. Lawrence S. Kaplan and Katherine A. Kellner, "Lemnitzer: Surviving the French Military Withdrawal," in *Generals in International Politics: NATO's Supreme Allied Commander, Europe*, ed. Robert S. Jordan, (Lexington: University Press of Kentucky), p. 104.

17. Lemnitzer to Adm. Harry W. Hill, June 22, 1965, box 42, 1–28–71, Lemnitzer Papers, National Defense University Library, Washington, D.C.

18. De Gaulle to Lemnitzer, February 7, 1967, box 48, L–355–71, Lemnitzer Papers; Lemnitzer to Lydia and Bill (Lemnitzer), March 20, 1967, box 66, Family, ibid.

19. Letter from de Gaulle to Johnson, March 7, 1966, *American Foreign Policy: Current Documents 1966* (Washington, DC: Government Printing Office, 1969), pp. 317–18; French memorandum to the fourteen representatives of the NATO governments, March 29 and 30, 1966, ibid., pp. 324–26.

20. Harlan Cleveland, *NATO: The Transatlantic Bargain* (New York: Harper and Row, 1970), p. 102; Charles E. Bohlen, *Witness to History* (New York: W. W. Norton, 1973). As U.S. ambassador to France, he admitted to being "fooled by de Gaulle," after being told in January that France would do nothing precipitate; reply made by the president of the French Republic to a question asked at a news conference, February 21, 1966, *American Foreign Policy: Current Documents 1996*, pp. 316–17.

21. March 29 memorandum, *NATO Letter* 14 (May 1966): 24; see also French memorandum to the fourteen representatives of the NATO governments, March 8 and 10, 1966, *American Foreign Policy: Current Documents 1966*, pp. 318–19.

22. Rostow memorandum to the president, March 7, 1966, IT 34 NATO, box 58.

23. Cleveland, *NATO: Transatlantic Bargain*, pp. 105–6.

24. Lyndon B. Johnson, *The Vantage Point: Perspectives of the Presidency, 1963–1969* (New York: Holt, Rinehart and Winston, 1971), p. 305; Leddy Oral History Interview, March 12, 1969, p. 12, AC 75–5; Gen. Andrew J. Goodpaster Oral History Interview, June 21, 1971, by Paige Mulhollan.

25. George Ball Oral History Interview, July 9, 1971, 2: 122.

26. Bator memorandum to the president, "Your Letter to de Gaulle," March 18, 1966, Papers of LBJ, IT 34 NATO, box 58. Letter from Johnson to de Gaulle; March 22, 1966, *American Foreign Policy: Current Documents 1966*, pp. 321–23.

27. *American Foreign Policy: Current Documents 1966*, pp. 321–23; *New York Times*, March 18, 1966.

28. French memorandum to the fourteen representatives of the NATO governments, March 29 and 30, 1966, *American Foreign Policy: Current Documents 1966*, pp. 324–26.

29. *American Foreign Policy: Current Documents 1966*, p. 320. For more detail, see Department of State *Bulletin* 54 (18 April 1966): 617–18.

30. These recommendations were largely the product of Working Group D on Relocation, undated memorandum to the secretary of defense, "Evaluations of Relocation Alternatives, Box 164, L–1502–7h; Lemnitzer letter to Secretary-General Brosio, May 3, 1966; Air Marshal MacBrien's memorandum to Lord Coleridge, July 26, 1966, "Broad Outline of the Requirement When Relocated in Belgium," all in Lemnitzer Papers.

31. Count Charles De Kerchove letter to Lemnitzer, 12 August 1966, box 45, 1–1502, Lemnitzer Papers.

32. Lemnitzer letter to Norstad, 8 July 1966, box 44, L–316–7, ibid.; *New York Times*, 22 August 1966; *Pourquoi Pas*'s comment was listed in a continental press summary, 11 August 1966, box 163, L–1495–71, Lemnitzer Papers.

33. Lemnitzer to Brig. Gen. Orwin C. Talbott, 28 August 1967, box 45, L–327–71, Lemnitzer Papers.

34. "The Crisis in NATO," *Hearings* before the Subcommittee on Europe of the Committee on Foreign Affairs, H.R., 89th Cong., 2d sess., 17 March 1966, p. 37. Testimony of Assistant Secretary of Defense John T. McNaughton, who noted that the Defense Department was looking for alternatives that would make efficient use of modern logistic knowledge and equipment and which "would bring the costs down."

35. News release, ODS (Public Affairs), statement by secretary of defense on relocation of U.S. forces from Europe, 3 April 1967.

36. "The North Atlantic Alliance," *Hearings* before the Subcommittee on National Security and International Operations of the Committee on Government Operations, U.S. Senate, 89th Cong., 2d sess., pt. 6, 21 June 1966, p. 187; McNamara's statement.

37. Quoted in Cyrus L. Sulzberger, *New York Times*, 8 June 1966.

38. Note Mansfield resolution on troop reduction, 19 January 1967, Sen. Res. 49, 90th Cong., 1st sess., in "United States Troops in Europe," *Hearings* before Subcommittee of Foreign Relations and Armed Services Committee, 26 April 1967, pp. 1–2; Henry H. Fowler, secretary of the treasury, memorandum to the president, 25 May 1967, "Problems ahead in Europe," NSC meetings, vol. 4, IAV51, box 2.

39. "The Atlantic Alliance: Unfinished Business," a study submitted by the Subcommittee on National Security and International Operations to the Committee on Government Operations, U.S. Senate, 90th Cong., 1st sess., 1 March 1967, pp. 2, 5, 7; McCloy to Walt W. Rostow, 17 February commenting on a paper by Assistant Secretary of Defense for International Security Affairs John McNaughton on proposed troop withdrawals from Europe, 17 February 1967, NATO Gen, vol. 4, box 38.

40. *New York Times*, 31 July 1966; Eliot R. Goodman, "De Gaulle's NATO Policy in Perspective," *Orbis* 10 (Fall 1966): 716–17; a background paper for an NSC meeting in December 1966 noted de Gaulle's willingness to permit NATO's use of facilities in peacetime "provided these are under French management." State Department paper, 10 December 1966, for NSC meeting, 13 December 1966, appended to summary notes of 566th NSC meeting, 13 December 1966, NSC meetings, vol. 4, box 2.

41. *Aviation Week and Space Technology*, 29 May 1967, p. 315; Michael Harrison, *The Reluctant Ally: France and Atlantic Security* (Baltimore: Johns Hopkins University Press, 1981), pp. 155–56.

42. NATO Facts and Figures (Brussels: NATO Information Service, 1976), pp. 219–20. Meeting of the North Atlantic Council (NAC) 8 June 1966, *Texts of Final Communiques, 1949–1974* (Brussels: NATO Information Service, n.d.), p. 171 (hereafter cited as *NATO Communiqués*).

43. Meeting of NAC, Paris, 15–16 December 1966, *NATO Communiqués*, p. 180.

44. Summary notes of 566th NSC meeting, 13 December 1966, NSC meetings, vol. 4, box 2.

45. *NATO Communiqués*, p. 165; Leddy Oral History Interview, 12 March 1969, p. 6; quoted in Jane E. Stromseth, *The Origin of Flexible Response: NATO's Debate over Strategy in the 1960s* (New York: St. Martin's Press, 1988), p. 80.

46. Schwartz, *NATO's Nuclear Dilemmas*, pp. 182–85; meeting of NAC, Paris, 15–16 December 1966, *NATO Communiqués*, p. 180.

47. Bator memorandum to president, "Your Meeting with McNamara and the NATO Nuclear Planning Group (NPG)—12 Noon, April 7," 6 April 1967, NATO Gen 5, box 37.

48. Ibid., with enclosure on "Background Material on the Nuclear Planning Group."

49. Meeting of NAC, Paris, December 15–16, 1966, *NATO Communiqués*, p. 177.

50. Remarks by McNamara, NATO ministerial meeting, Athens, National Security Archive, Washington, DC; McNamara draft memorandum to president, 15 January 1965, "Role of Tactical Nuclear Forces in NATO Strategy," ibid.; McNamara draft memorandum to president, 6 January 1967, "Thereafter Nuclear Forces," ibid., p. 6; Stromseth, *Origins of Flexible Response*, pp. 58–68.

51. Stromseth, *Origins of Flexible Response*, pp. 58–68; McNamara draft memorandum to president, September 21, 1966, "NATO Strategy and Force Structure," National Security Archive, Washington, D.C., Freedom of Information Act.

52. Ministerial meeting of NAC, Brussels, 13–14 December 1967, *NATO Communiqués*, p. 197.

53. Ministerial meeting of NAC, Paris, 15–16 December 1966, ibid., pp. 179–80; Cleveland, *NATO: Transatlantic Bargain*, p. 143.

54. Ministerial meeting of NAC, Paris, 11–14 December 1956, "Resolution of the Report of the Committee of Three on Non-Military Cooperation in NATO," *NATO Communiqués*, p. 104; ministerial meeting of NAC, Paris, 4–5 May 1957, ibid., p. 99.

55. Eugene V. Rostow Oral History Interview, 1 December 1968, by Paige Mulhollan, AC 74–72. Report of the council, "The Future Tasks of the Alliance," ministerial meeting of NAC, 13–14 December 1967, *NATO Communiqués*, p. 19.

56. State Department paper, undated, "Problems Ahead in Europe," pp. 5–7, NSC meetings, vol. 4, box 2.

57. Ministerial meeting of the NAC, Reykjavik, 24–25 June 1968, *NATO Communiqués*, pp. 206, 209–10.

58. Ibid., pp. 206–7.

59. Notes on emergency meeting of the National Security Council, 20 August 1968—President Johnson, Rusk, General Wheeler, CIA director Helms, vice-president, Ambassador Ball, Walt Rostow, Leonard Marks, George Christian, Tom Johnson, Notes of Meetings, box 2.

60. Summary notes, 590th NSC meeting, 4, September 1968, "U.S., Europe, and the Czechoslovakian Crisis," p. 2, Tom Johnson's Notes of Meetings, box 2.

61. Tom Johnson memorandum to the president, 22 August 1968, with notes of cabinet meeting of 22 August Tom Johnson's Notes of Meetings, box 2.

62. Rostow Oral History Interview, AC 74–72.

63. Trilateral Negotiations and NATO, undated, NSC paper, Background to the Negotiations, p. 1; Trilateral Negotiations and NATO, Book 1, NSC History, box 50.

64. Ibid., p. 2.

65. Ibid., pp. 2–6; Analysis of Major Decisions in Trilateral Talks, undated,

"The Decision to Offer the British $35 million in Purchases," Trilateral Negotiations and NATO, Book 2, NSC History, box 50.

66. Trilateral Negotiations and NATO, ibid., pp. 7–8; Eugene Rostow, Robert Bowie, John Leddy, and Jeffrey Kitchen, memorandum to secretary of state, and "OSD Proposal for Reducing U.S. Troops in Europe," Trilateral Negotiations and NATO, Book 4, NSC History box 51; Eugene Rostow, in a memorandum to the secretary, 30 January 1967, "Force Levels in Europe, ibid., believed that the risks of the plan "are out of proportion to the possible benefits." McCloy memorandum to the president, "Force Levels in Europe," Trilateral Negotiations and NATO, Book 2, NSC History, box 50; Bator claimed to prefer McNamara's position to McCloy's but "my bad dream is another Skybolt, with painful consequences at home" (Bator memorandum to the president, 23 February 1967, "U.S. Position in the Trilateral Negotiations," ibid.).

67. Trilateral Negotiations and NATO, Book 2, NSC History, box 50, pp. 8–9.

68. Bator memorandum to the president, 8 March 1967, "Your 12:45 P.M. Meeting with John McCloy on the Trilaterals," ibid. Bator was convinced that the promise not to convert German dollar holdings into gold was the more valuable part of the Bundesbank offer. (In effect, this would have put them on a dollar standard.) Johnson, Vantage Point, pp. 309–11.

69. Trilateral Negotiations and NATO, Book 2, NSC History, box 50, pp. 9–16.

70. Bator memorandum for the record, March 2, 1967, "President's Conversation with John McCloy Concerning U.S. Position in Trilateral Negotiations, 10:45–11:40 A.M., Wednesday, March 1, 1967," ibid.

71. Congressional Record, 19 June 1968, reprinted in "United States Troops in Europe, Report of the Combined Subcommittees of Foreign Relations and Armed Services Committees on the Subject of United States Troops in Europe to the Committee on Foreign Relations and Committee on Armed Services," U.S. Senate, 15 October 1968, pp. 88–89.

72. Johnson, Vantage Point, pp. 491–92; 475.

73. Ball Oral History Interview, 2, p. 17.

74. Richard Hart Sinnreich, "NATO's Doctrinal Dilemma, Orbis 19 (Summer 1976): 466.

75. Secretary of state to American embassy in Ottawa, no. 65140, 13 October 1966, for Harmel via the Belgian embassy, Trilateral Negotiations and NATO, Book 3, NSC History, box 51; Bator memorandum to the president, 12 October 1966, Bator memorandums, box 1—a voice for the Italian ambassador at Columbus Day parade.

76. The full text of President Johnson's letter of rebuke was published in the Turkish newspaper, Hurriyet, on 14 January 1966.

77. Memorandum for the record, summary of NSC meeting on NATO, 19 June 1968, NSC meetings, vol. 5, box 2.

8
NATO and the Nixon Doctrine: Ten Years Later

"NATO and the Nixon Doctrine: Ten Years Later," Orbis 24 *(Spring, 1980): 149–66, was drawn from a paper on "NATO: the Second Generation," delivered at a conference on "NATO after Thirty Years," organized by the newly established Center for NATO Studies at Kent State University in April 1980.*

"Doctrines" in American diplomatic history have never been satisfactorily defined. In their broadest form, doctrines are, says William Safire, "systematic statements on foreign policy" that provide some "guiding principles" for the administrations that formulate them. Safire notes, moreover, that doctrines are "policies that have hardened with acceptance," and he observes that "when the word is applied in retrospect it usually sticks; when it is announced as a policy, it usually fades."[1] The Monroe Doctrine is the pre-eminent exemplar of the nineteenth-century doctrine. In the twentieth century, doctrine proliferation has taken place as three successive presidents have had doctrines named after them—Truman, Eisenhower, and Nixon. Whether they all will remain fixed in the pattern of Monroe's doctrine is still moot; but from the vantage point of NATO, both the Truman Doctrine and the Nixon Doctrine have had vital roles in the evolution of American policy toward the Atlantic Alliance.

The Truman Doctrine originated in a presidential message of 12 March 1947, requesting Congress to help Greece and Turkey protect themselves from Communist pressures. It expanded into an elaborate system of military alliances in which the United States assumed a substantial responsibility for supplying military and economic aid to its allies.[2] In the 1950s and 1960s, the Truman Doctrine appeared to have been etched in stone: the United States assumed the endless burden of containing an ever aggressive communism. In this scheme, NATO was the grandest part of a "Grand Design," in the parlance of the Kennedy years. All the other treaties, even the Rio Pact, with its historic links to the Monroe Doctrine, appeared commonplace by contrast. The upheavals in the Middle East, from Suez in 1956 to the Six Day War in 1967, made CENTO appear either impotent or irrelevant, while the Vietnam War was the ultimate exposé of the hollowness of SEATO. NATO lived on, struggling with a defecting but not quite departed France and patching up various rents made by divisions among other uneasy allies.

No nation departed from membership voluntarily; no communist action forced an involuntary departure. Although the Brezhnev Doctrine, applied quickly and ruthlessly in Czechoslovakia in 1968, exposed NATO's inability to extend the values of the treaty's preamble to the Soviet zone of control, Soviet intervention pointedly refrained from threatening gestures against the Western allies. The survival of NATO became synonymous with the reconstruction of Western Europe, much as the Truman Doctrine had hoped, and "no revisionism," according to Uwe Nerlich, "will undo the fact that this reconstruction of the old continent was a historical achievement of American foreign policy."[3]

Because the Nixon Doctrine, introduced in 1969, was represented as a new direction in American foreign policy, NATO would inevitably be touched by it, even if its message was intended primarily for Asia. Containment was redefined. On the one hand, the Nixon Doctrine was to reflect an idea that Denis Brogan[4] raised in 1950, in the midst of the Korean War: namely, that there were limits to American power, that the way to achieve success lay in the realignment of objectives to resources. The failure of policy in Vietnam, in a war that seemed to make a mockery of containment, was the price of ignoring this wisdom. The Nixon Doctrine would retreat from apparently limitless support for anticommunist regimes everywhere. On the other hand, the United States would identify priorities, recognizing that some parts of the world are of greater concern than others. Through this new Weltanschauung, there could be disengagement from East Asia, a place of lesser priority. The Vietnamese would have to defend themselves, though with the continued blessing and material support of the United States. Thus, the concept of Vietnamization, which Kissinger had put forth in foreign affairs before becoming Nixon's national security adviser in 1969, was deliberately mingled with the Nixon Doctrine in the president's remarks during his summer 1969 visit to Guam.[5]

It would appear that some time had passed before the Nixon administration decided that its rationalizations for disengagement in Asia was a doctrine, which had its genesis in the president's informal remarks on 25 July 1969, in Guam. Part of a goodwill trip around the world, the stopover at Guam occurred a week after national attention was focused on the astronauts' lunar landing and on the tragic event at Chappaquiddick.[6] Not until November 3 did the president recognize that he had said something significant at Guam about "what has been described as the Nixon Doctrine."[7] More directly, in his State of the World address on 18 February 1970, the president referred to the Nixon Doctrine and amplified its meaning. In this speech, he distinguished NATO from all other commitments since "Europe must be the cornerstone of the structure for a durable peace." At the same time, he observed that the "central thesis" of the doctrine was that "America cannot—and will not—conceive *all* the plans, design *all* the programs, execute *all* the decisions and undertake *all* the defense of the free nations of the world. We will help where it makes a real difference and is considered in our interest."[8]

THE MANSFIELD RESOLUTIONS

With NATO as the first priority in American foreign policy, the new doctrine was expected to be well received in Europe. It signaled the end of the diversion of American energies and resources from the European arena, which had been brought about by the Vietnam War. It should have been welcomed, in the view of the new administration, as a means of reinvigorating the alliance as well as of responding to pleas made by the Europeans over the previous decade. Indeed, presidential candidate Nixon had lashed out at the Johnson administration the year before for ignoring NATO, particularly for Johnson's failure even to mention NATO in the 1968 State of the Union message. According to Nixon, "Actions have been taken by the United States which vitally affected the security of our European partners, without even the courtesy of prior consultation. . . . It's time we began paying Europe more attention. And if our ideals of Atlantic interdependence are to mean anything in practice, it's time we began lecturing our European partners less and listening to them more."[9]

To dramatize his desire for "genuine consultation," Nixon made a point of visiting Europe a month after his inauguration. Beyond this spirit of cooperation, he promised to present a plan to move "from crisis management to crisis prevention" as East and West emerge from a period of confrontation and enter into an "era of negotiation."[10] This commitment applied not only to relations within the alliance, but to relations with the Soviet bloc.

Presidential assistant Kissinger himself had a long record of absorption in European issues, from his doctoral dissertation on the Congress of Vienna to his perceptive book, *The Troubled Partnership*, published in 1965.

In this work, he considered a genuine Atlantic partnership with Europe to be vital for the success of NATO. He further advanced the importance of European unity as a pre-requisite to internal harmony, and he urged the United States to accept and even to support a supranational Europe without recoiling from its consequences.[11]

Repeatedly, over the next two years, the Nixon administration gave evidence of its concern for NATO in ways that should have been unmistakable to Europeans. The most critical support derived from its stand on the Mansfield resolution, Senate Resolution 292, calling for "a substantial reduction of U.S. forces permanently stationed in Europe."[12] (Resolution 292 was similar to a previous resolution proposed by Senator Mike Mansfield earlier in 1969 as the Vietnam crisis worsened.) The Mansfield arguments were numerous and weighty, the most important of which was that 315,000 American military personnel in Europe, along with 235,000 dependents and 14,000 civilian employees, exacerbated the "dollar gap" in foreign exchange to the extent of $1.5 billion a year. The intention of the resolution, according to Mansfield, was to induce the allies to make a larger and fairer contribution to NATO, rather than to indicate that the NATO military structure was overbuilt. In the event of an emergency, American troops could be quickly flown back to Europe. No changes were intended, he claimed, beyond reducing the size of the American contribution "without aversely affecting either our resolve or ability to meet our commitment under the North Atlantic Treaty."[13]

If ever there were a temptation to reduce costs through troop reduction, it was at its greatest in the early part of the decade. Inevitably, the national mood of disillusionment with the military investment in Southeast Asia found some resonance in the NATO arena. Not only could costs be pared, but anger over Europe's insensitivity to America's agony in Vietnam would be drained. Europe could and should do more for the common defense, particularly as a war-born inflation weakened the dollar while the economies of the Western allies flourished and their currencies strengthened at American expense.

The Nixon administration held firm, claiming that the United States would not reduce its forces unless reciprocal action were taken by the Soviet Union. Any unilateral action would create a military imbalance, which might induce the Warsaw bloc to risk provocations it would otherwise avoid, and would generate doubts among allies about the steadfastness of American commitments in Europe.[14] The doubts were unavoidable anyway as talk about neoisolationism flourished. If the United States could withdraw unilaterally from Asia, was there not a precedent that might apply to Europe, no matter what the Nixon Doctrine said?

The Nixon position was not simply a gesture of NATO solidarity. It was tested in 1971, when Senator Mansfield mounted his most powerful challenge in the form of an amendment to a bill extending the Selective Service

Act.[15] The amendment required that U.S. forces in Europe be halved to 150,000 men. To cope with the popularity of this amendment, the administration mobilized former NATO commanders Alfred Gruenther, Lauris Norstad, and Lyman Lemnitzer, along with such veteran Democrats as former secretaries of state George Ball and Dean Acheson, to express their opposition to Mansfield's plan. Nixon even won the endorsement of former President Johnson, who agreed that the drastic reduction of troop strength would have dangerous consequences for the alliance.[16] The amendment was defeated in the Senate on May 18, 1971, by a vote of 61 to 36.[17]

At the same time that it was warding off the Mansfield threat, the Nixon administration served Europe in another fashion: by maintaining, as Raymond Aron called it, "a low profile" on matters that in the past the American voice would have been loudly raised. Aron contrasted Washington's "ostentatious silence" since 1969 on the British candidacy for entry into the Common Market with the heavyhanded advocacy of British membership during the de Gaulle years.[18] Moreover, the United States chose not to speak out against Chancellor Willy Brandt's *Ostpolitik*, despite serious reservations about the terms that the Soviet Union might demand in return for improved relations with the Federal Republic of Germany. The United States confined its public concerns to negotiations with the Soviet Union over the section of the German accords that related directly to the American position in Berlin. This discreet behavior appeared to fulfill the Nixon Doctrine's resolution to allow Europeans responsibility for managing their own affairs in ways they regard appropriate without American interference.

In retrospect, Nixon and Kissinger won little credit from the European allies for their pointed abstention from internal European affairs or even for their firm championship of the American military presence on the continent. Some of the reasons for the ingratitude emerged from ambiguities within the Nixon Doctrine itself. The new "era of negotiations" that the president welcomed in his 1970 State of the World message meant no denigration of Europe's role in America's future, but the priority of the European partnership was interpreted to be subsumed under other unstated objectives. Implicit in the structure of the Nixon-Kissinger vision of the 1970s was a détente with the Soviet Union, a sentiment Europeans had valued in the 1950s and 1960s, but which, in the light of the Vietnam retreat, had become an object of suspicion. To many Europeans, a bilateral détente with the Soviet Union seemed to be a consequence of the scaling down of American commitments abroad, which, of necessity, would include Europe as well as Asia. A drive for a new modus vivendi with the Soviet Union was an admission of inferiority in the competition of East and West. To build the new "structure of peace," Americans might sacrifice the interests of the European allies.[19]

Fears of American weakness permeated Europe's perception of the Nixon Doctrine. If the United States and the Soviet Union managed mutual restraint over strategic-nuclear arms, the result might also subvert American nuclear protection of Europeans. De Gaulle may have departed by the 1970s, but his cry that America would not sacrifice its own security for the sake of Europe continued to be heard. Within this context, the call to Europeans to do more for themselves rather than to rely on American in-itiatives seemed to have arisen less from American respect for European sensibilities or for their equality in the alliance than from a desire to min-imize American responsibilities abroad. No matter what the guise may be, retreat from Asia could lead to retreat from Europe. The logic of the Nixon Doctrine was applicable everywhere in the world. "Its purpose," in the words of James Chace and Earl Ravenal, "was to assuage domestic op-position to costly interventionist wars through a limited military retrench-ment, yet at the same time remain politically engaged throughout the globe."[20]

The message dispatched from America's NATO allies was one of distrust in America's ability to maintain such a delicate balance. Partial disengage-ment in one part of the world veiled only imperfectly the weakness that would be felt in other parts of the world. Thus, the American push for SALT I or the Kissinger opening to China in the first Nixon administration symbolized not detente but serious American failings or loss of nerve that could damage NATO's sense of security.

EUROPEAN CONCESSIONS

If Europe was less than fair in judging the Nixon administration's posi-tive efforts to serve the alliance, it could point to other actions that eroded the credibility of the Nixon Doctrine, and of American relations with NATO in general, even as Nixon and Kissinger were congratulating themselves in turning aside congressional challenges. American international economic policy could not be separated from the rest of foreign policy, and it was in this area that European concern became manifest. As the dollar weakened, Nixon followed the advice of Secretary of the Treasury John Connally and, in August 1971, suspended the convertibility of the dollar into gold.[21] Moreover, a 10 percent surcharge was imposed on all imports. These acts shocked Europe partly by their unilateral nature, partly because of the con-fession of weakness they demonstrated in what had been a bastion of sta-bility for a generation.

The justification for America's defense of the dollar was not negligible: the dollar gap grew out of the massive American military expenses in Eu-rope, as well as from the burden of Vietnam. The devaluation of the dollar and the seeming end of trade liberalization as protectionist sentiment bur-geoned in the United States had an impact on the European economies that was sharp and immediate, and the European Economic Community was no help either in mitigating the force of Washington's actions or in mediating with the United States. Indeed, a principal focus of Secretary Connally's animus were the preferential trade agreements (especially on agricultural products), which discriminated against American interests.

Connally's initiative, however, did not have a long life. The December 1971 Smithsonian Agreement created an essentially floating exchange-rate system that helped to restore temporary equilibrium to the monetary system.[22] Indeed, the surcharge was lifted, the American troop level remained unchanged, and Europe's military contributions to NATO stayed the same; but the psychological damage could not be undone. Four years of the Nixon Doctrine had left Europeans as suspicious of American policy in 1973 as they had been in 1969.

The continuing drain of mutual recriminations accounted for the special exertions on both sides of the Atlantic to repair differences within the organization. The European Community opened the way for a new direction in its communique of October 1972, calling for a "constructive dialogue" with the United States.[23] With the Vietnam War behind them, Americans responded with at least a rhetorical concern for what Nixon labeled the "Year of Europe" in 1973.[24] Early in the year, Secretary of Commerce Peter Peterson led an exploratory mission to Europe and Japan after which he reported on the linkages between economic and political problems, urging that these problems be addressed as early as possible.

Kissinger's proposal for a new "Atlantic Charter," a rededication of the Atlantic Alliance, followed in a major address on April 23, 1973. Phrases such as "fresh act of creation" and "a revitalized Atlantic partnership" punctuated the speech.[25] Europe's reaction was cynical, for Kissinger's overture, despite the American avowals, contained many of the elements that contributed to the malaise in the first place. Laced with arrogance, the speech was drawn up without significant consultation either at home or abroad. Not even Secretary of State William Rogers had advance notice of Kissinger's terms. The message was that "the United States has global interests and responsibilities," whereas "our European allies have regional interests." The style of the speech, characterized by Wilfrid Kohl as "the royal-court model of foreign policy making," combined with the tone, could only grate upon European sensibilities.[26] This language accentuated the divisions between Europe and America and emphasized as well, if only by implication, the new and potentially dangerous bilateral relationship between the United States and the Soviet Union.

But a deeper source of continuing discord than the lordly manner of Kissinger's presentation was another by-product of the Nixon Doctrine: namely, the imperative of Europe's making greater sacrifices than before in building the military strength of NATO and in improving its financial infrastructure. Kissinger's new overture, inspired in part by the stirrings of the European Community, assumed a unity among some if not all its members that could make burden-sharing a reality. Indeed, President Nixon's

State of the World address of May 1973 emphasized the need for the European allies to redress the American balance-of-payments problem in Europe.[27] The assumption greatly exaggerated the reality of European unity.

That the United States was prepared to conceive of Europe as a coherent and effective unit, potentially dangerous to U.S. interests but also capable of carrying greater weight in the alliance, was not surprising. West Germany was able to conduct its *Ostpolitik* with the Soviet Union with reasonable success, defusing in the early 1970s the burning issues of a divided Germany. For its part, the United Kingdom finally brought its strength to bear in an enlarged European Community in 1973, marking, as Michael Howard has claimed, "the final transformation of a Western Europe from a collection of weak and frightened clients of the United States into America's most formidable adversary."[28]

That adversary was indeed impressive. The population of "the Nine" (the member-states of the European Community) was 260 million in 1973, compared with 210 million in the United States and 249 million in the Soviet Union. The Nine's gross domestic product was $1,061.4 billion, almost twice that of the Soviet Union, though approximately $250 billion less than the GDP of the United States. Particularly revealing was that the Nine spent $34.4 billion on defense, compared with U.S. spending of $90 billion, at a time when the Community had $43.9 billion in currency reserves convertible in gold and the United States had $13.19 billion. Seeing in these figures an inequitable distribution of the alliance's burdens, Washington was unhappy indeed.

The United States, however, did not recognize that Europe's strength was more potential than real, tied to a "United States of Europe" that did not yet exist. There was no simple way for Europeans to act—without a united Europe—that could raise troop levels or increase taxes for defense in the manner of the United States of America. For all the vocal opposition to many American policies in the early and mid-1970s, and for all the potential equality the foregoing figures suggest, Europe could neither respond to American demands nor do without American aid. Kissinger frightened as much as annoyed Europeans with his call for equality from the NATO allies.

Given this disarray among Europeans, they had no choice but to respect the continuing discontent in the Congress over the heavy costs that the alliance was imposing on Americans. The Mansfield resolution may have been contained and deflected in Nixon's first administration, but with the Vietnam War over, the administration was worried about neoisolationism arising from widespread, disillusionment with foreign affairs. Since détente with the Soviet Union was in the air, and since Europeans continued to complain without responding to American needs, Congress might have accepted the Senate plan in September 1973 to reduce American forces in Europe: first, by 40 percent; later, by an additional 23 percent. Only a belated recognition that a unilateral initiative of this sort would undermine the Mutual and Balanced Force Reductions (MBFR) talks stayed the legislators' hand.[29]

The European allies felt obligated to give at least lip service to American thinking, and so they accepted in place of Kissinger's new Atlantic Charter a "declaration of Atlantic principles."[30] Such public reaffirmation of European-American solidarity in the summer of 1973 was all the more important in light of the Nixon-Brezhnev accords of June 1973 in which the superpowers pledged to avert confrontations that would lead to nuclear war. The allies speculated that behind the high-minded words lay a Soviet-American nuclear stand-off, exacerbating Europe's vulnerability to Soviet political pressures. Europe's words were grudging, its mood suspicious, and its spirit resentful. The term "West-West dialogue" conveyed a message that Europe and America were as far apart as they had ever been in the past.[31]

In this heated atmosphere, it is hardly surprising that an American riposte would be made. The Jackson-Nunn amendment, a rider to a vital military appropriations bill, was the immediate reaction. Public Law 93–155, section 812, required the president to reduce U.S. forces in Europe by the same percentage that Europeans failed to offset balance-of-payment costs arising from the stationing of those forces in Europe for fiscal year 1974.[32] Fearing that a veto would trigger other more drastic legislation, the administration accepted the amendment, despite misgivings over the pall it would cast on negotiations with allies.

Officially, NATO had no alternative but to accede to American demands. At a December meeting, the NATO defense ministers spoke of an impending NATO examination of "how the share of the United States in the civil and military budgets of NATO and in the infrastructure program might be substantially reduced."[33] An "offset" agreement with Germany, involving $2.22 billion over a two-year period, embraced military procurement, loans, and German assumption of some of America's real estate costs in Germany.

The spirit on both sides, however, was still sour. In fact, the German concession was accompanied by Nixon's outburst in Chicago on March 12, 1974, in which he warned that "the Europeans cannot have it both ways. They cannot have the United States participation and cooperation on the security front and proceed to have confrontation and even hostility on the economic and political front."[34] So, on the eve of its twenty-fifth anniversary, the alliance looked shakier than ever. Titles such as "Unhappy Birthday" and "NATO: End of an Era" captured the mood of leading American newspapers,[35] and a Gallup poll taken in 1974 revealed that internationalist views dropped 45 percent, the lowest figure since 1945. Only 48 percent of those polled would approve the use of force to help Western Europe in a crisis.[36]

The Soviet press did not overlook the troubles of the alliance and took the occasion to note that the strains left from the Arab oil embargo proved that the Atlantic alliance was obsolete. TASS observed that "oil is only the upper layer of a compound and bitter cocktail of contradictions" between the United States and Europe. Europe could no longer be assigned a junior partnership. The solution was to assign NATO "to the archives."[37]

Even the official *NATO Review*[38] included in its twenty-fifth anniversary issue an essay entitled "Twenty-five Years of Ups and Downs." For the NATO Information Service to give equal weight to the "downs" indicates the magnitude of the distress. Yet, it could find solace in the fact that the organization seemed always to be in a state of crisis, and the editor was comforted by the knowledge that NATO, after all, had recovered from the shock caused by the building of the Berlin Wall in 1961 and from the high tension of the 1962 Cuban missile crisis.

AMERICA AND EUROPE: MUTUAL DEPENDENCE

The alliance did not collapse as anticipated by friends and enemies alike, and the "Finlandization" of Western Europe did not develop from the malaise of 1974. Indeed, the Soviet price for an East-West relationship remained unacceptable, a revived American isolationism never materialized, and the new bilateralism between the Soviet Union and the United States quickly revealed the limits of détente. If the alliance did not fade out in the subsequent years, in the manner of SEATO in 1977 or of CENTO in 1979, with little fanfare and no sense of loss, either the professional optimism of NATO officials was a matter of good luck or the bonds within the organization were less brittle than observers had credited.

The chief factor in NATO's resilience was the mutual dependence on both sides of the Atlantic that frequently went unrecognized or, when identified, was given grudging respect. The growing maturity of a European Community in which the NATO powers played a predominant role ensured friction between Americans and Europeans, if only because new strength required a reevaluation of older relations. The centrality of France's presence ensured, as well, a certain testiness in the Community's outlook on the United States. Nothing that the United States could do would appease French suspicions since the fundament of France's idea of a Community was its utility as an instrument in placing a distance between Europe and both the superpowers, whether on matters of relations with the Middle East, the attack on the dollar, or the projected restrictions on multinational companies. Even the rise of detente in the 1970s distressed the French, though they had been advocates of the concept the decade before; if successful, detente would be seen as devaluing the position of France and Europe as a mediating force.[39]

The separate status of a new Europe would seem confirmed as well by the Eurogroup, a forum for NATO defense ministers to articulate a coherent—and distinct—European voice. Not unimportant, Europeans contributed 90 percent of the ground forces of NATO, 80 percent of the navies, and 75 percent of the aircraft. Most of the Eurogroup's activities centered on furthering military cooperation, particularly in coordinating purchases of U.S. weaponry.[40]

But for all the collaboration among Europeans in the direction of a single European entity, no "United Europe" has yet appeared. The subcommittees of Eurogroup—Eurotraining, Europmed, or Eurostructure—helped to support a European Defense Improvement Program in the 1970s but did not conceal a continuing painful dependence on the United States. All their activities were still defined by a relationship with the Americans. For the past quarter of a century, much of the debate over European unity was "as much about the relationship of Europe to America," according to William Pfaff, "as about the relations of Europeans to one another."[41] As Kissinger expressed it, "They favored unity in the abstract, but they feared that the attempt to articulate a European identity within NATO might give the United States an excuse for reducing its military establishment in Europe."[42] At least psychologically, this condition has not changed. Without America, Europe found itself unable to cope with Soviet power. As the decade ended, NATO's importance to the European partners remained the single vehicle for ensuring security.

For its part, the United States, while experiencing as many frustrations from the alliance as its allies, was no less bound to the alliance. The ambiguities of our relationship with Europe frequently obscured NATO's importance. European unification has never been fully conceptualized in the American mind. Though sincerely wishing for a "United States of Europe," patterned on the American model, every administration harbored fears of nurturing a Frankenstein's monster that would run amok as soon as it was created. A Gaullist Europe was one apprehension; a Eurocommunist Europe susceptible to Finlandization was another. But just as with the Europeans, the bonds of a generation could not be broken without traumatic effects. On the one hand, the American multinational corporations that had invested in Western Europe and had bloomed with the expansion of the national economies presented a hostage of considerable significance. On the other hand, that U.S. disengagement might lead to Soviet pressures on the West would be as intolerable to the Americans as to the Europeans. Perhaps the most important factor in keeping NATO together was the absence of alternatives.

The Nixon Doctrine seems to have slipped away into history with Nixon himself. It no longer has much resonance in American politics; the term even disappeared from the index of the *U.S. Department of State Bulletin* in 1972.[43] Yet, it had a meaning for Europe that deserves in retrospect more attention than it has received to date. "Partnership" and "era of negotiations" were too quickly identified as code words to indicate abandonment of Europe, just as Vietnam had been abandoned. Nixon's NATO record, like his Vietnam record, certainly invited suspicion; but if NATO has survived the Nixon years, it was in part because the Nixon Doctrine's statements on Europe could be taken at face value. Its emphasis on adjusting commitments to resources, on requiring an increasing European share of NATO responsibilities, and on reaffirming the priority of Atlantic interests in American foreign policies continued to characterize the American position on NATO long after Nixon's resignation.

TOWARD A REVITALIZED NATO

In 1980, the compartmentalized universe of the Nixon Doctrine appears as remote as the doctrine itself. The collapse of imperial Iran in 1979 as the surrogate American policeman of the Middle East directly challenged the policy of military disengagement from Asia. The overthrow of the shah seems also to have removed much of the trauma remaining from the Vietnam War, at least with respect to popular revulsion against potential American military intervention abroad. Even before the Soviet occupation of Afghanistan in January 1980, President Carter had implicitly abandoned the use of regional allies to keep order in their areas, calling in late 1979 for a Rapid Deployment Force to intervene, if necessary, in global trouble spots. Whatever the future of a "Carter Doctrine," with its "cooperative security framework" for South Asia, the challenges of 1980 assume the demise of the Nixon Doctrine.[44]

The importance of the NATO allies has increased, rather than decreased, since the promulgation of the Nixon Doctrine. Western Europe occupies the front line of an intensive Soviet military challenge to NATO. As such, it is a key to congressional acceptance of SALT II and a goad to the pursuit of SALT III. Hence, the priority assigned Europe by the Nixon Doctrine has assumed a higher place than had been anticipated in 1969, returning NATO to the predominant position it had enjoyed among American policymakers in the late 1940s and the mid-1950s.

At the same time, the rapid expansion of Soviet influence in Africa and Asia, combined with the rising power of the Third World through its control over oil resources, have made more imperative than before concerted NATO positions on issues beyond defense against possible Soviet nuclear attack in Europe. NATO's stability has been damaged by the Western world's increasing dependence on external energy sources, as well as by the anti-Western thrust of the former colonies. The alliance displayed disconcerting divisions when most European members denied bases to the United States during the 1973 Yom Kippur War and when, in 1979, they hesitated to deny themselves Iranian oil in support of U.S. policy toward Iran. Understandable though their behavior may have been in both instances, the fissures must be closed if NATO is to survive the decade. NATO will have to consider as appropriate to its vital concerns the very parts of the world toward which the Nixon Doctrine had sought to reduce American commitments.

There is considerable doubt in 1980 that the United States can continue to base its policies in Asia and Africa on the lessons of Vietnam. The Nixon Doctrine had identified limits to American commitment on the assumption that others would pick up the burden of peacekeeping. The upheaval in the Islamic world, the apparent willingness of the Soviet Union to spread into the southern hemisphere, and the inhibited NATO responses to these challenges have shaken this assumption. The direction for the 1980s lies not in a unilateral revival of the Truman Doctrine, but in a reinvigorated and unified NATO in which both authority and responsibility are more widely shared than in the past.

NOTES

1. *The New Language of Politics: An Anecdotal Dictionary of Catchwords, Slogans, and Political Usage* (New York: Random House, 1969), p. 114.

2. See Truman Message to Congress, March 12, 1947, in *Public Papers of the Presidents, 1947* (Washington DC: GPO, 1963), p. 178ff.

3. "Europe's Relations with the United States," *Daedalus*, Winter 1979, p. 87.

4. "The Illusion of American Omnipotence," *Harper's,* December 1950, pp. 21–28.

5. Henry A. Kissinger, "The Viet Nam Negotiations," *Foreign Affairs,* January 1969, pp. 211–234; Informal Remarks on Guam with Newsmen, July 25, 1969, in *Public Papers of the Presidents, 1969* (Washington: GPO, 1971), p. 544ff.

6. Warren F. Kuehl, "The Nixon Doctrine: A New Strategic Concept," unpublished MS, 1977, p. 5.

7. Marshall Green, "The Nixon Doctrine: A Progress Report," *U.S. Department of State Bulletin*, February 8, 1971, p. 161.

8. First Annual Report to the Congress on Foreign Policy of the 1970s, in *Public Papers of the Presidents, 1970,* 18 February 1970 (Washington DC: GPO, 1971), pp. 118, 119, 126. (Emphasis in the original.)

9. Radio address, 13 October 1968, "The Time to Save NATO," in *Atlantic Community Quarterly*, Winter 1968–1969, pp. 481–82.

10. Remarks to the North Atlantic Council in Brussels, 24 February 1969, in *Public Papers of the Presidents, 1969,* p. 106. In his memoirs, Nixon says he "felt that the European trip had accomplished all the goals we set for it." (*RN: The Memoirs of Richard Nixon* [New York: Warner Books, 1978], vol. 1, p. 463.)

11. Henry A. Kissinger, *The Troubled Partnership: Reappraisal of the Atlantic Alliance* (New York: McGraw-Hill, 1965). See, also, John G. Stoessinger, *Henry Kissinger: The Anguish of Power* (New York: W. W. Norton, 1976), p. 137ff. Kissinger underscores his case for European unity in his memories, *White House Years* (Boston: Little, Brown, 1979), pp. 81–82.

12. *Congressional Record*, Vol. 115, 91st Congress, 1st Session, December 1, 1969, pp. 36147 and 36167.

13. Ibid., pp. 36147–36149.

14. Wilfrid Kohl, "The Nixon-Kissinger Foreign Policy System and U.S.–European Relations: Patterns of Policy Making," *World Politics*, October 1975, p. 28.

15. *Congressional Record*, vol. 117, 92nd Congress, 1st Session, May 11, 1971.

16. *New York Times*, May 13 and 16, 1971.

17. *Congressional Record*, vol. 117, 92nd Congress, 1st Session, May 19, 1971, p. 15960.

18. "Richard Nixon and the Future of American Foreign Policy," *Daedalus*, Fall 1972, p. 18.

19. Werner Kaltefleiter, "Europe and the Nixon Doctrine: A German Point of View," ORBIS, Spring 1973, p. 94.

20. Jame Chace and Earl C. Ravenal, *Atlantis Lost: U.S.–European Relations after the Cold War* (New York: New York University Press, 1976), p. 52.

21. *New York Times*, August 15, 1971.

22. Text of Communique, Smithsonian Agreement, December 18, 1971, in *U.S. Department of State Bulletin*, January 10, 1972, pp. 32–34.

23. European Community Communique, October 21, 1972, in *Keesing's Contemporary Archives*, vol. 18, p. 25542.

24. News Conference, January 31, 1973, in *Public Papers of the Presidents*, 1973 (Washington DC: GPO, 1975), p. 57.

25. Henry Kissinger, "A New Atlantic Charter," address delivered to the Associated Press Editors' Annual Meeting, New York, April 23, 1973, in *U.S. Department of State Bulletin*, May 14, 1973, pp. 593–98.

26. Kohl, "Nixon-Kissinger Foreign Policy," p. 18.

27. Fourth Annual Report to the Congress on U.S. Foreign Policy, in *Public Papers of the Presidents, 1973*, pp. 402–4.

28. "NATO and the Year of Europe," *Survival*, January-February, 1974, p. 21.

29. James Reston, *New York Times*, September 28, 1973. For the debate on troop reduction, see the *Congressional Record*, 93rd Congress, 1st Session, September 26, 1973, p. 31507ff.

30. Final Communique of North Atlantic Council, June 15, 1973, in *Atlantic Community Quarterly*, Fall 1973, p. 387; *New York Times*, August 6, 1973.

31. *New York Times*, August 5, 1973.

32. *U.S. Statutes-at-Large, 1973*, vol. 87, pp. 619–20.

33. Final Communique, Defense Ministers Meeting, North Atlantic Council, December 7, 1973, in *Atlantic Community Quarterly*, Winter 1973–1974, p. 17.

34. Question and Answer Session at the Executives' Club of Chicago, 15 March 1974, in *Public Papers of the Presidents*, 1974 (Washington, DC: GPO, 1975) p. 276.

35. Cyrus L. Sulzberger, *New York Times*, 4 April 1974, and *Wall Street Journal*, 16, November 1973.

36. Leslie Gelb, *New York Times*, 17 June 1974.

37. Christopher Wren, ibid., 12 March 1974.

38. April 1974, p. 3.

39. Robert S. Lockwood, "NATO Gaullist Policy: NATO Withdrawal and Systemic Change," doctoral dissertation, George Washington University, 1976.

40. NATO Information Service, "The Eurogroup," *Atlantic Community Quar-*

terly, Summer 1976, pp. 76–79. See, also, the communiqué of the conference of Eurogroup defense ministers, Brussels, December 8, 1975, ibid., pp. 121–24.

41. "Unity of Europe," *The New Yorker*, 12 April 1976, p. 124.

42. *White House Years*, p. 386.

43. Kuehl, "The Nixon Doctrine," p. 8.

44. George C. Wilson, "Arms Policy: Farewell to Nixon Doctrine,"*Washington Post*, 13 December 1979; President Carter's State of the Union address, 23, January 1980, in the *New York Times*, 24 January 1980.

9
The INF Treaty and the Future of NATO: Lessons from the 1960s

"The INF Treaty and the Future of NATO: Lessons from the 1960s," was a chapter in Lawrence S. Kaplan, ed., American Historians and the Atlantic Alliance *(Kent, Ohio: Kent State University Press, 1991), pp. 135–53. The book developed from a symposium on the role of NATO in American history held in Brussels in May 1969 and jointly sponsored by the U.S. Mission to NATO and the Lyman L. Lemnitzer Center for NATO Studies.*

As the North Atlantic Treaty approached its fortieth anniversary, the United States and the Soviet Union signed an Intermediate-Range Nuclear Arms Reduction Treaty in December 1987. On one level this action represented a striking triumph for the West, and a vindication of the promise inherent in the North Atlantic Council's dual-track decision of 1979. America's firmness over deploying the cruise and Pershing II missiles in Western Europe led initially to a confrontation with the Soviet adversary in 1983, when its delegates walked out of the arms talks in Geneva. But it ultimately led to an agreement that would remove both the newly deployed American missiles and the Soviet SS-4 and SS-5 as well as the SS-20 missiles. An elaborate system of verification would follow over the next thirteen years. The signing of this treaty, with its Memorandum of Understanding and Protocols, and its subsequent ratification in 1988, seemed to testify to the validity of a major NATO assumption: that a strong defensive posture was a prerequisite to genuine détente with the East bloc.

On another level, however, the INF treaty raised a host of new questions about the future of the alliance that could lead to its dissolution if its members could not respond to new challenges:

1. Would the new agreement produce a normalization of East-West relations that would permit American troops to be returned to the United States? If so, there might not be a further need for the alliance to continue.

2. Would the new agreement be a prelude to denuclearization of Europe, which would leave the allies vulnerable to the Warsaw bloc's superiority in conventional arms? If so, the treaty would have produced less rather than more stability in Europe.

3. Would the new agreement become a symbol of superpower collaboration at the expense of the European allies? If so, longstanding suspicions of American commitment would rise again, to the detriment of the alliance's solidarity.

In short, a detente between the United States and the Soviet Union could carry in its wake the decoupling of America from Europe. If this were to be the result, the treaty of Washington of 1987 could lead to the dissolution of the treaty of Washington of 1949.

Predictions of NATO's demise had been abundant in the late 1980s, even before the INF treaty was signed. Some of the commentators coming from the neoconservative Right, such as Irving Kristol and Melvyn Krauss, cite the lack of support given by the allies to American efforts on their behalf. Rather than carry the load for the allies, they say the United States would serve the Europeans better by withdrawing from the alliance and encouraging the Europeans to make their own security arrangements. Two of their themes that fall upon receptive American ears are: (1) unfair sharing of the burden of defense, and (2) the potential but untapped strength of an almost but not quite united Western Europe.[1]

But if this is the view from the Right, there is equal ardor for withdrawal from some pundits of the Left. Richard Barnet, for example, supports the termination of NATO on grounds that the Soviet threat is no longer valid and that Europe is capable of handling its own defense while the United States uses its good offices to continue its efforts toward demilitarizing the Continent. On the Left also appear European critics who see in NATO an American obstacle to peace in Europe, from the Greens of Germany to the radical wing of the British Labour party. Rand analyst Robert Levine has called the American opponents "withdrawers" and their European counterparts "removers."[2]

Most critics of the alliance, whatever their political orientation, share many of these views. David Calleo, in his case for "devolution," urges the reduction of the U.S. presence in NATO and its replacement by Europeans hitherto excessively dependent upon U.S. assistance. Calleo approaches the subject from an economic standpoint, pointing to the enormous cost that the United States has borne. What was bearable in the time of American preeminence is dangerous in time of relative decline. The idea of a decline, if not a fall, in American power was given wide circulation in Paul Kennedy's comparative studies of empires, ranging from sixteenth-century Spain to twentieth-century America. Each had its period in the sun, and each found its underpinnings distorted by economic strain. The "imperial overstretch" cited by Kennedy in each imperial power would apply to the American role in NATO.[3]

The arrival to power of Mikhail Gorbachev in the Soviet Union has helped to bolster arguments of critics. General Secretary Gorbachev seemed to herald a new foreign policy in which the Soviet Union would face inward, reduce its military establishment, and become a regular, if still powerful, member of the nation-states of the world without the revolutionary engine of Communist expansion to threaten its neighbors. Since it was Soviet aggressiveness that brought the Western European states together in alliance, a reversal of that behavior could make the alliance in 1989 unnecessary. According to these critics, it has fulfilled its purpose and should disband.

Although most of the voices responding to Gorbachev's invitation were from the Left, they found resonance throughout the West, notably among Germans and other West Europeans eager to change the status of the long Cold War. The air of relaxation in Europe matched the mood of those in the United States whose various grievances over burden sharing or lack of appreciation for the American presence in Europe impelled them to look to the Pacific as the major focus for American foreign relations in the 1990s.

The rise of Japan and the Asian nations reminds many Americans that the United States is a Pacific as well as an Atlantic power. Should the United States continue to pour its resources and its energies into Western Europe when increasingly its vital interests are involved in a Pacific connection— with Japan, Korea, and the ASEAN group? On two fronts the traditional American connections with the Far East are reawakening. First, with the increased trade with Japan and the other Asian powers on the Pacific rim; and second, with the steady westward movement of the American population from the East to the West Coast, from the Rust Belt to the Sun Belt. Asia is the focus of California, the most populous of the American states, not Europe. If this trend continues, Europe's position on the American horizon will inevitably be diminished.

The 1987 INF treaty between the United States and the Soviet Union gave credence to European concern that the United States was turning away from its allies. Like the abortive Reykjavik plans of 1986, the INF arrangements might be a Soviet-American trade-off at the expense of Europeans. Despite the demands that the NATO allies had made for a Western counteraction against the SS-20s, and despite the obvious success of the dual-track initiative of 1979 in effecting their removal—and moreover forcing the Soviets into serious negotiations for reductions in nuclear weapons—there was fear that disengagement for American forces from Europe would be the end product of de-escalation efforts. Inconsistent though this sentiment may be with the new confidence Europeans have in living alongside a restructured Soviet Union, it was nonetheless a factor in straining the Western alliance. After more than thirty-five years of an American military presence in Europe, many wondered if the removal of intermediate nuclear weapons would lead to the removal of American troops as well. If so, what effect would this action have on the security of the West?

As a result of Europe's reexamination of both the American ally and the Soviet foe, there is a new sense of European unity abroad. For half a generation, since the *Wirtschaftswunder* of the 1960s, Europe has had the potential of equalling both America and the Soviet Union in economic power. In 1992 the remnants of economic nationalism are expected to fall. And with them the idea of a United States of Europe could become a reality. Political and military integration could be built on the infrastructure of the Western European Union, enlarged to serve the European Community as a whole. Two of its members—the United Kingdom and France—are already nuclear powers. There is reason to anticipate the flowering of a genuine third force in Western Europe in the 1990s.

In light of the challenges of 1989, critics have a right to suspect that the alliance is on the threshold of dissolution. As one acute observer has written:

> The Atlantic Alliance, which has been the keystone of American foreign policy during three administrations, has begun to founder under the impact of Europe's new nationalism and the apparent decline of the Russian military threat. There is no longer any agreement on how NATO shall be organized, where it is going, or what its purposes are . . .
>
> This disarray within the alliance is more than simply a dispute among allies as to the proper means toward a commonly desired end. It is the ends themselves which are now in question. The problem facing the Atlantic Alliance today is not so much how it shall protect Europe from Russian invasion—an invasion no one now believes in—but what kind of political settlement will be made between Russia and the West in Europe. The collapse of Atlantic unity is merely the result of the transformation of the old military impasse into a period of diplomatic fluidity where Europe's political future is at stake.[4]

The extended quotation above encapsulates most of the issues that would account for the "end of the alliance," the title of the book from which the quotation was taken. They include: Europe's new nationalism, decline of the Soviet threat, lack of agreement over the purpose of the alliance, and the consequent irrationality of stationing American troops in Europe. These are lively issues in 1989. But they were equally valid in 1964, when Ronald Steel published this book. In the foregoing paragraphs only the reference to "three administrations" instead of "eight" anchor this passage in time. In other words, all the generalizations made in 1964 about the impending termination of the alliance were as pertinent in the early 1960s as they are in the late 1980s.

Given these constants why did NATO survive its twenty-fifth anniversary and live on to commemorate its fortieth anniversary? One possible answer might lie in the force of bureaucratic inertia. By 1962 NATO had in place a large and politically powerful establishment, both civilian and military. Both headquarters were located in Paris and included influential soldiers and politicians from all the allied nations. The supreme allied commanders, Europe, were all men of distinction and status, with ranking that rivaled positions in the Joint Chiefs of Staff in Washington. Although the offices of the secretary-general and the permanent representative to NATO lacked Americans with comparable visibility, the American ambassadors were diplomats or politicians of superior intellectual ability, as in the cases of Thomas Finletter and Harlan Cleveland in the 1960s. The Europeans in NATO were drawn from the summits of their respective national political communities: Paul-Henri, Spaak and Dirk Stikker—the secretaries-general between 1957 and 1964—had been premiers of Belgium and the Netherlands respectively.

Today there are approximately thirty-nine hundred people employed in the political headquarters in Brussels; another twenty-five hundred military personnel, along with seven thousand dependents, are located thirty miles away in SHAPE's headquarters at Casteau.[5] When local employees are included in the figures, the numbers mount to twelve thousand people. The numbers employed in Paris a generation ago were not substantially fewer. Could it be that the weight of this apparatus was too heavy to dissolve? Could NATO's survival be a product of a bureaucratic mass that has taken on a life of its own? Could NATO personnel comprise a formidable factor in keeping the organization alive?

Comparisons with other such organizations that outlived their usefulness and eventually dissolved do not give much credibility to this thesis. SEATO and CENTO, products of the Dulles chain of alliance organizations in the 1950s, disappeared in the late 1970s without many ripples. Their headquarters, however, were modest affairs, not comparable in prestige or numbers with NATO's. A better example may be the League of Nations, with an apparatus and branches more closely approximating NATO's. Despite its visibility, its impotence in the 1930s caused it to collapse in the wake of World War II, to be succeeded by the United Nations. Even though the successor organization incorporated some of the league's subunits into its own organization, the size of the league did nothing to prevent it from dwindling into irrelevancy and dissolution. One needs more than the self-preserving nature of a large bureaucracy to explain the survival of the organization and alliance in the 1960s. A more pertinent question would be to ask if and how the alliance addressed some of the pressing problems that seemed to be bringing it to the brink of disintegration a generation ago.

From the American side in the 1960s, a major issue was burden sharing, particularly in the form of the six U.S. divisions in Europe. These divisions had been the fruits of the great debate of 1951, when General Eisenhower used his influence to win over a restless Senate to accept the administration's decision to send four divisions to the support of the newly established SHAPE. The Truman administration succeeded, but not without dissenting voices over the limits of executive right to send troops without the explicit permission of the Congress.

In 1951 the defense of Europe demanded the American contribution, as plans were made to build up allied forces to provide a deterrence that had been absent in Korea the year before. Even when nuclear weaponry reduced the numbers of ground forces necessary to maintain the deterrent, the American forces remained in Europe, now more as a trip wire than a conventional force. The Eisenhower administration continued the policies of the Truman administration.

But with the amazing economic recovery in the West, questions arose over the ability of Europeans to provide a greater share of the economic burden of maintaining troops in Europe. These questions were made all the sharper because the older fears of invasion had lessened in the Khrushchev years. While such questions could be deflected by observing the continued threats from the East, given Soviet behavior in Berlin or in Cuba, another question was not so easily answered. In 1960 there was danger of excessive outflow of the American gold reserve, blamed—fairly or not—on the drain on the U.S. dollar. If that drain was caused in good measure by the enormous cost of maintaining the divisions abroad—250,000 to 300,000 troops, then why should not the Europeans pick up those costs?

This was a concern that the Kennedy administration had to cope with. It was a legacy of the Eisenhower administration, and one that the new secretary of defense, Robert S. McNamara, was more than willing to manage. There was a potential $3 billion drain that he intended to bring down to no more than $1 billion as quickly as he could. If the Eisenhower solution—bring home American dependents in Europe—aroused too much opposition, other answers would have to be found. McNamara had them, and they disturbed the European partners.

The Kennedy administration in 1961 was looking as much—or more—to Asia and Latin America as it was to Europe. The crises points were as much in Laos and Vietnam as in Berlin, and the Kennedy administration undertook a sweeping revision of both the strategic thinking and the strategic emphasis of the Eisenhower administration. In the course of its evaluations, the heavy expenses of maintaining forces in Europe came under review.

High on McNamara's list of priorities was an emphasis on the need for highly mobile task forces to engage in low-intensity warfare, to strike out through counterinsurgency at the kinds of forces threatening American interest in Southeast Asia. It is noteworthy that the budgets for fiscal years 1962 and 1963 placed a premium on aircraft capable of lifting troops to areas of conflict with dispatch and with limited costs. The dangers of conflict with the Soviet Union were to be encountered in areas where wars of national liberation were sponsored or supported by the Soviet Union, rather than in Europe where NATO and the Warsaw Pact were in a static confrontation.

The consequences for the European partners were quickly apparent. If U.S. troops could be airlifted in a crisis, why should the United States maintain such a large standing army in Europe? If the allies wanted U.S. forces to remain in place, they should be prepared to pay a larger share of their expenses. They could afford the costs after a decade of rising prosperity. Although it is unlikely that there was a Machiavellian design in the Defense Department's development of a new strike force with a fleet of aircraft and ships to undergird it, it was equally unlikely that once conceived and implemented, the designers of foreign military policy would not be reluctant to press their advantage.

All of these actions helped to account for German and Italian willingness—and even French acquiescence—to enlarge their contributions to NATO in 1961. An aide-mémoire of 17 February 1961, less than a month after the Kennedy administration was in office, prepared the way. While directed at all the allies, it pointedly was delivered to the West German delegation in the course of bilateral talks on the balance of payments. The document made clear, though, that the issue was not bilateral: "The deficit of the United States arises wholly from the common defense of the free world," it stated. "Without these freely assumed obligations the United States would now be running a heavy surplus in its commitments and action in balance of payments."[6] Hence it was reasonable to expect a better balance to the partnership that would ease the balance of payments problem.

While the Europeans could resist the logic of this American assumption—including the long-term reality of the gold drain—they could not resist the tide of events. The Berlin Wall crisis of the summer of 1961 undercut German objections. It led to a rapid buildup of U.S. troops in Europe that forced the German hand as the projected U.S. dollar deficit rose to almost $3 billion. America insisted and received compensation from the Federal

Republic. Germany could hardly do otherwise, since the United States was sending forty thousand additional troops to bolster NATO's defenses in Germany.

To soften the blunt edges of its demands, the United States avoided direct payment for U.S. troops. Instead, it accepted the purchase of American goods and equipment to offset U.S. expenditures in Europe. Direct sale of U.S. equipment was probably the least objectionable way of achieving results without offending German dignity.

Similar negotiations followed with other NATO allies, and although the results were more modest, there was some easing of the problem. It took time, however, before the extent of European cooperation entered into the congressional psyche. As late as February 1963, at hearings on military procurement authorizations for fiscal year 1964, Senator Richard Russell, chairman of the Armed Services Committee, was still asserting that "the NATO allies had been riding free and that the $50 billion establishment that you preside over, over there, has been the shield not only for Great Britain but for France and Germany. They got years behind in furnishing their troops." McNamara was able to respond that "We have signed agreements with the West Germans under which they are buying $650 million of equipment from us. We have signed an agreement in the last 90 days with the Italians under which they are buying initially $125 million of equipment from us."[7]

Offset agreements did not settle the issue. Europeans were concerned as well over a new U.S. emphasis on East Asian affairs that stemmed from problems in Laos and Vietnam.

Many of the fissures in the alliance in the early 1960s grew out of the confluence of two elements of change: (1) the successful launching of the first earth satellite, Sputnik, in 1957; and (2) the dramatic economic recovery of most European powers, reflected in the signing of the Treaty of Rome in the same year. Sputnik aroused alarm in the United States over Soviet advances in missile technology, which in turn stimulated the development of America's ICBM. Yet Sputnik raised fears that the United States soon would be vulnerable for the first time to direct Soviet attacks. Would the United States come to the aid of a missile attack on Paris or Bonn if their own cities were at stake?

This question was answered negatively by France, particularly after General de Gaulle assumed the presidency in the Fifth Republic. France assumed that it was unnatural for any nation to place another's security ahead of its own, and it was equally unnatural to expect that the United States would remain indefinitely in Europe. When the United States rejected a reorganization of NATO that would have made France part of a triumvirate controlling the organization, de Gaulle's course of subversion and separation was set. As earnests of what would come to pass, the French fleet in the Mediterranean in 1959 and in the Atlantic in 1963 were removed from SHAPE and SACLANT authority.

It was obvious that de Gaulle's stand appealed to many Europeans. They might not necessarily agree to French leadership, but most Europeans could respond favorably to complaints about charges of American hegemony. Certainly the American pressures to assume more financial burdens bred irritation over the preeminent position of the United States. But the availability of intercontinental ballistic missiles coinciding with the conception of a more flexible nuclear response raised a variety of suspicions among Europeans. A less rigid reliance on nuclear defense could mean that America's new vulnerability to nuclear weapons dictated the Kennedy administration's new emphasis on conventional forces. Part of the reason for this pressure rested on the need for forces to cope with outbreaks where nuclear weapons might be counter-productive. To ask, as Secretary of Defense Mc-Namara did, at the North Atlantic Council meeting in Athens in May 1962 (and then more publicly at a commencement address at Ann Arbor, Michigan, a month later) that Europeans prepare defenses on the basis of more troops on the ground was unsettling.

While McNamara actually spoke of a variety of weapons and a flexible response to the problem at hand, Europeans heard the implication of raising the nuclear threshold and the prospects of a conventional war on the ground. The allies, with the obvious exception of West Germany, considered the Berlin Wall crisis to be an aberration, a problem primarily for the Warsaw bloc, and not a reason to abandon the successful deterrent system of the past decade. To Americans the Berlin crisis of 1961 reinforced views that NATO required conventional forces to meet any level of nonnuclear aggression.

The result of these divergent views was European resistance to both the building of conventional defenses and the principle of flexible response. Europeans were unimpressed with McNamara's claim that the West had exaggerated the extent of Soviet military power. The new team of systems analysts at the Department of Defense was convinced that the figure of 150 divisions was unrealistic. The size of a Soviet division was smaller than those of the West, and the equipment was inferior. There should be no reason why a modest conventional buildup of NATO forces should not be sufficient to hold off aggression from the Warsaw Pact bloc, at least long enough for other means of coping to come into play.[8]

The allies did not accept this judgment. What they saw was a rationalization for American willingness to subvert the security of the West, which had been constructed under a nuclear umbrella. European discontent centered on the illogic of conventional defense. It could invite conflict by raising the nuclear threshold to excessive heights. If the Soviets knew that American nuclear power would not be employed immediately, they might be tempted to employ tactics that could lead to protracted land warfare in Europe. No matter how vigorously the United States asserted that a flexible response would increase not decrease, the deterrent capacity of the West, Europeans could not erase from their memories images of World Wars I and II. Nor could they ignore the prospect of a war that would destroy Europe but leave the superpowers intact. On the other hand, they were much less vocal about their unwillingness to bear the financial burdens that raising conventional armies would incur.

The allies had forums outside NATO where their discontent with American leadership could be expressed. Although the Western European Union was a sham, the European Economic Community developed from the Treaty of Rome in 1957 was a reality, even if its accomplishments were more in the future than in the present. It contained a potential for a third force between America and the Soviet Union, which would be independent of both. This was President de Gaulle's vision of the future, when Europeans would not be second-class citizens with their fate decided by superpower politics. If there were tactical and intermediate nuclear weapons in Europe, they were controlled by the United States not by Europe. The result was pressure for development of national *forces de frappe*, particularly in France.

It is noteworthy that Europeans were successful in resisting American pressure to raise their troop strengths. It was the United States that gave way. By the late 1960s, Secretary of Defense McNamara had accepted these constraints on conventional forces. In fact, he converted the 1966 withdrawal of France from the organization into an asset, or at least into a circumstance "in no way disabling" to the military posture of the alliance.[9]

The secretary of defense used Europe's reluctance to increase its forces to justify the thinning of American troops in Europe during the Vietnam War. He was convinced that the combination of the NATO forces in place and the reduction of a Soviet threat would still permit a flexible response to any Soviet challenge.

Just as Europeans had to make repeated financial concessions to keep American troops in Europe, so American leaders had to make serious efforts to appease Europe's increasing insistence on equality within the alliance, particularly with respect to the control of nuclear weapons. De Gaulle's challenge had to be met, Germany's unhappiness with its inferior status in NATO could not be left unheeded, and the smaller powers' sense of isolation from policy making required attention as well.

The major effort was a multilateral force, which began under SACEUR Norstad's auspices in the Eisenhower administration and terminated in disarray under Johnson in 1964. Norstad's plan was to make NATO a fourth nuclear power in a way that would appease German if not French demands for equality and would dissolve doubts about America's dedication to the defense of Europe. The concept won adherents, particularly among American supporters of European unification. The multilateral force (MLF) eventually took the form of twenty-five surface vessels carrying eight Polaris A-3 missiles, each with mixed manned crews and nuclear warheads under joint ownership and custody. Each participating nation could veto the use of nuclear weapons, although the United States would retain final control of the weapons.

The MLF won some enthusiasm among dedicated American supporters of European unification. Robert Bowie, former director of the State Department's Policy Planning Staff, urged the United States "to concede to a European or NATO force the same degree of ultimate autonomy as it has already accepted in assisting the British force."[10]

But it was always an illusion, never becoming reality. If the United States kept its veto intact, nuclear sharing was a charade. If it did not, there would be the prospect of fifteen fingers—or at least thirteen if France and Iceland were discounted—on the nuclear button. France was going its way with its *force de frappe*; Britain was smarting over the Skybolt debacle. This left Germany as the major enthusiast for the MLF, and Germany's enthusiasm had a dampening effect on the other allies. The multilateral force disappeared from the NATO communiqués by the end of 1964.

Like offset agreements, the MLF was an action on the part of Americans and Europeans to take into account the other side's concerns. If the MLF failed, at least it bought time for the alliance to sort out paths for survival. It represented a spirit of accommodation, even if the results were mixed or negative.

Admittedly, the MLF has gone down in NATO's history as a fiasco, while the offset agreements have been identified as an example of American blackmail. Neither served its intended purposes for very long. The American monopoly on the control of nuclear warheads led to the departure of France from the organization in 1966 and the demand for détente on the part of the other allies, as demonstrated in the Harmel initiative in 1967. And the need for further offset measures became more urgent as the Vietnam War diverted American troops and American attention from its NATO obligations. Pressures for more burden sharing increased by the end of the decade. Yet each concession in its way postponed the dissolution foreseen by pundits at the beginning of the decade. And each represented the continuing importance NATO represented for the allies. After all, in 1969 under the treaty terms Article 13 any member nation could have issued a "notice of denunciation" to leave the alliance. None of the members, not even France, followed this pattern.

The answers may be found in part in a transformation that occurred without fanfare in the mid-1960s. On the surface the organization was essentially unchanged; SACEUR and SACLANT and the secretary-general remained in place. But with France's departure there was a subtle increase in the influence of the smaller nations of the alliance. NATO's Defense

Planning Committee, created in 1963, assumed greater authority, with consequent lessening of American influence over military affairs. Similarly, the Nuclear Planning Group, founded in 1967 after France's withdrawal from the organization, brought nuclear questions more closely into the purview of the secretary-general. If the nuclear warhead remained an American monopoly, nuclear planning became more oligopolistic after the secretary-general moved from Paris to Brussels.

An unintended and perhaps unexpected by-product of that move was a diminution of the powers of the SACEUR. The old Standing Group, composed of the three major NATO powers in Washington, was replaced by a military representative system with a wider NATO membership and with its center in Brussels. With the Standing Group dissolved, the smaller nations had a greater voice in military planning at the expense of the supreme allied commander, Europe. Even the locus of his headquarters, thirty miles away from Brussels, helped to reduce the stature and influence that the SACEUR had enjoyed in Paris. While none of these changes was advertised as American responses to complaints against its dominance over NATO, they helped to elevate the role of the junior partners in the organization.

Nonetheless, these alterations in the NATO structure may be labeled as cosmetic. America's commitment in 1969 remained as important as the American "pledge" of 1949. The centripetal force through much of this decade was the continuing fear of a powerful and still dangerous Soviet Union.

The Berlin Wall crisis of 1961, the Cuban missile crisis of 1962, and the Czech crisis of 1968 reminded Europeans of the reasons for the founding of NATO, even as they noted with ambivalence American reactions to those crises. Contradictions continued to abound. The strength of the Soviet superpower—and its willingness on selected occasions in the 1960s to display it—generated pressures to keep American forces in Europe where they served as a guarantor of NATO's stability. At the same time there was a sense of a new era dawning in which the Soviets had moderated their ideological drive and were ready to coexist with the Western democracies. This manifested itself in the Harmel Report of 1967, calling for steps toward détente to accompany military preparedness, and a subsequent declaration—the "Reykjavík signal" on mutual and balanced force reductions at the Reykjavík meeting of the North Atlantic Council in 1968.[11]

The Reykjavik declaration was announced in June 1968, before Soviet intervention in Czechoslovakia. While the council at Brussels in the fall of that year determined that Soviet action "has seriously set back hopes of settling the outstanding problems which still divide the European continent," it also supported "continuing consultations with the Warsaw Pact bloc," preparing for a time when the atmosphere for fruitful discussions would be more favorable.[12] In this tense situation, even Europeans most optimistic about detente and most hostile to the American role in NATO would be reluctant to risk destabilizing NATO through altering the force structure, let alone through a major reduction in the American presence in Europe. NATO itself remained vital for both defense and detente.

Was NATO still a vital force in 1989? The parallels of the 1980s and the 1960s have considerable validity, but how compelling are they? No historical situation can be completely replicated. There are obvious differences over the twenty-year span, if only in emphasis. European unity in the 1960s was still undeveloped; the United Kingdom's effort to join the European Community had failed in 1963. De Gaulle, the dominant personality in Western Europe, was also a disruptive force. In 1989 the United Kingdom was a full member of a considerably enlarged European Community. Europe appeared closer to an integrated whole than it had ever been before. Given this evolution Europe could develop into a third force as readily as it could become a genuine second pillar of the Atlantic alliance. Is NATO needed any longer, as it obviously was two decades ago? Cannot Europe stand alone at last?

These questions take on a special relevancy in light of the new spirit animating the Soviet Union under Mikhail Gorbachev. His challenge to the Soviet past appears far more credible than Khrushchev's. The latter may have demonized Stalin's image and opened the way to detente, but his own volatile personality stood in the way of full confidence in the West's relations with the Soviet Union. His aggressiveness in supporting "wars of national liberation" in the Third World and the risks he took in installing missiles in Cuba diminished expectations among the European allies. The Brezhnev succession did little to support a belief in a fundamental change in Soviet foreign relations, even though Brezhnev's conservative style encouraged hopes for detente.

Gorbachev, however, has made *glasnost* and *perestroika* concepts that inspire much more than simple relaxation of tensions. He has recognized fundamental flaws in communism as an economic system, and has moved to make the Soviet Union a partner rather than enemy of a peaceful world order. Wherever one looked in 1989—the United Nations, Afghanistan, southern Africa, the Middle East—and notably U.S.–U.S.S.R. relations—Gorbachev appeared to have changed the face of the Soviet Union. A new order had arrived. The projections of George Kennan about the future of communism forty years before appear to have been realized. Containment has worked. NATO in this case may be an anachronism, an alliance that has fulfilled its functions of protecting the West against Communist ambitions.

After forty years of confrontation, the alliance might be dismantled on the prospect of a new Soviet leader infused with what the North Atlantic assembly has accepted as "benign" intentions.[13] But undermining this acceptance are doubts of at least two varieties. One is over the question of the Soviet Union's new foreign policy objectives. With all the openness and reconstruction that has been exhibited, the Soviet Union remains a superpower whose military strength plays a role independent of its ideological bent. Gorbachev's objectives in many respects resemble those of his predecessors, namely, the removal of the United States from Europe. Gorbachev's posture could achieve this goal through the dissolution of the alliance. Are the members of NATO certain that destabilization would not result, leaving Europe exposed, as it has not been since the 1940s, to the influence of the strongest military power on the continent? Denuclearization of Europe increases the imbalance in conventional weapons between East and West.

There is, however, another consideration. What if Gorbachev fails to maintain control of the Soviet Union? The pull of conservative forces is strong, and resistance to his reforms could result in his departure, even without a failed policy such as marked Khruschev's removal. And if Soviet conservatives cannot stem the tide of change, what new tensions would the dissolution of the Soviet Empire generate? NATO remains an insurance against such a turn of events.

If uncertainty about Soviet goals and about the Soviet political system remains alive, even though less intense than in the 1960s, the condition of Western Europe as a political entity remains equally uncertain. European unity does not rest on the number of members in a community, nor even in the promises of an economic union in 1992. The major question centers on its willingness to compromise national sovereignty in favor of a united Europe. Despite periodic expressions of common purpose, in the Western European Union as well as in the European Community, centrifugal forces remain strong. Nationalism still survives. The community could come apart over economic issues alone. As long as there is no United States of Europe in place, the termination of the alliance risks not only a political and military imbalance with the Warsaw bloc but also new divisions within the West that could set back accomplishments of the past generation.

These cautionary notes are on one level of concern about the future of Europe. There is another level that is rarely aired. This involves a post-NATO Germany. Where will it fit into a united Europe, or a divided Europe? What role would it have in East-West relations? Unfettered by NATO ties, a unified Germany would stay inside the European Community to dominate the West and shape its foreign policy toward an *Ostpolitik* that neither its fellow members nor the Soviet bloc welcome? These considerations are alive, though unspoken. They bring to mind the assumption, going back to the 1950s, that a West Germany inside NATO was more acceptable to the Soviet Union than Germany armed and outside. Could conflict break out in Europe, not from the Soviets moving in on a weakened West after the departure of the United States, but from ambitions, real or imagined, or German irredentism?

Do any of these considerations affect the United States? If the anger over unfair burden sharing is fueled by an economic recession, or if the anti-American sentiment in Europe reaches a new volume, it would be understandable if a new administration should wish to leave the organization. Even if there are sufficient brakes against such a crisis, America in the 1990s—for all the reasons that surfaced in the 1980s, or in the 1960s—could lead NATO into dissolution. The Pacific emphasis, the troops issue, the relative decline of American power could all work toward a devolution into irrelevance, even if there is no violent crisis to mark its end. Yet, it is unlikely that any administration will take this path to dissolution.

Scenarios of this sort have never been a part of any administration's agenda, for the obvious reason that NATO figures as a fixture in the late twentieth century with as much force as isolationism did a century ago. Disengagement from Europe into a fortress America poses too many disruptive prospects for any political figure or political party to take seriously. It would mean, among other things, leaving Europe to a Soviet influence of an order that the Soviet Union itself would not have dreamed possible in the last two generations. Furthermore, a breakdown of Europe's will to survive as an entity could follow from the loss of American presence. As Colin Gray has put it, "The geopolitical realities of European security are such that the security-producing potential of NATO-Europe is far less than is the sum of its several columns of national assets."[14] America's vital interests would be endangered by a recrudescence of the nationalist passions of the past, not least of which would be the revival of a German problem. Third, does the technology of the twentieth century permit a withdrawal of the United States into its hemisphere in the fashion of the Monroe Doctrine? If it does not, in the world's interrelated, interlocked economies and polities of the 1990s, America's own security would be affected by a breakdown in an important part of the world.

Europeans recognize these possibilities even as they chafe against American controls, or against American bases, training exercises, or mistakes in statecraft. They show this by responding to charges of unequal burden sharing with evidence of their contributions. They urge the United States to look beyond superficial statistics. Colin Howgill of the British Embassy in Washington observed that the overall contribution to Atlantic security defensive capability should be identified not merely by the amount of money spent; toleration of noise pollution caused by thousands of low-level jet fighters flying in maneuvers over Europe's countryside was itself a sharing of the defense burden not to be measured in dollars and cents. A report from the nonpartisan Center on Budget and Policy Priorities in Washington made the same point by noting that "the European states are carrying a substantial share of the alliance's military burden."[15]

What is significant about these reports and Europe's efforts to rebut American criticism is not the number of governmental and private bodies and individuals criticizing Europe but the need Europe still feels to satisfy the United States about its activities. Equally significant, the repetitive American complaints always stop short of genuine action. There have been no formal withdrawals of troops, although division size has varied over the years, particularly in the Vietnam period. In 1987 when the question once again arose in Congress, the Senate passed an amendment to keep American forces intact in Europe.[16]

The most eloquent evidence of American response to the need for stability in Europe derives from the silence in the presidential campaigns themselves. In 1984 Europeans were aroused by Senator Nunn's variation on troop withdrawal in June of that year—phased withdrawal would follow from failure of Europeans to increase their share. But even then the resolution was watered down to a pious hope for change.

Just as Europe fears that American exasperation over military costs could lead to American withdrawal of forces, so the United States fears the exclusionary potential of a United States of Europe. A united Europe was a goal of the founding fathers of NATO, but if achieved it could damage America's economy. Even more that this, a genuinely united Europe could challenge the United States politically as well. Is this then a reason for cutting loose? The consensus among American leaders has always been that European unification was in the long-term interest of the United States, if only because a united Europe would block Soviet expansionism. There was little prospect for change in 1989, no matter how high the level of frustration over policies, political and economic, a united Europe might make.

Looking ahead to the 1990s, a bipartisan panel of former policy makers that included former secretaries of defense Republican Melvin Laird and Democrat Harold Brown, as well as former SACEURs Alexander Haig and Bernard Rogers, concluded that after forty years the original vision of the wise, skillful, and determined founders who understood mutual benefits that would result from a coupling of both sides of the Atlantic has been confirmed again and again. Changes such as greater efforts to reduce duplication through specialization, or greater increases in defense expenditures on the part of smaller members, or the "progressive takeover of Europe's defense requirements by Europeans should be gradual and progressive."[17] Whatever changes take place over the next generation should be made through multilateral, not unilateral, action, same. Even if the more extravagant hopes of 1989 should come to pass and the Cold War between East and West should be permanently terminated, NATO will still have functions to perform. The alliance has always been more than a military organization, and West-West relations more often than not have figured more prominently than East-West confrontations. Removal of American troops could follow the reduction in arms and tension in Europe without necessarily ending the alliance. Even if the machinery of SHAPE were dismantled, wholly or partly, the transatlantic ties could keep the treaty if not the organization intact, not as an empty shell but as a bond of reassurance to both sides of the Atlantic. But until this happier climate among nations becomes a reality, there is no serious alternative to the relationships in the West that NATO has built over the past forty years.

NOTES

A different version of this essay was published by the Woodrow Wilson International Center for Scholars as " 'The End of the Alliance': Lessons of the 1960s," in the series "Beyond the Cold War," *Current Issues in European Security*, September 1990.

1. Note for example Irving Kristol, "Does NATO Still Exist?" in Kenneth A. Myers, *NATO: The Next Thirty Years* (Boulder, CO: Westview Press, 1980), 361–71; Melvyn Krauss, *How NATO Weakens the West* (New York: Simon and Schuster, 1986).

2. Richard J. Barnet, "Reflections: The Four Pillars," *New Yorker* (9 March 1988), 80–83; Robert A. Levine, *NATO: The Subjective Alliance: The Debate Over the Future* (Santa Monica, CA: RAND, 1987), 215–20.

3. Paul Kennedy, *The Rise and Fall of the Great Powers* (New York: Random House, 1987), 515, 518–19; David Calleo, *Beyond American Hegemony: The Future of the Western Alliance* (New York: Basic Books, 1987), 215–20.

4. Ronald Steel, *The End of the Alliance: American and the Future of Europe* (New York: Viking Press, 1964), 15–16.

5. SHAPE pamphlet "Supreme Headquarters Allied Powers Europe (SHAPE) at a Glance," 1987.

6. Aide-Mémoire, 17 February 1961, in the *New York Times*, 21 February 1961.

7. Military Procurement Authorization 1964, *Hearings* before the U.S. Senate Committee on Armed Services, 21 February 1963, 88th Cong., 1st sess., 342–43.

8. Alain C. Enthoven and K. Wayne Smith, *How Much Is Enough? Shaping the Defense Program, 1961–1969* (New York: Harper and Row, 1971), 147FF.

9. McNamara testimony, "The Atlantic Alliance," *Hearings* before the U.S. Senate Subcommittee on National Security and International Operations of the Committee on Government Operations, 21 June 1966, 89th Cong., 2d sess., pt. 6, 187.

10. Robert Bowie, "Tensions Within the Alliance," *Foreign Affairs* 42 (October 1963): 68.

11. The Future Task of the Alliance (Harmel Report), 13–14 December 1967, Brussels, North Atlantic Council, *Final Communiqués*, 198–202; ibid., 24–28 June 1968, Reykjavík, North Atlantic Council, *Final Communiqués*, 216.

12. Ibid., 15–16 November 1968, Brussels, 214.

13. "NATO in the 1990s: Special Report of the North Atlantic Assembly, 1988," 26.

14. Colin S. Gray, "NATO: Time to Call It a Day?," *The National Interest* (Winter 1987–1988): 24.

15. Quoted in Bernard E. Trainor, "Sharing the Defense Burden: Allies Are Listening," *New York Times*, 6 September 1988.

16. *Congressional Record*, 100th Cong., 1st sess., 8 May 1987, 3329–31. The amendment to a military authorization bill in support of maintaining U.S. troops in Europe was sponsored by Bill Richardson, and was accepted by voice vote.

17. "The Future of NATO," Policy Consensus Reports, The Johns Hopkins Foreign Policy Institute, August 1988.

IV
NATO in the Third Generation, from 1991

The decade of the 1990s is both easier and more difficult to evaluate than the two preceding generations. Unlike older milestones, the break with the past was more dramatic and far clearer than the Harmel report of 1967. While acceptance of that document, along with the concept of flexible response, suggested a major change in the nature of the Cold War, the war went on. There was a détente of sorts in the mid-1950s under Khrushchev, and the military buildup under Reagan had its precedent in the activities following the outbreak of the Korean War. But the toppling of the Berlin Wall, followed rapidly by the unification of Germany, the breakdown of the Warsaw Pact, and the implosion of the Soviet empire were unprecedented in NATO's history.

How to cope with success was a major concern of the 1990s, and it had not been solved at the alliance's fiftieth anniversary. Indeed, the end of the Soviet Union raised the question of the need for the continuation of the alliance. As the first two chapters in this section indicate, NATO devoted much of its energy in this decade in seeking ways to justify its survival, in identifying new strategic concepts, and in finding new missions for the impressive infrastructure built up during the Cold War. The third chapter is an apologia for the long years of NATO's existence since the end of World War II. Conjectures about what might have been the history of the West if the alliance had not been fashioned conclude this volume.

10
NATO after the Cold War

"NATO after the Cold War," covering the period from 1989 to mid-1995, was the product of a collaboration between the Lyman L. Lemnitzer Center for NATO and European Union Studies of Kent State University, USA, and the International Relations Society of the University of Kent, UK. It was published in Jarrod Wiener, ed., The Transatlantic Relationship *(London: Macmillan, 1996), pp. 26–43.*

It has been a quarter of a century since the Johns Hopkins scholar David Calleo wrote that "the Supreme Allied Commander has never been the first servant of the Council, but the viceroy of the American president." The North Atlantic Treaty Organization itself, he asserted, was "the rather elaborate apparatus by which we have chosen to organize the American protectorate in Europe."[1] This was the language of revisionism in 1970, articulating a judgement that NATO was little more than an instrument of America's imperial power. Whether that power was exploitive, as the foregoing statements imply, or benign, as the United States and many of its Allies believed, the Alliance under American leadership was a success.

From the time that the Alliance was founded in 1949, Europe's fear of communism spreading under the wings of the Soviet Union kept it intact and gave meaning to the military organization it had created. Although less fearsome in 1970, Soviet power still sent shivers down the collective spine of Western Europe. And, even though detente between East and West had been in the making since the end of the Cuban missile crisis in 1962, it was a fragile coexistence always subjected to such shocks as the brutal snuffing out of the "Prague spring" in the summer of 1968. At the same time that the Soviet Union accepted the Federal Republic's *Ostpolitik* and engaged in confidence-building SALT talks in the 1970s, it accelerated its nuclear capabilities and challenged the Western European allies with medium-range missiles targeted on their major cities. The result was what Norwegian historian Geir Lundestad has labelled the American "empire by invitation."[2] Only France was prepared to revoke the invitation—for itself but not for its allies; France was not unhappy with American troops remaining in neighbouring countries. Notwithstanding mutual displays of annoyance, Europeans regarded the American commitment to the Alliance for almost two generations as a guarantee of stability in the West.

It was on the strength of this assumption that over 300,000 Americans enjoyed a welcome in Europe that deserves more attention than it has received in the past. These forces enjoyed favors and concessions which in other circumstances would have been insults to national sovereignty. American villages blossomed in Germany, Italy, England, and even in France before 1966. Germany in the 1960s allowed gasoline stations on the autobahns to serve only American servicemen, with signs in English along the highways. While there was increasing restiveness as time went by over the American economic presence in Europe in the form of soft drinks, automobiles, or computers, these were acceptable while the Soviet menace loomed large. As long as the Soviet arsenal of nuclear weapons and superior manpower on the ground remained in place NATO's solidarity was assured.

The disbanding of the Warsaw Pact and the subsequent dissolution of the Soviet Union in 1991 seemed to remove almost overnight NATO's raison d'être. It no longer had the mission to defend the West from the communist East when the latter ceased to exist. To bowdlerize Dean Acheson's words, which so aggravated the British in 1962, NATO had lost its "empire," and had not yet found a new role.[3] The sudden self-destruction of the adversary instantly made irrelevant much of the allies' military planning. As late as September 1989, six weeks before the Berlin Wall collapsed, NATO planners were concentrating on the most pressing problem of the day, namely, the modernization of the Lance nuclear missile in Germany. This had been a sensitive issue with Germans, since the tactical weapon would be usable only on German soil, East or West. West Germany's reaction was part of its growing rebellion against NATO's intrusions on the quality of life from noise pollution by low-flying planes to tanks on manoeuvre ripping up arable fields. But no matter how much distress these activities caused and no matter how much assurance Gorbachev-inspired reforms in the Soviet Union gave to the Western Allies, the reality of Soviet power dividing Europe continued to be a centripetal force holding the Alliance together. Had the unexpected events of the following year not occurred the Allies in all likelihood would have accepted the improved missile.

Instead, President Bush cancelled without fanfare the Lance Program on 3 May 1990.

What was left for NATO to do when the enemy had left the field? Even if the "end of history," in the words of State Department official Francis Fukuyama,[4] had not been cancelled almost as soon as it was proclaimed, the future was expected to be one of harmony between former enemies, and consequently of stability in a world formerly caught up in the rivalry of the superpowers. There were hopeful auguries in 1990 and 1991. The new Russia seeking entry into capitalist society looked to the West for support, and in turn appeared prepared to be part of a consensus in the Security Council. The immediate results of this dramatic change was the empowerment of the United Nations to fulfill peacekeeping functions which had been hampered by the cold war. There was even a prospect of a UN police force to keep the new world order. The Gulf War of 1991 was an example of the kind of co-operation, although at a minimal level, that could have set a precedent for suppressing disorder around the world. If this was to be the future, what need was there for an alliance directed against a threat that no longer existed? Any threats to European security should be managed by Europeans themselves through one or more of the military agencies associated with the European Union. In light of the expectations of the European Union after its meeting in Maastricht in 1992, there hardly seemed to be a need for an American-led alliance to defend the West.

There were other serious after-effects of the collapse of NATO's former mission. The most immediate from an American standpoint was the size of the American presence in Europe, or even the very existence of an American military presence. This was not a new issue. Pressure to reduce American forces in Europe had been building over time, in large measure as a by-product of Congressional unhappiness over burden-sharing in the organization. For years complaints had been raised over the contrast between American costs and the European contribution, particularly in light of Europe's prosperity in the last generation. The Europeans retorted that the costs of supporting American troops had increasingly become part of the host's responsibility. In addition, the Germans were more frequently asking the question that the French had always raised: How reliable was the American commitment? Would the end of the Cold War mean the departure of American troops from the continent?

There was some justification for Europe's uneasiness. The figure of 326,414 American troop strength which SACEUR General John Galvin had identified when he took office in 1987 was deemed too high even before the disbanding of the Warsaw Pact. The minimal cuts begun by President Bush in 1989 culminated into a 20 percent reduction in Army and Air Force personnel, from 305,000 to 270,000. The reductions continued. In May 1991 the Congress called for a troop reduction from 250,000 then in place to 100,000 by 1995. This remains the figure under the Clinton administration. At this size at least a "medium" army corps could be formed in place of a "large" corps, according to a Congressional Research Service (CRS) study in September 1992.[5] While this would be a lesser combat force it could be supplemented by contingency units airlifted from the United States.

Will the momentum be checked at 100,000? The CRS survey observed that at 50,000 the most that could be extracted would be an army division, much like the force currently on the line in South Korea. Below this figure the United States would have to think solely in humanitarian terms, or, more likely, to leave Europe to the Europeans. If the reduction of U.S. forces in Europe should come to pass, the assumptions of France and the hopes of the Soviets would finally be realized. There has always been a strain in French thinking about NATO which held that the United States was an alien presence in Europe, at best only a temporary one. America would leave when its interests changed. The Soviets as early as the 1950s worked to convince Europe that the continent could enjoy peace and security if only the American troops departed, as the Rapacki proposals of 1958 had postulated. An American military withdrawal from Europe is not beyond the realm of possibility. The disillusionment with European behaviour in Bosnia, a preoccupation with domestic problems and a rise of aggressive unilateralism, if not isolationism, under resurgent Republicans in 1995 could lead to this. If the U.S. were to withdraw, NATO in all probability would cease to exist.

There would be no need for NATO without the United States (or Canada, which would follow the American lead). Any potential security threats to Western Europe should be manageable by the European security organizations, such as the Western European Union (WEU) or Organization for Security and Co-Operation in Europe (OSCE). The onset of the 1990s had witnessed a quickening of the pace of European unification, and with it a diminution of the American connection. With the Maastricht agreements of 1992 the Europeans appeared ready to go beyond the economic framework of the Treaty of Rome and to move into a political unity symbolized by the change of name from European Community to European Union.

Although the expectations of Maastricht were extravagant, the aspirations of a United States of Europe have not disappeared. Divisions between those members who want immediate expansion and those who want to deepen existing ties have slowed the movement. Nevertheless, the enlistment of new members such as Sweden and Austria as well as the anxiety to join on the part of a waiting list that includes Turkey and Poland attests to the EU's vibrancy in 1995. If the European movement ultimately embraces a military component, it could be the final act in NATO's history. Not only was there no superpower to frighten Europeans in the mid-1990s, but in the event of a potential threat Western Europe had the power and equipment to cope with it. The U.S. and NATO would be irrelevant to the security of Europe.

Not surprisingly, France has been the leader in furthering both the removal of the United States and the empowering of Europe as it presses its campaign for an "independent" Europe. One French commentator saw the Brussels meeting of the North Atlantic Council in January 1994 which featured the American sponsored Partnership for Peace, as "la dernière fois, sans doute"—that the United States would impose its will on the Council.[6] In place of the American superpower, indeed, in place of NATO itself, there would be a variety of alternatives available for the defense of the West. They ranged from the Franco-German Eurocorps to the incorporation of the WEU as the military arm of the EU.

THE BOSNIAN CONFLICT

The Bosnian war seemed to possess all of the foregoing elements which should have attended the imminent demise of the Atlantic Alliance: the transformation of the Soviet Union into a quasi-ally of the West, the decline of American military power in Europe, and the assertiveness of the European partners. Serbian aggression was a challenge that the Europeans could meet alone. But from its inception the major European allies, Britain and France, regarded the Bosnian conflict as a civil war in which neither side was blameless. While conceding the aggressive designs of Serbian leaders, the allies saw their primary role as helping the United Nations to maintain a neutral presence, and supporting innocent civilians—but not the warring parties—of either side. Indeed, if there was a bias it was not against the Serbian aggressor but against the Muslim state in the Balkans. Opposing this position, the United States made an effort to aid the Bosnian government by asking for an end of the arms embargo which had only served the well-armed Serbs and for the use of NATO air power to protect Bosnian enclaves. The American refusal to accept Serbian territorial conquests was undergirded by its moral revulsion against Serbian behaviour, particularly its ethnic cleansing policies that forced thousands of Muslims from their homes in the course of the war.

Europeans and Americans had not been so divided since the Suez debacle of 1956. While Americans pointed to Europe's unwillingness to take charge of a matter in its own backyard, Europeans refused to accept lectures from a country which would not provide troops for the UN mission. Reluctantly, the allies accepted in principle the use of NATO air power to enforce UN safe zones, but then did as little as possible to make the threat credible to the Serbs. The principle of consensus in NATO appeared to be failing as America's authority dwindled and as Europe failed to take up the leadership that the United States seemed to have been abdicating. Three years after the Bosnian war had begun the only bond holding together the Alliance over the Bosnia issue was the common ground of the "contact group," and with it the concept of a federal Bosnia. Under this arrangement the Muslims would receive 51 percent of the territory, which required considerable concessions by Serbs who held 70 percent of Bosnia-Herzegovina. How firm would this "contact group" be, consisting of Russia along with NATO members United States, Britain, France and Germany?

Superficially, the problem lies with the role of the United Nations, to which the Alliance seemed to defer. The reason for this may be traced to the Gulf War when the UN, with the moribund Soviet Union reluctantly agreeing, gave its sanction to the war against Saddam Hussein. Among other consequences of the end of the Cold War was the potential for a united Security Council to exercise a military function which had eluded it for two generations. While peacekeeping missions had been conducted in the Middle East and Cyprus during the Cold War, it appeared in 1991 that an expanded mission was possible and that NATO could be an instrument in achieving the UN's objectives. Correspondingly, the UN could serve NATO by legitimizing out-of-area operations which otherwise might be open to criticism. Although the Gulf war was not a NATO action, there were enough NATO nations engaged—the United States, Britain and France in particular—to offer that impression to the world at large.

What worked in Iraq was a dismal failure in the Balkans, however. The allies' inability to act together undermined NATO's new mission as crisis manager which had been a vital part of the "Strategic Concept" developed at the North Atlantic Council meeting in Rome in November 1991. By invoking Article 4 of the North Atlantic Treaty,[7] they did have a reason to be involved in this particular out-of-area region, which was neighbor to more than one member. What better example of the Rome message than in Bosnia where the threat could arise not from "calculated aggression against the territory of the Allies but rather from the adverse consequences of instabilities."[8] Moreover, the Allies had ample warning of trouble in Yugoslavia ever since the death of Tito in 1980. Slobodan Milosevic, the former communist apparatchik turned nationalist, foreshadowed his intentions to convert multiethnic Yugoslavia into a greater Serbia by his repressive policies towards the formerly autonomous region of Kosovo, which was populated mostly by ethnic Albanians. The United States did, however, take the preventive step of stationing an army battalion in Macedonia to prevent a potential intra-NATO conflict between Greece and Turkey.

Notwithstanding, the extent of European involvement was to offer peacekeepers under a United Nations umbrella, and to provide safe-havens to shelter civilians caught between the Bosnian Serb aggressors and the Muslim-controlled Bosnian government forces. NATO was brought into the picture, only to make a travesty of its potential role as a military arm of the United Nations. Its plans for enforcing a "no-fly zone" were never implemented. The confused lines of communication between the UN and NATO inhibited decisive action and encouraged Serb resistance. The British and French were unwilling to jeopardize their peacekeeping forces in Bosnia and were ambivalent about supporting the territorial integrity of Bosnia.

As these events unfolded, the position of the United States was in sharp contrast to that of its European allies. Aroused by televised scenes of Serb brutality the Clinton administration initially demanded a NATO response. Here was an opportunity for Europe to exercise a leadership role. The fruits of unification could have been displayed through the EU's activation of one or more of the European security organizations to manage the problem without major American involvement. Such a solution would have fitted the Clinton administration's agenda in 1993 when domestic issues were its first priority. This explains Secretary of State Christopher's missions to Europe in 1993 to urge the Europeans to act, if not by sending forces into Bosnia alongside the Bosnian government, at least by lifting the embargo on arms which was only serving the Serbian side. These missions failed, and in their failure underscored the loss of status that the United States enjoyed in the alliance during the Cold War. The U.S. position was further undermined by its persistent unwillingness to station its own troops as part of the UN's peacekeeping force. The memories of loss of life in the Somalian operation in October 1993 seemed to inhibit an American initiative in Bosnia. Europe's rejection of American advice caused the U.S. Congress to sound a unilateralist if not isolationist note. The American action in removing its ships from a naval embargo in the autumn of 1994 was an important answer to Europe's obdurate refusal to heed American advice.

Actually, NATO had used air power against Serb positions in Bosnia and with apparent effect in February 1994 when it was first exercised after international outrage over deaths in a crowded marketplace. This intentionally consisted of only a warning strike, and it succeeded in deterring Serb attacks temporarily. When the Serb leadership recognized the extent of the disarray between the UN and NATO and between the United States and the European allies, subsequent strikes lost even symbolic value. The Bosnian Serbs rejected the "contact" group's division of the nation with impunity. Not even the putative influence of Milosevic or his Russian ally made a difference.

Granting that Yugoslavia is not Czechoslovakia, the scene in Europe in 1995 resembles the 1890s more than the 1930s, when Western Europeans moved towards the creation of the Triple Entente. The European parties are the same, particularly as Russia finds common ground with Britain and France. The object of their attention, however, is different; it is the United States, not Germany. But despite the differences over the Balkans, the war is regional, not continental or global. There are centripetal forces countering the American impulse to withdraw and Europe's annoyance over American behavior. There is also room for compromise over the Bosnian tragedy without wholly abandoning the victims of that conflict. The United States refrained from lifting the arms embargo unilaterally, and the Europeans moved toward enforcing access to protected zones in Bosnia. The Clinton administration's offer to supply up to 25,000 troops to help extricate, if necessary, UN peacekeepers from Bosnia reflected an effort towards accommodation in December 1994 that was not present the month before. And Europe's intention to provide more effective lines of communication and supply to their forces in Bosnia suggests that the "two-key" rule on use of NATO air power could be changed. NATO remains in 1995 a symbol of stability which none of the Allies wished to risk abandoning.

However, the fact remains that there has been no "NATO method" to deal with Bosnia, as the Allies pursued their national interests in dealing with that Balkan conflict. In doing so they have inflicted more damage upon the alliance than any specific Soviet measure in the years of the Cold War. The mid-1995 crisis over the Bosnian Serb aggression against the Britain and French UN peacekeepers risked the dissolution of the alliance. American pressure for air strikes against the Bosnian Serbs had jeopardized British and French forces whose governments resented an American leadership which demanded action but withheld troops. The United States in turn has never concealed its annoyance over European unwillingness to identify the Serbs as aggressors, and to act accordingly, The outcome could be the end of the alliance with the United States washing its hand of a "European" problem, and Europe convinced that American isolationist sentiment had proven the unreliability of the transatlantic partner.

Yet, in the grand scheme of things, notwithstanding the intra-NATO conflict over Bosnia, the post–Cold War objective of maintaining the stability of Europe has not changed. No matter how morally repugnant the Allied behavior—of both Americans and Europeans—has been over war-torn Yugoslavia, that war has not moved out of the Balkans, or spread to Albania or Macedonia (or to Greece or Turkey). NATO solidarity has been in silent agreement on these issues at meetings of the North Atlantic Council. If this has been international, it has been a wise judgment.

Less sensible has been the language of communiqués, both from NATO headquarters and from the White House. As inter-allied tensions flared in the summer of 1994, and as the Bosnian Serbs flaunted their defiance of NATO and the UN more flagrantly, the White House trumpeted NATO's success in ending the Serb shelling of Sarajevo and restoring calm to the capital. A White House press statement read: "We have led the way in NATO's decisions to enforce the no-fly zone, to protect UN troops if they are attacked, to enforce the economic sanctions against Serbs on the Adriatic and, most recently, to end the Serbs assault on Gorazde."[9] What is striking about this string of achievements is the general inaccuracy of the claims. Sarajevo continued to be shelled periodically throughout 1994, the no-fly zone had been violated repeatedly by Serb aircraft, and the United

States pointedly withdrew its few ships enforcing the blockade in the Adriatic. True, it mentioned the Contact Group and its comprehensive settlement, but this was hardly an American achievement. The settlement represented a scaling down of the Bosnian government's ambitions and a softening of the requirements that the United States had earlier laid down. While some credit may legitimately be taken for the peacekeeping troops in Macedonia the most likely reason why the conflict has not spilled over there is Milosevic's absorption with the Bosnia conflict.

The White House's overstated claims have been matched by NATO communiqués. Of some thirty paragraphs in a lengthy communiqué issued after the ministerial meeting of the North Atlantic Council at Istanbul in June 1994, only three dealt with Bosnia. The Council expressed its concern that the conflict should be settled "at the negotiating table and not on the support efforts towards an early and durable political settlement." Words such as "negotiated compromise" and a "viable, realistic and reasonable territory" for the "Bosnia-Croat Federation" may be found as well as the urging of parties to accept a settlement that preserves Bosnia and Herzegovina as a single Union within its internationally recognized borders. These were vague phrases with little meaning. Nowhere was there condemnation of either side for violating the UN/NATO safe zones. Nor was there any identification of the violation of UN/NATO safe zones as a source of aggression. The only mention of Bosnian Serbs appeared in a hope for a settlement "providing for constitutional arrangements that establish the relationship between Bosnian-Croat and Bosnian-Serb entities."[10]

What both the United States and NATO did in their public statements was to paper over the differences in the Alliance and to pass off with meaningless phrases the cancer in the Balkans which should have been central to their meetings in 1994. The bulk of NATO's attention dwelled on the commitment to a strong transatlantic partnership through the development of a European Security and Defence Identity. This entity may be as irrelevant to NATO's survival as the OSCE which "remains central to European security." How the OSCE can ensure security if NATO itself fails is in no way clear. Too much attention is paid to the Combined Joint Task Force, as if by simply mouthing this term, NATO can put aside the more specific issues that need redress.

Where there has been more substance in NATO deliberations there arose the question of relevance. Among the achievements of the Brussels summit in January 1994 was the establishment of the aforementioned Combined Joint Task Force (CJTF). The very linking of such loaded terms as "combined" and "joint" evoked expectations that a panacea had been found. "Combined" meant that two or more military services would be involved, and "joint" meant that two or more nations would contribute to the task force. Even the term "task force" reinforced expectations; it implied a limited operation in the post–Cold War world where NATO's power could be concentrated on contingencies of all kinds, inside or outside NATO borders. The CJTF could be the vehicle for allowing Europe to handle its own problems without America being part of any particular combination.[11]

The trouble with the CJTF is how to put it into effect without conflicting with older NATO institutions. In January 1994 the North Atlantic Council bestowed its blessings on the CJTF, noting that the military capabilities of the WEU and NATO would be "separable but not separate,"[12] thereby encouraging a flexibility that could be of vital importance in the new function of crisis-management. But what does "separable" but not "separate" mean? Some elements of a potential task force, such as the Eurocorps, have shown signs of being competitive with NATO. If the test is in practice, there has been no sign of its presence in the most obvious proving ground—Bosnia. The problem with the CJTF is not with its mechanics; it offers a genuine means of fulfilling the aspirations of the Rome agreements in 1991. Rather, it lies in the lack of consensus on the part of the political leaders of the alliance. Flaws in the management of the alliance, not in the composition of CJTF accounted for the failures in the Balkans.

NATO ENLARGEMENT

While it may be too late to manage the Bosnian crisis satisfactorily, it is not too late for NATO to act in unison in its relations with Eastern Europe and the Russian Federation. In fact, this may be more significant in the long run than the consequences of the irresolution of the Bosnian conflict. Yugoslavia was, and remains, an out-of-area location. The nations of Central and Eastern Europe may become members of the Alliance, with far-reaching impact on its organization as well as its mission. The key questions revolve around the admission of new NATO members on the eastern flank of NATO, particularly the Czech Republic, Poland and Hungary. Ever since they had won their freedom from the Warsaw Pact they had been campaigning for membership in the alliance. Their primary champion had been Germany, pressing for early admission much as it had pressed for recognition of Croatia, Slovenia and Bosnia to further its traditional influence in Central Europe. Opposing the German initiative were Britain and France. Those allies had other concerns as well, ranging from suspicion of German ambitions in Eastern Europe to France's concern that an eastward expansion of NATO could divert attention from the threat of Muslim fundamentalism on the southern flank of NATO. In this instance the Western powers had support from the Clinton administration, which had its own worries about the admission of former Warsaw Pact states upon the new and fragile Russian-American friendship. Conceivably, precipitate action could arouse Russian fears of NATO intentions, jeopardize President Boris Yeltsin's efforts to westernize and democratize Russian institutions, and push the nation down the road towards extreme nationalism.

As 1994 opened the Clinton administration felt that it had just the right mix of encouragement for the Eastern Europeans and comfort for the Russians. American enthusiasm for the "Partnership for Peace," unveiled at the summit meeting of the North Atlantic Council in Brussels in January 1994, prevailed over the scepticism of the European Allies. The new "partners" would be "allies," but not in the beginning. While they would not be offered membership immediately they would be able to participate in a host of confidence-building activities, such as military exercises, would have access to certain NATO technical data, and would exchange information on defence planning. Full membership is possible only after some major qualifications are met, among which are an irreversible commitment to democracy, civilian control of the military and the development of the nation's military capability to a level of interoperability with those of NATO members.[13]

Such stiff requirements, if enforced, could make the partnership the kind of sham that the Multilateral Force has been in the 1960s. The MLF had promised a nuclear capability to Europeans while keeping the nuclear warhead firmly in American hands. Under the PfP the qualifications for membership might make it impossible for any Central or Eastern European country to fulfill. While the records of NATO's or the U.S. administration's deliberations are not available, it is likely that the illusion of membership without actually being able to realize it was precisely what the designers of the Partnership had in mind. The Czechs and Poles would have the assurances they wanted, while the Russians would not have NATO immediately at their doorstep. Indeed, the Partnership was held out to Russia itself.

The program went forward in 1994, but not quite as its planners had envisaged. The Poles among others were not satisfied; they wanted immediate admission to NATO. American friends of the former Warsaw Pact nations were also unhappy. Influential voices, both Democratic and Republican, insisted on the vital necessity of expanding membership without worrying about its impact on Russia. The new Republican majority in the Congress in 1995 made an issue of President Clinton's coddling of the Russians, of being excessively concerned with Russian sensibilities at the expense of its beleaguered neighbors. Within a week of each other Zbigniew Brzezinski and Henry Kissinger, writing Co-Ed columns for the *New York Times* and the *Washington Post*, respectively, in December 1994, urged the administration to bring the Czech Republic, Poland and Hungary into the Alliance as quickly as possible.[14]

Even as the Central European powers grudgingly went along with the Partnership as at least a first step towards membership, Russia was suspicious of its implications. Yeltsin warily agreed to join provided that Russia was accorded a special status. But this was effectively revoked in December 1994 at the Budapest meeting of the CSCE when Yeltsin denounced the

Partnership as the onset of a "cold peace." It is obvious that the hopes of the Brussels summit have not been realized. NATO's offer of expansion, carefully qualified as it was, seemed to do precisely what the Administration had hoped to avoid; namely, to tip the balance of power in Russia away from democrats and economic reformers and towards nationalists and supporters of a command economy.

There may be a way out of this dilemma which could quell the anxieties of the East Europeans without stoking the paranoia of the Russians and without inviting the many new problems which the expansion of NATO would bring. Current plans to grant full membership to Czechs or Poles or other East Europeans could be abandoned. The chances that they would fulfill the Partnership requirements are minimal at any event. Given the fragility of their economies, how realistic is it to expect that they could afford to modernize their military establishment to meet NATO standards in the near future? And how sensible is it to ask them achieve this goal? Diverting funds into a military buildup could threaten the modernization of their economies which undergird the strength of their new democracies. One of their major objectives is to make themselves attractive to the European Union which all the countries of the former Warsaw bloc aspire to join.

This course need not mean the scuttling of the Partnership, even if NATO could convince East European States that Russia poses no immediate danger to their future, or that Russian military action against Chechnya would not be translated into a revival of the Soviet empire. Instead, the Partnership could be redesigned to permit early membership under Article 5 of the North Atlantic Treaty. Such an arrangement would offer assurance to new members that an armed attack against any one or more of them "shall be considered an attack against them all" to be responded to by individual and collective action of other members, "including the use of armed force" to protect their territorial integrity. There would be no need for joint exercises or the involvement of SHAPE or the creation of a military machine to win this security.

Article 5 represented the "pledge" which comforted Western Europeans in 1949 when only a guarantee of American membership could ensure security against a Soviet invasion. The Korean War a year later changed NATO's perception of the threat, and opened the way for a military buildup which lasted to the end of the Cold War and remains in place in attenuated form today. But it is unnecessary for armies to be stationed on Russia's borders in 1995 when the Russian military is in disarray. Should this situation change in the future Article 5 should deter aggression as long as NATO's military posture is prepared to meet such a challenge. And if NATO is to survive, with or without new members, the new techniques of crisis management should be able to cope with this possibility. Assistant Secretary of State Richard Holbrooke identified a variation of this model in his statement before the House International Relations Committee hearing on U.S. Policy in Europe. Full membership in NATO, he noted, would mean guarantees under Article 5: "That doesn't necessarily means American troops on their soil. There are countries in NATO today which have no American troops on their soil but have the guarantee. Is it a nuclear guarantee? Of course, it's a full guarantee. Do I ever see a reason for that to be revoked? No, I don't."[15]

This arrangement would not set a precedent. The history of the Atlantic Alliance will always make France's departure from the organization in 1966 a traumatic milestone. France left SHAPE but did not renounce the treaty. Article 5 continued to cover France was well as its neighbors in the alliance even though the French military was no longer involved with the defense of Europe. But the French precedent has its limitations; France was a major military power with its own nuclear component when de Gaulle acted. A more useful precedent would be the examples of Iceland, a charter member of the Alliance, and Spain, a member since 1982. Iceland had no army in 1949, and has none today. Yet it is fully protected by the terms of its membership. Similarly, Spain's army is not integrated into the SHAPE command, and has abstained from troop commitments to the organization. There is no reason why Poland or Hungary or the Czech Republic, or other neighbours of Russia might not enter NATO under the same terms.

What impact, then, would the expansion of NATO to the Russian border under these conditions have upon that former superpower? There would be no reason for Russian leaders to complain, as Foreign Minister Andrei V. Kozyrev did in December 1994, that membership of East European neighbors would place a potentially hostile military on Russia's doorstep. NATO would be no farther east then it had been in the past. And the rapid pace of downsizing NATO's military should give little excuse for nationalist posturing.

Conceivably, this outcome could be the occasion for Russia to return to its earlier interest in potential membership in the alliance. There would be no specific barrier. But it is unlikely that Russian leaders, Yeltsin or his successors, would accede to this arrangement. Yeltsin's agreement was an aberration, as was made obvious in his insistence on a special status befitting a nuclear power. It is difficult to envision Russia accepting parity with Poland or Hungary. Instead, having given evidence of good faith in its treatment of the East European powers NATO could fashion a new relationship with the Russians that would recognize Russia's special position without arousing alarm once again among its neighbours. The relationship could take a number of forms. One of them might be to exploit the OSCE to serve as a vehicle for a comprehensive treaty between NATO and the Russian Federation. The OSCE embraces both the United States and Russia, and has often been cited by Russian leaders as the instrument they would prefer as a guarantor of European security. Such a mechanism would be preferable to a United States–Russian arrangement that would revive Europe's old concerns over superpower negotiations in the Nixon-Brezhnev mode. If it were adopted, clear understandings would be necessary to clarify the future of the Baltic states and the Caucasian republics. The former could be included under the NATO blanket while the latter would remain inside the Russian Federation. But if Latvia or Estonia should become a member of NATO, the position of the Russian minority would have to be monitored strictly. And there must be no more Chechnya incidents. The Chechens would enjoy autonomy within the federation. The alternative could be the secession of Islamic states along Russia's southern tier which could lead to much instability in Eastern Europe.

The benefits of a stabilized Europe would be substantial. Russian pride would be respected through its role in the "near abroad." The smaller neighbors would relax through NATO membership. Rather than looming as a menace the Russian presence in the Balkans could soothe tensions. Most importantly, steps towards democracy and a market economy could proceed without being burdened by dangers of a military coup, a communist revival, or a new wave of imperial expansionism. While there would be many unsettling issues in any grand resolution of Europe's security they need not be insoluble. A small volatile nation such as Moldova, with its breakaway Russian minority could be incorporated into Partnership by establishing ties with both NATO and the Russian Federation. More difficult would be the place of such a large nation as the Ukraine in this new Europe. Conceivably, a special relationship between the two Slavic powers might be an answer. But small signs of cooperation between Russia and the Ukraine were evident in 1994 over Crimea and over nuclear issues. Whatever the Ukrainians may wish, it is difficult to envision them inside the Atlantic Alliance without tipping the delicate balance that a NATO-Russia agreement would create.

If any of these optimistic scenarios should come to pass, one then could make a case for NATO itself to be discarded. Without a revanchist Russia, without fearful Poles and Baltics, and without turmoil in the Balkans and the Caucasus, the European Union with the aid of one or more of the European units currently associated with NATO should be able to maintain the stability of the continent. It is the European Union, after all, which presumably will be the engine of Europe's prosperity. For the former Warsaw Pact nations membership in NATO would be the instrument of their own *Wirtschaftswunder* in the 1990s, much as NATO was for Western Europeans in the 1990s. NATO could disband, and the United States could work out a new cooperative but not necessarily entangling relationship with Europe.

Regrettably, it is unlikely that such happy outcomes will be realized in the near future. There are too many variables that cannot be controlled by even the most solid of arrangements. Given the fluid political and economic condition of Russian society, Russian democracy could be the victim at any time of a military coup or an anti-Western government, coming into power by ballot or by force. The centrifugal currents operating in the old Soviet empire have not run dry, and the potential for more conflicts between Moscow and the former Soviet republics remains alive in 1995. NATO's presence, even in an attenuated military form, is an insurance against a new anti-Western campaign on the part of inflamed Russian nationalists.

CONCLUSIONS

Even if Russia becomes comfortable with NATO next door and accepts a supportive treaty with the Western Allies, security in Europe does not automatically follow. The rising militancy of Islam not only might topple secular Arab regimes but could affect the northern as well as the southern littoral of the Mediterranean. France and Italy may be affected. And it is not beyond the realm of possibility that Greece and Turkey, both members of NATO, might fall out in an even more dangerous fashion than they did over Cyprus in 1974.

But there is another centripetal force undergirding NATO in the mid-1990s and that is the role of a powerful united Germany. While German democracy is as assured as that of any of its neighbours, its very size creates problems. Its dominant role in the European Union is one fact for slowing the unification of Europe. In this context the American component of NATO is a counterbalance to the authority of Germany in the alliance. The allies rarely publicize this issue, but the allies in NATO remember the "pledge" of 1949, and show no signs of wishing to remove this link. The downsizing of American and European forces in the alliance is not accompanied by demands for the expulsion of American troops. Nor is there any sign that any member intends to exercise its right to remove itself from the treaty under Article 13.

If the American connection remains important for Europe today, does it follow that the European entanglement is still in America's national interest? While there are voices in the United States which from time to time speak out about the Pacific region replacing the Atlantic, or about the high cost of the Atlantic burden, the consensus of both political parties is that a return to isolationism, even if possible, would be self-destructive. The American stake in European stability is as vital today as it was during the Cold War. The mechanisms within the Alliance may change. It is not unreasonable to assume greater European responsibility in the future, possible symbolized by a European SACEUR, as some American commentators have observed over the past generation. But such changes need not involve an abandonment of Europe. Breaking entangling ties with Europe now would threaten what historian John Lewis Gaddis has called "the long peace."[16] There is no longer the balance of terror which had discouraged conflict during the Cold War. What NATO balances today is the threat of disorder that has accompanied the intensification of ethnic and religious conflict in the 1990s.

The American component of NATO gives it credibility to cope with uncertainties of the future. Despite failures regularly thrust onto the front pages of newspapers, there is no evidence that the alliance will be relegated to the back pages and then be reduced to the small print of an obituary column in the manner of the Southeast Asian Treaty Organization (SEATO) and the Central Treaty Organization (CENTO). NATO is the only institution with the capacity to keep order, if not quite a new world order, as the century comes to an end. But capacity may be an insufficient guarantor of European security if the Allies lack the will to act in concert. A happier outcome of the Bosnian crisis might be NATO's recognition that this sort of out-of-area issue deserves the unified attention of all the Allies. There is an opportunity to demonstrate a European unit that the European Union has been seeking over the years. And, without dissolving the Alliance the United States would recognise a diminished but not insignificant role for the future, not only in southeastern Europe but also across the Mediterranean where the troubles of the Maghreb could spill over onto its northern shores. America's infrastructure in Europe as well as the important psychological impact of a continued partnership would retain its importance, particularly in East-West relations, but the United States would have to identify a new role for its European partners that hitherto neither Americans nor Europeans have been willing to conceive since the end of the Cold War.

NOTES

1. David Calleo, *The Atlantic Fantasy: The US, NATO, and Europe*, Johns Hopkins University Press, Baltimore, MD, 1970, pp. 27–28.

2. Geir Lundestad, "Empire by Invitation? The United States and Western Europe, 1945–1952," *The Society for Historians of American Foreign Relations Newsletter*, Vol. 15, September 1984, pp. 1–211.

3. See "Our Atlantic Alliance: The Political and Economic Strands," speech delivered at the U.S. Military Academy, West Point, New York, 5 December 1962. Reprinted in *Vital Speeches of the Day*, 1 January 1963, pp. 162–66.

4. Francis Fukuyama, "The End of History," *National Interest*, Summer 1989, p. 4.

5. CRS Report for Congress, 28 September 1992, Edward F. Bruner, "U.S. Forces in Europe: Military Implications of Alternative Levels," pp. 1–2.

6. See editorial, "L'Otan obsolète, freine la politique européene de défense," *Le débat stratégique*, No. 12, January 1994, p. 1.

7. Article 4 authorizes members to "consult together whenever, in the opinion

of any of them, the territorial integrity, political independence, or security of any of the parties is threatened."

8. "The Alliance's New Strategic Concept," agreed by Heads of State and Government participating in the Meeting of the North Atlantic Council in Rome on 7–8 November 1991, *NATO Review*, Vol. 39, December 1991, p. 26.

9. The White House, "A National Security Strategy of Engagement and Enlargement," July 1994, p. 21.

10. Ministerial Meeting of the North Atlantic Council, Final Communiqué, Istanbul, *NATO Review*, Vol. 42, June 1994, pp. 25–28.

11. Stanley R. Sloan, CRS Report for Congress, "Combined Joint Task Forces (CJTF) and New Missions for NATO," 17 March 1994.

12. Declaration of the Heads of State and Government participating in the meeting of the North Atlantic Council held at NATO Headquarters, Brussels, on 10–11 January 1994, *NATO Review*, Vol. 42, February 1994, p. 31.

13. Partnership for Peace: Invitation Issued by the Heads of State and Government participating in the meeting of the North Atlantic Council held at NATO Headquarters, Brussels, from 10–11 January 1994, ibid., pp. 28–30.

14. Zbigniew Brzezinski, "NATO—Expand or Die?" *New York Times*, 28 November 1994; Henry Kissinger, "Expand NATO Now," *Washington Post*, 19 December 1994.

15. Testimony of Assistant Secretary of State Richard Holbrooke to the House International Relations Committee hearing on U.S. Policy in Europe of 9 March 1995.

16. John Lewis Gaddis, *The Long Peace: Inquiries into the History of the Cold War* (New York: Oxford University Press, 1987).

11
NATO at Fifty

"NATO at Fifty," which updates the preceding chapter, was prepared specifically for this volume.

As the North Atlantic allies celebrate the fiftieth anniversary of the signing of the North Atlantic Treaty, they wonder about the direction of the alliance in the twenty-first century. This is not a new concern. In fact, the uncertain future of the alliance was an acute issue at the time NATO's fortieth anniversary. The language of *perestroika* and *glasnost* in the late 1980s, and particularly the toppling of the Berlin Wall in the fall of 1989, gave rise to a hope for a new age in which the Hegelian conflicts of history would be at an end, as Francis Fukuyama anticipated. At the least, there would be no need for the continuation of NATO. A flurry of publications in this period, with titles like *Beyond Hegemony: The Future of the Western Alliance* and *Search for Enemies: American Alliances after the Cold War*, relayed this message.[1]

While postmortem reflections on the alliance and organization were premature, questions about a viable future for an organization designed to contain the menace of Soviet communism were understandable. If the Cold War was the raison d'etre for the alliance, what purpose would be served by its existence after the threat had dissolved? This was a major question in the 1990s, and the alliance's existence at the end of the decade may have answered it. Or, is NATO's survival more a matter of bureaucratic inertia, a structure without meaning or purpose? The League of Nations, after all, may have been essentially dead by the mid-1930s, but it lived on through

World War II. Such may be the fate of the alliance, but, if so, its demise has been warded off with mixed success so far. NATO is alive even as it still seeks a rationale for its role in the future.

The civil war in Bosnia, which NATO had addressed so inadequately in the mid-1990s, is showing signs of becoming a legitimate focus of NATO's attention at the end of the decade. On the other hand, the much-heralded Partnership for Peace, which led to the admission of three new members in 1998, is a source of potential destabilization of Europe. There are other centrifugal forces to threaten the future of the alliance, not least of which is Europe's—and particularly France's—wish for more authority in NATO. France has yet to resume its membership in SHAPE; specifically, it wants command of the southern flank. Fifty years after the signing of the Treaty of Washington, the strains caused by European resentment over its trans-atlantic dependence have not been resolved despite major efforts to close the gap between America and Europe.

The most notable effort to share power with the European allies was the American acceptance of a European Security and Defence Identity (ESDI), "the overarching term," as Charles Barry has expressed it, "to refer to the various collective arrangements among European members of NATO that are more than national but less than trans-Atlantic."[2] The ESDI arguably was best reflected in the Combined Joint Task Force concept put forth at the Brussels meeting of the North Atlantic Council in January 1994. Europeans would be able to manage crises of more pressing concern to them than to the United States. NATO facilities would be available to a European-led task force "as a means to facilitate contingency operations with participating nations outside the Alliance."[3]

The breakup of Yugoslavia and the bitter civil wars that followed from 1991 to 1995 should have been just the right venue for almost all the scenarios of 1991 to be played out. The Organization for Security and Cooperation in Europe (OSCE) could provide services, as it did in elections in 1997. And the strategic concept of crisis management seemingly settled in the Rome meeting had direct applicability to the potential war between the rump Serb-dominated Yugoslavia and Slovenia in 1991 and then to the short-lived war between Serbia and Croatia putatively over Croatia's discrimination against its Serb minority in the Krajina region. Failing to contain those brief outbreaks—the former ending in an independent Slovenia and the latter in the attachment of Krajina to Serbia—the NATO allies considered a variety of actions to take in the triangular war in Bosnia among the Muslims, Croatians, and Serbs.

The record from 1991 to 1995 was one of failure and embarrassment. None of the components of ESDI—WEU or Eurocorps, or the Rapid Reaction Force—took the leadership in a military intervention in the Balkan catastrophe. The United States, absorbed initially in a domestically-centered presidential campaign and then led by an administration with other priorities, deferred to Europeans on the Bosnia problem. Unlike with the Persian Gulf War of 1991, there were no natural resources to attract Americans. Nor was there a sense that the national interest was at stake. This was essentially a European problem, particularly because it was the initiative of the European Union, under German pressure, that lent legitimacy to the separated republics of former Yugoslavia.

It was left to the United Nations once again to provide a fig leaf for Western action. The televised scenes of brutality gnawed at the consciences of the NATO allies and inspired the Security Council's Resolution 781 in October 1992, which banned all flights over Bosnia not approved by the UN. While the allies vetoed the American recommendation to shoot down violators of the resolution, they did accept U.S. AWAC aircraft as monitors. The Europeans, in turn, provided peacekeeping operations under United Nations auspices "for the first time" in NATO's history as the NATO communiqué of December 1992 noted.[4]

This distinction between Americans in the air and Europeans on the ground had been a source of continuing tension within the alliance until the massive air assault against the Bosnian Serb forces surrounding Sarajevo in August 1995. The lightly armed and British and French forces working with the UN in Bosnia were vulnerable to the belligerents' retribution if NATO followed American advice to use air power to force the Bosnian Serbs to the peace table. The United States chafed over the refusal of the UN to take the bold steps Americans wanted. But, if the Security Council did not respond to America's impatience, it was because the NATO allies on that council recognized that casualties from such action would be borne by Europeans in Bosnia not by Americans safely in the air above Bosnia.

The ongoing conflicts between beleaguered and inadequately armed UN peacekeepers and the warring parties in Bosnia, between the United States and its NATO partners over the American role in the areas, and between NATO's strategy and tactics, all ended abruptly with a Serb mortar attack on 30 August 1995, killing thirty-eight people in an outdoor market in Sarajevo. This brought on massive NATO air strikes over a three-week period that not only removed heavy weapons from the heights overlooking Sarajevo, but pushed the Bosnian combatants to the negotiating tables. Serb compliance was facilitated by an assault from rearmed Croats that resulted not only in the retaking of Krajina but also occupying a large swath of Bosnian Serb territory. Unlike the spasm that followed a similar marketplace massacre in Sarajevo a year and a half earlier, the belligerents recognized that there was no alternative to external mediation.

From the American perspective, the factors that unleashed at long last a powerful reaction to the communal war in Bosnia had been building up over the years. Efforts at partition through NATO or UN mediation had failed, as had efforts to press the man who set in motion the Balkan War, President Slobodan Milosevic. But the combination of the violation of such

UN safe zones as Srebenica and the inability of NATO commanders to function under UN leadership ultimately drove NATO to act outside UN control. As Senator John McCain noted in December 1994, it was incredible that no air strike could be made without final approval of the UN secretary-general. He asked rhetorically if NATO could "ever operate, frankly with a U.N. master who has neither the equipment, training, background, staff, or support to make that kind of tactical battlefield decision?"[5] The answer to this question was given in August. It was NATO alone that determined the course of events that ended the bloodshed in Bosnia. This included keeping in check a Croat-Muslim offensive that took advantage of the NATO bombing of Serb military positions to regain lost ground.

The air assaults became a twenty-two-day campaign, Operation Deliberate Force, which included twelve days of actual bombing; this broke the siege of Sarajevo and convinced Milosevic that the only way out for his country and his Bosnian Serb clients was to position himself as a peace broker. NATO South's air commander, General Michael Ryan, observed that precision-guided missiles made the operation possible: "Precision weapons gave NATO airmen the ability to conceive and execute a major air campaign that was quick, potent, and likely would not kill people."[6] Understandable as Air Force exuberance was, it was unlikely that the bombing campaign was the decisive factor in ending the bloodshed in the summer of 1995. The parallel Croat ground offensive and the diplomatic skills of Assistant Secretary of State Richard C. Holbrooke, the chief U.S. negotiator in Bosnia, played important roles as well. Yet, it may be claimed, as Colonel Robert Owen, dean of the School of Advanced Airpower at Maxwell Air Force Base, observed, "I can't say that airpower was *the* decisive factor in bringing the war to an end in the shape and form it was, but airpower catalyzed the end of the war in September 1995. . . . It was the factor that tipped the balance toward peace."[7]

When the Dayton (Ohio) agreement was initialed in November 1995, the UN was conspicuous by its absence, with the exception of unarmed UN international police monitors to watch Bosnian police forces. And even in this limited area, NATO had to replace the UN presence. But although the North Atlantic Council congratulated itself in its communiqué of 5 December 1995, welcoming "the agreement initialed in Dayton for peace in Bosnia and Herzegovina,"[8] the Dayton agreement was not a council action. The meeting of Croat, Muslim, and Serb leaders was held in an American midwestern city.

The arrangement was obviously a patchwork designed to end the fighting but with no assurance that its components would endure. No indicted war criminal could hold political office in the new state, but there was no provision for requiring the constituent governments to turn over war criminals for prosecution. A major component of the Dayton accords was the return of refugees uprooted by the war, some 2.7 million, who would either be returned to their homes or compensated for their lost properties.[9] But while there would be a human rights commission to monitor the treatment of refugees, there was no machinery created to facilitate their repatriation.

Skeptics who doubted the viability of the Dayton agreements found their doubts realized over the next few years, as Serb leaders Radovan Karadzic and General Ratko Mladic remained free from trial despite indictment as war criminals. Even though Karadzic did step down as formal head of the Serb government, he continued to exercise power through his followers, not least of whom was the Serb member of the presidential triumvirate. Nor was there progress in repatriation. Elections took place that permitted the original residents to vote, but few Muslims in Serb-controlled territory and few Serbs in Croat-controlled territory dared to take up their old lives in their old homes. In 1998 the lines had hardened, with few Muslims in the Serb republic and few Serbs in Croat-controlled territory.

The Bosnian federation was a fiction. To make matters worse, the Muslim-Croat relationship left the Muslims fearful of Croat power and ready to use U.S. military aid along with arms from the Islamic world to resume fighting once the peacekeepers departed. Bosnian Croats were only waiting for the right moment to join neighboring Croatia, a sentiment they shared with supporters of Greater Serbia. Arguably, the most foreseeable conflicts arose from the Serb wish to keep the territory around Brcko connecting the Serb territory in northwest Bosnia with the eastern enclaves and Serbia proper while the Muslims insisted on the return of Srbrenica and Gorazde, formerly a UN-protected "safe zone" seized by Bosnian Serbs.

Given these flash points, the keeping of peace among these factions through the next few years was itself a minor miracle. Its guarantor was a military presence under NATO leadership that involved 60,000 troops, including 20,000 Americans, in the Implementation Force (IFOR). In light of an earlier pledge by the Clinton administration to make 25,000 troops available to cover the removal of lightly armed British and French peacekeepers operating ineffectively under UN auspices, the American commitment seemed modest. Yet, it required political courage for American leadership to confront an uneasy public by committing military force to Bosnia. It was not the Vietnam syndrome that was the problem; presumably the Gulf War had laid that ghost to rest. Rather, it was the more recent memory of the failed Somalian operation in which the U.S. and the UN were blamed for being caught up in an unwinnable domestic conflict that had converted a mission of mercy into a "mission creep" to rebuild the nation.

To avoid this fate, IFOR's mission was to last only year, to give time to the former warring parties to work out peaceful solutions among themselves. To the surprise of many skeptics, all parties accepted the NATO force, and the year passed without casualties. But the unworkable assumptions of the Dayton accord made it obvious that an abrupt departure could lead to an immediate resumption of hostilities. Consequently, IFOR's name was changed to SFOR (Stabilization Force) after IFOR terminated in December 1996; and, with fewer troops (8,000 in the U.S. contingent), the mission continued with another terminal date, June 1998. There was a faint hope, nourished primarily by the United States, that SFOR could be the testing ground for the Combined Joint Task Forces (CJTF) system, under which Europeans in the Western European Union could use NATO facilities to command an all-European organization. The North Atlantic Council endorsed the CJTF concept in June 1996, six months before IFOR's mandate was to expire. But the challenge was never accepted. There were too many unsolved problems about the CJTF, not least of which was who would command the task force. Europe's failure to accept the system rested primarily on an unwillingness to move ahead without the United States as a participant. Stabilization Force (SFOR) became the son-of-IFOR with few changes and fewer expectations.

Finally recognizing that there was no viable exit strategy, President Clinton early in 1998 gave up the idea of a deadline for withdrawal and relinquished as well the vain hope that Europeans would carry the military burden while Americans would provide only communications and logistical services. The numbers would be somewhat smaller but not substantially changed. The NATO contribution would have to "be sufficient in number and in equipment," as the president put it on 18 December 1997, "to achieve its mission and to protect itself in safety."[10] But the Dayton accord did not make clear just what that mission was, and the experience of IFOR and SFOR offered little help. The underlying assumption behind the dispatch of troops was that everything else would fall into place once NATO made its appearance, and that a peaceful Bosnian federation would make the presence of troops unnecessary in the future.

This happy end to the Balkan story has not yet taken place. For much of the time, NATO troops, with American blessing, interpreted their mission narrowly. They would keep the former belligerents from breaking the peace, but would take no steps toward arresting indicted war criminals, or force unwilling Serbs or Croats to return Muslim refugees to their homes. Instead, the ethnic cleansing that the Serbs and Croats (to a lesser extent) had practiced so brutally doing the war was played out in the refusal of occupiers to relinquish their homes and in the unwillingness of refugees to live in a hostile environment. Sarajevo, formerly a model of civilized interaction among all ethnic groups, was converted almost entirely into a Muslim city. Radicals of all three communities seemingly controlled the political scene in Bosnia, with NATO looking the other way.

By the winter of 1998 there were some signs of impending change. The fact that the United States and its allies had abandoned the self-imposed deadlines might have been interpreted as an acceptance of a permanent presence in Bosnia and a surrender of hopes for a harmonious federation. But it may also have given a signal to dissidents on all sides that they should give up their expectation of resuming hostilities once the peacekeepers departed. Even before the president made his announcement, NATO leadership was exhibiting more vigor. It took the side of Bosnian president Biljana Plavsic in her power struggle with Karazdic, with money and periodic shows of strength, and was rewarded with the selection in January 1998 of a new government under Prime Minister Milorad Dodik that excluded Karazdic's party for the first time. These developments, along with the increasing number of indicted war criminals dispatched to the Hague for trial, suggested that SFOR was gradually bringing order to Bosnia.

But these steps were not irreversible. The divisions between the Croats and Muslims remained deep; there was no common currency in Bosnia or even common number plates on automobiles. Bosnian Croats, with periodic winks from Croatia, still looked forward to joining the mother country. And the victory of Dodik in the Bosnian Serb republic was paper thin; the division there between Banja Luka and Pale was not healed. While some of the indicted leaders were captured, the most notorious remained free and influential.

Another dimension to NATO's Bosnian experience deserves a close examination: namely, the experience NATO allies had in working together as a military organization. Although the United States provided the largest share of troops, the United Kingdom and France were well represented, with 14,000 and 10,000 troops respectively. When IFOR became operational, Bosnia was divided into three sectors in which troops from the U.S., Britain, and France would take responsibility for keeping order. NATO contributions were not confined to the three major allies. A fourth leading member, Germany, whose constitutional restrictions and memories of a shameful past had hitherto limited its involvement in the Balkans, sent some 5,000 noncombat personnel to the NATO command and later included combat troops in its mission. Smaller allies, such as Belgium and Spain, were also present, and Italy has served as a major staging area for U.S. forces. A positive force behind NATO's commitment has been SACEUR general Wesley Clark, who had been deeply involved in working out the Dayton agreements.

The success that NATO has had in keeping the lid on violence in Bosnia without suffering casualties arguably has obscured the ability of the allies to work together under SACEUR in a major military operation. Such difficulties as those connected with communications and command-and-control responsibilities seemed not only soluble but solved with minimal friction among the allies. But the Bosnian operation engaged more than just the NATO allies. A major element in "Operation Joint Endeavor," as IFOR was labeled in 1996, was the long list of non-NATO countries from the Partnership for Peace (PfP), that participated in the operation. Eighteen countries, ranging from former members of the Warsaw Pact to current members of the Arab League, sent troops to serve under a NATO command.

The most visible, and most important, of these non-NATO powers has been Russia, which had dispatched an airborne brigade to Bosnia. In deference to Russian pride, its brigade nominally has an autonomous status, but in reality serves in the American sector under a NATO commander. The experience of collaboration in this peacekeeping effort—disarming the belligerents and preventing renewal of hostilities—was a valuable by-product of the Partnership for Peace program, which had been instituted at the Brussels meeting of the North Atlantic Council; and, in a more distant connection, this collaboration was a link to the concepts behind the ineffective North Atlantic Cooperation Council (NACC). Military collaboration within an integrated operation could have a political impact as important as that of the formal Charter of 1997, which linked Russia to NATO.

There is still another element in NATO's role as peacekeeper. It is not alone in Bosnia. The United Nations, with all its shortcomings, remains an important player in the Balkans. Alongside NATO in Bosnia are the UN secretary general's special representative, the UN high commissioner for refugees, and the UN International Police Task Force. NATO's mandate in Bosnia is the UN Security Council Resolution 1088 under Chapter VII of the UN Charter. Moreover, the OSCE has become an agent in the deescalation of tension by its service as organizer and inspector of election proceedings. Just as Russia and other non-NATO nations have participated in the military operation, the OSCE, which is composed of many of the same nations, including Russia, has become part of the process. Unlike the UN, which is not mentioned in the Dayton accords, the OSCE was specifically requested to supervise the preparation and conduct of municipal and national elections. Not coincidentally, this has been the one organization to which Russia has given its enthusiastic endorsement as a successor to NATO. While this prospect is unlikely in the near future, it has been through informal modes of collaboration performing complementary tasks or through informal integration of non-NATO military units rather through formal charters with Russia and the Ukraine that the new missions of the alliance may develop.

If the alliance succeeds with management of this crisis, it will have fulfilled one of the major expectations of the 1991 Rome meeting of the North Atlantic Council. In this process, NATO would be *primus inter pares* among regional organizations that include the WEU and EU as well as the OSCE, while the American presence would serve as the rubric beneath which positive change could take place. Rather than the out-of-area being a distraction to the alliance, it has the potential of becoming its raison d'etre and a prototype of future activities. Managing ethnic conflict in Kosovo or coping with the challenge of a radical Islamic movement on the southern rim of the Mediterranean may be the central mission of the alliance in the new millenium. As such, it could serve as the regional organization under Chapter VIII of the UN Charter.

But a more immediate prospect might well be a review of the North Atlantic Treaty's articles, particularly Article 4, which provides for consultation among the allies "whenever, in the opinion of any of them, the territorial integrity, political independence or security of any of the Parties is threatened." It is under this broad provenance that "out-of-area" problems have been addressed. A clearer mandate on the order of Article 5, in which an "armed attack against one or more of them in Europe shall be considered an attack against them all," could deal more satisfactorily with the parameters of such operations as Bosnia—or the Middle East.

The foregoing scenario was inspired by the actions of the North Atlantic Council at its Brussels meeting in January 1994. And, like many scenarios, it may never materialize. The obstacles are numerous and obvious, beginning with failure to keep the peace in Bosnia and extending to divisions among the allies and American withdrawal from the area—if not from Europe. But, arguably, the most prominent impediment to new strategic concepts for NATO was self-inflicted.

At the Brussels meeting in January 1994 that implicitly at least opened the way for SHAPE to execute "out-of-area" missions, the primary attention of the allies was on the Partnership for Peace (PfP). This was a program that was intended, as the NATO communiqué noted, to invite non-NATO nations "to participate in political and military bodies at NATO headquarters with respect to Partnership activities." In some respects there was no conflict between tying the former Warsaw bloc states into NATO operations and supporting the CJTF in an out-of-area action. The example of PfP states working with NATO in Bosnia bears out the potential of both initiatives. The problem arises from the language in an accompanying communiqué. In paragraphs 12 and 13, the Declaration of Heads of State and Government made a point of noting that Article 10 of the North Atlantic Treaty kept the alliance "open to membership of other European states in a position to further the principles of the Treaty and to contribute to the security of the North Atlantic area. We expect and would welcome NATO expansion that would reach to democratic states to our East, as part of an evolutionary process, taking into account political and security developments in the whole of Europe."[11]

This was not a specific invitation to membership in the alliance. Initially, it was a promissory note to be redeemed sometime in future. In the meantime, the "welcome" should be enough to comfort the new democracies anxious to develop market economies and to enjoy the sense of security that NATO provided its members. The council did promise to consult with any "partner" if it perceived "a direct threat to its territorial integrity, political independence, or security." Permanent liaison officers were invited to reside at NATO headquarters as joint military activities were coordinated in the Partnership framework. But none of these warm invitations involved Article 5 of the North Atlantic Treaty or assumed the obligations and responsibilities of a member state.[12]

A year later the scene was very different. The language of some of the allies, particularly the United States, contained the idea of "expansion" or the more neutral term, "enlargement," sooner rather than later. The former term after all was embodied in the council communiqué of January 1994 wherein Article 13 concluded with the statement that "active participation in the Partnership for Peace will play an important role in the evolutionary process of the expansion of NATO." If this sentence was meant to satisfy potential new members with involvement but not alliance in NATO, the intention was a failure. In December 1995, the council spelled out in considerable detail the steps the partners for peace (PfP) should take to "facilitate their ability to assume the responsibilities of membership." While the communiqué emphasized that these steps would not apply to all partners, it was understandable if those waiting for an invitation would be heartened by the tone of the NATO statement issued less than two years after the PfP program was inaugurated.[13]

Where does responsibility for NATO enlargement lie? A facile answer places it with the United States and, specifically, with the presidential election campaign of 1996 in which the two major political parties competed for ethnic votes by their devotion to bringing Poland and the Czech Republic into the alliance's fold. Undoubtedly, this political element accelerated the movement, but the centripetal forces were more complicated than the exigencies of an American election.

The United States was by no means alone among the allies concerned with expansion. Helmut Kohl's Germany had a stake in this outcome. Kohl himself saw in Poland's adherence an opportunity to end once and for all the ugly history of German-Polish conflict as well as to advance German economic interests in Central Europe. It was not unlikely that Chancellor Kohl saw himself emulating Konrad Adenauer's successful rapprochement with France.[14] While other allies may not have shared his enthusiasm, they recognized that attention to NATO could divert the former Warsaw Pact nations from pressing for membership in the European Union. Given the absence of a threat from the East, economic rather than military integration should have been the first priority of Poles and Czechs. Even as the European Union recognized this reality, its members were concerned with the potential impact of eastern expansion on their common currency; the potential members would not be prepared to take on the obligations of the euro. Not only would the incorporation of Central European countries threaten EU with an unwelcome flow of labor and competition in farm products, but this would raise the specter of a financial burden reminiscent of the problems that arose when Ireland, Portugal, and Greece joined the EU.

There was another element in the push for expansion that played on the sensibilities of all the allies: namely, the promise of completing the unification of a Europe, which had been divided artificially by the Iron Curtain during the Cold War. Inclusion of Eastern Europe would remove the stain of the Yalta agreement. Even though the Soviets did not live up to their agreement to free elections in the occupied lands, the West seemingly had betrayed the cause for which they had fought in World War II. Restoring victims of Soviet expansion to the West was simple justice. And it had immediate beneficial effects in the form of mitigating conflicts between Hungary and Romania over ethnic Hungarians in Transylvania or between Hungary and Slovakia over ethnic Slovaks in Hungary. The prospect of joining NATO seemed to reduce problems that might have jeopardized their admission to the alliance.

No statesman expressed the civilizing function of NATO enlargement better than Vaclav Havel, president of the Czech Republic and hero of Czech resistance to communism. A poet and playwright, Havel felt that the arguments for enlargement of NATO were "often mechanical, somehow missing the real meaning of the alliance. The process of expansion must be accompanied by something much deeper: a refined definition of the purpose, mission, and identify of NATO." For him the alliance was an instrument of democracy, a defender of political and spiritual values, "not as a pact of nations against a more or less obvious enemy, but as a guarantor of Euro-American civilization and thus as a pillar of global security." He deplored the stereotyped thinking in which Russia was still the enemy. While Russia could not become a member of NATO because of its position as "a Eurasian superpower, with its own diverse interests, it should be a partner in the cultivating of common values." He was convinced that "if the West does not stabilize the East the East will destabilize the West. If principles of democracy win in the East, the peace and stability of all Europe will be insured."[15]

Ever since the peaceful Velvet Revolution in Czechoslovakia, Havel's was a voice above the fray, respected in the way Nelson Mandela's was in South Africa. Both men suffered for their idealism and prevailed. But the irenic future Havel envisioned in NATO's expansion, particularly in the relationship with the Soviet Union, was a major source of debate in 1995 and 1996 as invitations to at least three of the former Soviet satellites appeared to be a strong possibility. That Russia was opposed to any expansion of the alliance that would encompass former Warsaw Pact members, would bring NATO to its borders, and would exclude any possibility of its participation, was anticipated and discounted. Professions of NATO cooperation through NACC, PfP, and IFOR would calm Russian concerns. Or so NATO leaders hoped.

The initial Russian reaction was sharply negative. At a conference in Washington on NATO enlargement in the spring of 1995, Alexander E. Pushkov, director of Political and Public Affairs of the Public Russian TV, presented a sharply critical view of what he saw as inevitable. Essentially he recognized that Russia was too weak to prevent Poland or the Czech Republic from joining NATO but was unwilling to accept the promises of cooperation and the disclaimers of any hostile intention on the part of the Western allies. His preference was to replace NATO with the OSCE. "NATO enlargement," he asserted, "risks poisoning the relationship between Russia and the West for a long time."[16]

This line of reasoning carried weight with opponents of enlargement who worried about needlessly antagonizing a former enemy. Russia was moving toward a market economy, fitfully and painfully, as it gingerly accepted a democratic polity. The fear was that these advances would be jeopardized by a nationalist reaction that would damage relations with the West. This could take the form of a return to dictatorship, neo-Communist or Fascist; a refusal to ratify START II or reduce its still powerful nuclear arsenal; and in general an indulgence in a passive-aggressive pursuit of foreign policies hostile to NATO's interests. The intervention of Foreign Minister Yevgeni Primakov in the Iraqi standoff in 1997 reflected anger over Russian impotence in the face of NATO's eastward thrust.

Recognizing its apparent inevitability, President Boris Yeltsin attempted to make the best deal he could in view of NATO's eagerness to appease Russian suspicions. He oscillated, at least in public, between reluctant acceptance and outright rejection. NATO leaders tried to make the case that greater stability in Central Europe should serve Russian as well as Western interests. In 1997, as the North Atlantic Council prepared to offer membership to Poland, the Czech Republic, and Hungary, Russia pressed for as many concessions as it could extract from the Western allies. At a meeting with NATO Secretary-General Javier Solana in February 1997, Primakov asked for Russian involvement in developing theater missile defense capabilities as a price for acquiescence in NATO's enlargement.[17]

The result of the complementary efforts of Russians to press NATO for as many concessions as they could win and of the allies to soften the impact of eastern expansion with as many blandishments as would appear credible was the Founding Act on Mutual, Relations, Cooperation and Security between NATO and the Russian Federation on 27 May 1997. Citing the UN and particularly the OSCE as common bonds, the founding act promised that "NATO and Russia will seek the widest possible cooperation among participating States of the OSCE, with the aim of creating in Europe a common space of security and stability, without dividing lines or spheres of influence limiting the sovereignty of any state."[18] A Permanent Joint Council would provide the mechanism for consultation, coordination, and even "joint decisions and joint actions with respect to security issues of common concern." Arguably, the most sensitive issue was the commitment not to station permanent foreign ground troops on the territory of member nations that did not already have them—not that this was a new commitment. The text noted that NATO member states "reiterate that they have no intention, no plan and no reason to deploy nuclear weapons on the territory of new members, nor any need to change any aspect NATO's nuclear posture or nuclear policy"[19]

The elaborate language of the text, with its insistent references to the UN and OSCE, was designed to give the Russians and the world the impression that the relationship between Russia and NATO would be closer after expansion than before. Whether or not it was illusory, the mantra employed by the Clinton administration in celebrating the Founding Act— the Russians would have a voice but not a veto in NATO affairs—created difficulties with some critics. Former Secretary of State Henry Kissinger, a strong advocate of expansion, was concerned that Russia would have both a voice and a veto and would have them before ratification of the enlarged NATO was completed. His fear was that a revived Russia in the future— and even a weakened Russia in the late 1990s—could follow policies dangerous to the alliance.[20] It did not escape the notice of critics that the Russian nuclear arsenal remained largely intact and that progress on the START II agreement, which should follow logically from the Founding Act, remained stalled in the Duma. Russian nationalism was still a threat to the West.

For critics opposed to NATO enlargement, the problem with Russia took on another aspect. What about countries left out of the enlargement process? As the time grew closer for an invitation to be preferred, the voices of other East European countries were heard—and championed. At the Madrid summit in August 1997, France threw in Romania as a worthy addition. Other partners in the PfP program were anxious to join the parade of new members, including the former Yugoslav republic of Slovenia. But the most difficult and embarrassing suitors were the Baltic states, former republics in the U.S.S.R., which the United States had never recognized since Soviet occupation in 1940. Now Lithuania Latvia, and Estonia hoped that the steadfast support the West had given under foreign occupation would be translated into NATO membership. Only an application by Ukraine would be more difficult to manage, and the Ukraine matter was solved for the time being by the new charter tying it to NATO along the lines of the Russian-NATO Founding Act.

Of greater immediate concern to American legislators was the cost of NATO enlargement, and this would be known only after the new members had been incorporated into the organization. The figures circulated in 1997 ranged from modest to extravagant, depending upon who was doing the calculation. The watchdog Congressional Budget Office estimated a cost of $125 billion, while the Rand Corporation projected figures between $42 billion and $110 billion. The administration was more interested in a State Department estimate of $27 to $35 billion spread out over the next twelve years. What made these figures all the more palatable was an assumption that most of the cost should be borne by European allies, with the U.S. share to be no more than $2 billion.[21]

By the summer of 1997 the secretary-general was downplaying the cost of enlargement, which was presumably confirmed by a NATO study claiming that the Clinton administration estimate of $30 billion over the next decade was much too high. More likely the cost would be less than $2 billion over this period. Such was the soothing estimate of a NATO study designed to relieve Europeans, disturbed as they were over domestic agendas requiring cuts in military budgets. If accurate, the modest cost of enlargement would have a beneficial effect on the ratification prospects in the U.S. Senate.

Despite the positive assurances of such NATO leaders as Secretary-General Javier Solana, an examination of the state of military preparedness in the three countries suggested that none of their military establishments was strategically interoperable with NATO's systems. At the same time that NATO civilian officials were downplaying the cost factor, Defense Planning Questionnaires submitted in October 1997 and evaluated in November found that their equipment, combat readiness, and training levels were well below NATO's operating standards. In light of the major deficiencies in their military infrastructures, Solana's insistence on the manageability of costs, perhaps as little as $1.3 billion, sounded hollow. One of the West's major military journals had laid out some of these future problems in the summer of 1997 before the concerted campaign to minimize costs of expansion was mounted. Left unexamined were the implications of Poland's plan to increase its defense budget by 3 percent annually for five years, with 40 percent of defense spending going to procurement.[22]

Inevitably, these questions, particularly those centering on cost, arose in the U.S. Senate debate in the spring of 1998. But a bipartisan majority, assuming a comfortable margin of at least the minimal two-thirds of the Senate to modify the North Atlantic treaty, brushed off opponents and defeated amendments that would have limited costs of enlargement and restricted enlargement to the three countries already invited. Senator Tom Harkin's amendment on 28 April 1998 to confine military subsidies to the prospective members to 25 percent of total NATO aid to those countries was resoundingly defeated by a vote of 76 to 24.[23] This was only one of more than a dozen amendments that would be tacked on to the resolution on bringing new members into the alliance.

But in the context of the Senate's business, the debate over enlargement seemed to have started as a way to fill spare time in March 1998 when the Senate majority leader, Trent Lott, was frustrated over Democratic obstruction to a Republican-sponsored education bill. Senator Lott then casually introduced the NATO issue and just as casually postponed it to April. It seemed that the administration had no need to create a special Office for NATO Enlargement Ratification, given the apparent lack of public interest in this issue. The voices of such distinguished diplomats as George Kennan and knowledgeable legislators as former Senator Sam Nunn opposing the resolution seemed to have had little resonance in 1998. The vote on 30 April 1998 was 80 to 19, with 35 Democrats joining 45 Republicans in support of the revised treaty and 10 Democrats joining 9 Republicans in opposition. It was a resounding victory for an otherwise embattled president.

What might have been a momentous debate in the spring of 1988 over the extension of the alliance to include former members of the Warsaw bloc was trivialized in the Senate. Compare the visibility of the ratifying process in 1998 with the "great" debates over the American relationship with NATO in the past—in 1949 when three volumes of hearings reflected the emotions of the day, requiring almost four months to elapse between the signing of the treaty and its approval. Note the heated arguments in the Senate over the dispatch of U.S. troops to Europe in 1951 as well as the panic in 1971 when the Nixon administration barely beat back Senator Mike Mansfield's resolution to reduce drastically American forces in Europe unless Europeans shared the financial burden of the alliance more equitably. The enlargement of NATO at the end of the century may be as critical an issue as the foregoing had been in the past.

Such attention as was given to the enlargement process in the U.S. Senate and in the deliberative bodies of the member nations centered on relations with Russia, the admission of new members beyond the three in 1999, and the cost of the enterprise. Almost entirely ignored, has been the impact on NATO as a defense organization if it continues to enlarge. With the addition of Poland, Hungary, and the Czech Republic the alliance will have nineteen members. There was some sentiment in the Senate to postpone new admissions for a few years, or at least until the consequences of enlarging the alliance to 19 could be evaluated. But the concerns of expectant candidates, such as Romania and Slovenia, not to mention the Baltic states, prevented any such delay to be made a matter of NATO law, which meant that the Baltic question remained open. It also meant that Russian fears of NATO as too close a neighbor seemed justified, the Foundation Act notwithstanding.

Granted that the movement of NATO's border eastward to include membership in NATO of nations that were once part of the Soviet Union raised serious questions. And it was hardly surprisng that the vague estimates of cost would engender controversy. But were they the most critical issues before the Senate? More to the point, how can a defense organization based on consensus function with 20 or 25 members. It was difficult enough with 16. There may come a time in the near future when NATO's enlargement will be of such girth that it becomes a collective security organization indistinguishable from the OSCE. At such a time the two organizations could be fused, with one or the other dissolving. In this context the argument that NATO's expansion would only move the dividing line between Russia and the West farther to the east would disappear. Russia would be part of what might be considered a united Europe. But how serious is this prospect? It would be based on two assumptions: (1) had that there would no longer be a need for the intricate military machine NATO had created over fifty years, and (2) that the American presence would be gratuitous.

Neither of these assumptions appeared valid in the alliance's fiftieth year. NATO as a military entity remains an important element in the security of the West. Its capabilities help to keep such peace as is possible after the civil war in Bosnia and serve to inhibit further outbreaks in such potential points of conflict as Kosovo in Serbia. Greek-Turkish relations, always volatile, are constrained by their membership in NATO, while tensions on the southern rim of the Mediterranean make all allies, particularly the French, aware of the benefits the alliance's military power confers. As for the American presence, France's frustrated hopes for new European commands notwithstanding, no ally would welcome an American departure from Europe. Only the United States has the military technology to manage out-of-area crises in the Middle East, and only the United States provides reassurance against German predominance in Europe. If the U.S. were removed from the scene, which ally would replace its leadership? Intra-European rivalries could destroy the effectiveness of a rump NATO. Even if European economies would permit the requisite military investment, American withdrawal would seriously damage their military capabilities.

Or, are there other answers in the future? A case can be made for an expansion that gathers nations under the protection of Article 5 without committing them to building up their military capacity, or even stationing NATO forces within their borders. Such a solution would go far toward reducing the costs of enlargement and alleviating Soviet fears of American hegemony. Elements of this approach were evident in promises made to Russia as Poland entered the alliance. And certainly there are members of the alliance and organization who have never made troop commitments; Iceland is a case in point. Such an approach might soften but not terminate Russian opposition. Nor would it satisfy the aspirations of new members Ideally, the answer would have been to have made the Partnership for Peace a genuine substitute for membership. In brief, it is questionable if enlargement of the alliance was necessary in 1998, particularly since it diverted attention from the more pressing activities of NATO in the Balkans.

But the reality is that, wisely or not, NATO made its decision in 1997 and had it ratified by the constituent members in 1998. Enlargement has moved along without serious challenge in any of the member states. Even if drawbacks outweigh advantages, the deed was done, and the alliance will have to live with its consequences. Are they fatal? They may not be if no further immediate efforts are made to extend the alliance eastward. It is likely that all members will recognize that NATO is the only organization among the many that can provide a military contribution to crises. And only the United States can be the instrument to implement military decisions. The arenas will not be within the organization, despite the ongoing Greek-Turkish tensions. There will be out-of-area situations in which NATO finds vital interests at stake and where, as in Bosnia, the OSCE and UN may collaborate as "partners for peace." In this environment there is little incentive for any NATO members to abandon the alliance or to separate Europe from America. Such appears to be the state of NATO at the end of the twentieth century.

NOTES

1. David Calleo, *Beyond American Hegemony: The Future of the Western Alliance* (New York: Twentieth Century Fund/ Basic Books, 1987); Ted Galen Carpenter, *A Search for Enemies: American Alliances after the Cold War* (Washington, DC: CATO Institute, 1992).

2. Charles L. Barry, "ESDI: Toward a Bi-Polar Alliance?," Charles L. Barry, ed., *Reforging the Trans-Atlantic Relationship* (Washington, DC: National Defense University Press, 1996), p. 64.

3. Declaration of the Heads of State and Government Participating in the Meeting of the North Atlantic Council, Brussels, 10–11 January 1994, *Texts of NATO Statements, Declarations, and Communiqués, 1994* (Brussels: NATO Office of Information and Press, 1994), p. 11.

4. Ministerial Meeting of the NAC, Brussels, Final Communiqué, 17 December 1992, *Texts of Statements, Declarations, and Final Communiqués 1992* (Brussels: NATO Office of Information and Press, 1992), p. 48.

5. Hearing, U.S. Senate Committee on Armed Services, 103 Cong., 2 sess., 1 December 1994, p. 10.

6. *Defense Week*, 6 November 1997.

7. Ibid.

8. Ministerial Meeting of North Atlantic Council, Brussels, Final Communique, 5 December 1995, *Texts of NATO Statements, Declarations, and Communiqués, 1995* (Brussels: NATO Office of Information and Press, 1995), p. 69.

9. Highlights of Bosnia Peace Agreement, 14 December 1995, *Facts on File*, vol. 55, p. 921.

10. *New York Times*, 18 December 1997.

11. Partnership for Peace Invitation Issued by the Heads of State and Government Participating in the Meeting of the North Atlantic Council, Brussels, 10–11 January 1994, *Texts of NATO Statements, Declarations and Communiqués, 1994* (Brussels: NATO Office of Information and Press, 1994), p. 5; Declaration of the Heads of State and Government Participating in the Meeting of the North Atlantic Council, 10–11 January 1994, ibid., p. 12.

12. Partnership for Peace Framework Document: Annex to Invitation, 10–11 January 1994, ibid., p. 8.

13. Brussels Meeting of NAC, 10–11 January 1994, ibid., p. 12; Ministerial Meeting of the North Atlantic Council, Final Communiqué, 5 December 1995, *Texts of NATO Statements, Declarations, and Communiqués, 1995* (Brussels: NATO Office of Information and Press, 1995), p. 73.

14. Martin Seiff in *Washington Times*, 6 April 1995.

15. Vaclav Havel, "NATO's Quality of Life," *New York Times*, 13 May 1997.

16. Alexei K. Pushkov, "A View from Russia," Jeffrey Simon, ed., *NATO Enlargement: Opinions and Options* (Washington, DC: National Defense University Press, 1995), p. 139.

17. Brooks Tigner in *Defense News* 3 March 1997.

18. *NATO Review*, July–August 1997, p. 7.

19. Ibid., p. 8.

20. Kissinger Testimony before Senate Foreign Relations Committee, 30 October 1997, *Washington Times*, 31 October 1997.

21. Report to Congress on Enlargement of NATO, 23 February 1998. News Release, Office of Assistant Secretary of Defense (Public Affairs), Washington, DC.

22. *Jane's Defence Weekly*, 6 August 1997.

23. *New York Times*, 29 April 1998.

12
NATO: A Counterfactual History

The last chapter in this section, "NATO: A Counterfactual History," was delivered as a dinner address at a conference held in April 1994 at the Lyman L. Lemnitzer Center for NATO and European Union Studies. It was published in S. Victor Papacosma and Mary Ann Heiss, eds., NATO in the Post–Cold War Era: Does NATO Have a Future? (New York: St. Martin's Press, 1995), pp. 3–21.

There are not many appropriate occasions for a historian to play with counterfactual history. To put it charitably, it is unreasonable for a scholar to venture into a realm where there are no records to provide guidance. For me to attempt to reconstruct a past for the Atlantic Alliance that might have been but never was invites ridicule, if not contempt, on the part of reputable scholars of the past. Despite the stigma attached to such an enterprise, I want to present a history of Europe and America with the North Atlantic Treaty Organization (NATO) after World War II and then to examine the difference that the alliance has made to its members over its forty-five-year history.

Before presenting this counterfeit history, I should like to note that the pundits who evoke a future rarely meet with the same suspicions that attach to the historian whose imagined past is no more preposterous than many an imagined future. "Futurology" even has a quasi-academic veneer of respectability; universities offer courses in the subject. And futurologists' projections are taken seriously in the press and podium, if not in the classroom, even if their counterfactual history proves to be mistaken or wrong-headed.

The triumph of the West in the Cold War opened the way for a host of predictions, most of which have not been realized; their authors have not been reproached for anticipating events that never happened. One of the most prominent visions, Francis Fukuyama's "end of history" in 1989, seemed absurd even as it was pronounced. Even granted that the afterglow of the destruction of the Berlin Wall could generate dreams of a new world order, it seems incredible four years later that Fukuyama's ideas were taken seriously. "What we are witnessing," he observed, "is not just the end of the Cold War, or the passing of a particular period of Cold War history, but the end of history as such: that is, the end point of man's ideological evolution and the universalization of Western liberal democracy as the final form of human government." This statement gives a special pejorative meaning to "counterfactual."

Other predictions made as late as September 1989 became suddenly irrelevant after the dramatic events that followed later that year and in 1990. Such was the fate of the conference convened at NATO headquarters in Brussels to instruct the youth of NATO's member-nations about the problems facing the alliance as the decade of the 1980s ended. The key issue, according to NATO officials, was not how the West should match the deescalation of tensions initiated by Soviet General Secretary Mikhail Gorbachev, but how to win European, particularly German, approval for a modernized Lance missile. This was a short-range nuclear missile that would be employed in combat only on German soil. As a result, the Lance met with understandable resistance from its potential victims. The prospect of a unified Germany coming into being in the immediate future was raised only once, when one member of the conference, with mischievous intent, asked a German general dispatched to the conference from Casteau how much thought he was giving to the possibility of unification, and of its impact on NATO. With a broad smile the general responded that he and his colleagues were giving as little thought as possible to such an unlikely future. Less than two months later, the Berlin Wall fell; less than a year later, Germany was reunited; less than two years later, the Soviet empire dissolved. Meanwhile, the Lance missile itself became irrelevant.

But even when predictions go wildly astray their authors are readily forgiven. One distinguished authority, Ronald Steel, whose work is always worth reading, began predicting the demise of NATO as early as 1964. Its mission, the defense of Europe, was completed in Nikita Khrushchev's time, he claimed, as normal, if often hostile, relations prevailed between the Western and Eastern blocs. NATO had lost its function and should dissolve. Steel still anticipates its termination, although the date remains uncertain.

Other commentators are more dogmatic about the necessity for immediate termination of the alliance. Political scientist Amos Perlmutter entitled a think piece in December 1993 "NATO Must Face the Fact It Is Obsolete" and judged that "the realities of contemporary international relations, with the United States on an inward retreat and Germany unwilling to become Europe's America, leave NATO with no reason to exist." Newspaper editorials and columns played with variations of "obsolete" before and after the January summit meeting of the North Atlantic Council. The *New Statesman and Society* declared on 7 January 1994, that "NATO is Obsolete." *Newsday* (New York City) said the same thing more delicately by noting on 16 January that "A Treaty Becomes an Heirloom."

THE STATE OF WESTERN EUROPE, 1948–49

Responding to these pessimistic judgments, I shall venture to predict a past that might have come into being had NATO not been created. Knowing what we do about the state of Europe in 1948, some of my predictions may carry more weight than others. What can be said without hesitation is that Western Europe was on edge that year, fearful not of a Soviet invasion as such but of a Communist sweep into power through Soviet intimidation or through well-organized political parties. Despair over the economic future of a still-devastated Europe was a factor in the power of communism. Memories of Communists as the heroes of World War II resistance movements also gave an authority to the position of European Communists. Even though the Truman Doctrine had been pronounced and the Marshall Plan finally passed into law by the spring of 1948, the distance between the promise of those initiatives and their realization seemed vast. The former represented American unilateralism, a promise of aid for nations threatened by Soviet imperialism that could be unilaterally revoked. The latter was an economic program with great promise for the revival of Europe, but it would be wasted if political insecurity undermined the economic benefits among the beneficiaries. The American tradition of nonentanglement with European politics was still alive.

It required the combined efforts of American statesmen, such as Robert Lovett and Dean Acheson, and their European counterparts, Britain's Ernest Bevin and France's Georges Bidault, to break down American resistance to a binding alliance with Western Europe. In retrospect, the signing of the North Atlantic Treaty on 4 April 1949 was a logical evolution of American-European collaboration. This cooperation began with American support for the Brussels Pact in March 1948 and the Vandenberg Resolution in June of that year and continued with the Washington Exploratory Talks with the Brussels Pact powers and the expansion of that alliance's scope in the winter of 1949. However, this was no easy transition. The path to the "pledge" of Article 5 had to overcome resistance from those in the American military fearing European raids on their own limited resources, from internationalists fearing the impact of a military alliance on the United Nations, and from traditional isolationists fearing infection from a close connection with the diseased Old World.

But what if the path toward the alliance had met with the insuperable obstacles that in the end would have doomed the North Atlantic Treaty? What would have been the fate of Europe—and the United States—if the Washington talks had collapsed in the summer of 1948, or if the Senate had succeeded in February 1949 in scrapping Article 5 of the treaty? The history of the West might have been very different from its actual experience in the first forty-five years of NATO's history.

THE NORDIC PAST

My speculations about what might have been begin with the "stepping-stone" countries on the periphery of the Western Union—Norway and Denmark—and then move to the Benelux countries and Italy before considering the major allies: Britain, France, and Germany. Scandinavia was an irritating afterthought for most of the European allies, considered in early 1949 only when the United States forced the allies to accept Norway and Denmark as stepping-stones valued for their position in the North Atlantic. Greenland and Iceland would provide bases for American aid to Europe. Norway, more than Denmark, was eager for the NATO connection as it worried about periodic pressure from the neighboring Soviet Union to enter into a bilateral nonaggression pact. For Norwegians these invitations were both an uncomfortable reminder of the Nazi invitation of 1939 and an incentive to come under the protection of the Western alliance. Denmark was more tempted to join a Nordic pact linking it and Norway with Sweden that would be independent of NATO and presumably less threatening to the Soviets. The Nordic pact never materialized, and Sweden remained outside the Atlantic Alliance. When Denmark joined Norway in accepting NATO membership, it nonetheless reflected its continuing concern over Soviet intimidation by not permitting NATO military bases on Danish territory.

Had NATO not come into being, what might have been the history of Scandinavia? First, the Nordic pact would have been signed. But how much security would it have given its members? Their combined military power was considerably less than even the skeletal military establishments of Western Europe. NATO had the potential to equal if not surpass the forces of the Soviet Union. Sweden's addition to Denmark and Norway would hardly be a deterrent to aggression. The future of Scandinavia without NATO would have been similar to that of another Scandinavian country, Finland. While there were worse fates than "Finlandization" under Soviet domination, the price to be paid for keeping the Soviet army at bay would have been high, both in a sense of freedom lost and very likely in prosperity unachieved. Of all the Scandinavian countries only Iceland might have managed well with or without a NATO relationship. It had no army and would have made a bilateral connection with the United States, whether or not it wanted it, similar to its position during World War II.

DISSOLUTION OF THE WESTERN UNION

The fate of the Benelux nations would have been somewhat different from Scandinavia's, but no less depressing. The Low Countries were physically separated from the Soviet Union, unlike Norway or Finland. They also had an existing alliance as an alternative, the Brussels Pact, out of which NATO developed. But the Western Union established under the pact was always a sham. It was essentially a device to lure the United States into a European entanglement. How long would have the fifty-year alliance survived with each of its "High Contracting Parties" affording, in response to treaty obligations, a "party so attacked all military and other aid and assistance in their power"? Given the rivalries among its leaders, the alliance would have broken up without even an external challenge to nudge it. The behavior of one of its major committees, the Commander-in-Chiefs Committee, suggested that it could not even decide on a military commander. But even if it had, the elaborate plans for economic and military coordination were all on paper and depended on an infusion of American funds that would come with American membership.

Without the rubric of the Atlantic Alliance, the strains within the Western Union would have become visible immediately. Even before the Brussels Pact was completed, American pressure was required to induce Britain and France to give Belgium and the Netherlands equality within the five-nation union. The Belgians and Dutch disapproved in particular of the larger members' intentions to have the lesser members sign a separate treaty with the two major powers. These fissures would have destroyed the pact had not NATO been present to subsume the core group under its aegis.

Among the casualties in a divided West would have been the Marshall Plan. If the Western Union had dissolved through impotence and mutual ill will, the self-help and mutual aid that Americans had asked as a price for their assistance would have been lacking. There would have been no European Economic Community developed to lift all of Western Europe into prosperity in the 1950s. In its place would have been a dispirited, disunited Europe, reminiscent of the 1930s, providing added opportunities for increasing the influence of domestic Communist parties. The Soviet Union could have then played the role of Nazi Germany a decade earlier; or even worse, a resurgent nationalist Germany could have taken its place.

For Belgium there was another price to be paid in the absence of an Atlantic alliance. While postwar Belgium was a leading advocate of European unity, it was also a nation divided by language, if not by culture and religion. Linguistic division was inextricably linked to class division. Since the nation had received its independence in 1830, French had been the language of government, of the military, and of industry. The beneficiary of the new industrial revolution had been Francophone Wallonia, not Flanders. French was also the language of the Flemish elite; the many dialects of Flemish reflected the parochialism of the peasant class. Flemish nationalism burgeoned in the twentieth century, aimed at the wealth and privilege of the Francophones. Nazi occupation during World War II had elevated Flemings above Walloons. In the postwar era, Flemings came into their own: Economic power shifted from the depressed coal regions of Wallonia to the north; the Flemish population rapidly outstripped its Francophone counterpart; and the government passed over to Flemish leadership.

A clash between the two Belgian populations had the potential to destroy the nation unless they were contained within a larger structure. With the failure of the Western Union, the demand for separation would have been irresistible, if only because Francophone Brussels was in the middle of the Flemish countryside. Consider that the distinguished bilingual University of Louvain split into two sectors, with the French-speaking wing moving across the linguistic line to build its Louvain-la-Neuve. The breakup of this ancient university occurred at a time when Belgium had a greater stake in unity than did any of its neighbors; Brussels, after all, was the capital of both NATO and the European Community. It hardly requires a great leap of imagination to envision the creation of two antagonistic nations emerging from a dissolved Belgium.

RED ITALY

Italy's history would have differed from that of Norway or of Belgium, if only because of the power of its native Communist party. The party commanded 25 percent of the voting population of the country, having won the reputation—fairly or not—of being the most effective opponent of Mussolini and his Nazi allies during World War II. Although the success of the Christian Democratic Union in the elections of April 1948 had eased American concerns about the Soviets seizing Italy through the polls, there still remained the possibility of Italy going Communist. It had taken a massive political campaign, orchestrated in the United States with the help of the new Central Intelligence Agency, to mobilize Italian-American influence in Italy. The prospect of failure in Italy had so shaken the composure of as cool a diplomat as George Kennan that he ruminated about American military intervention to prevent such a Communist victory. Without the benefit of the NATO ties, would the defeated Communist party have remained in the background? Defeated nationally, it still controlled a so-called Red Belt across the industrial center of Italy.

The Italian center parties succeeded in containing domestic Communist power, due to the split within Italian socialism between those who would accept the Western alliance and those who would follow Communist leadership. But it required NATO and the strong American connection to maintain a Western orientation. Italian communism never faded away. It assumed a putatively benign form in the 1970s under the name of Eurocommunism. Although its leader, Enrico Berlinguer, inspired considerable suspicion in Henry Kissinger's State Department, Eurocommunism won adherents in Europe because of its acceptance of NATO and its promotion of détente with the Soviet Union.

But what if NATO had not been in the background? Italy would have moved quickly into the Soviet camp, with serious consequences for the West. Where the Soviets were effectively removed from the Italian peace treaty in 1947, their continuing interest in a trusteeship over Tripolitania would have been intensified; and with the encouragement of a Communist government, they might have succeeded in establishing a Soviet presence both in Italy and in North Africa. Without NATO, the Mediterranean would have been as much a Soviet as a Western sea. The Adriatic would have been affected as well. The crisis over control of Trieste, which ended in Italy's regaining of the city, could have ended in war between a Communist Italy and a Yugoslavia that had escaped Soviet domination. Even if Italy rejected a Communist government, it would have had to attend to the warning that the leader of the party, Palmiro Togliatti, issued in 1949: namely, that if the Soviet army were to enter Italy, the Italian people would be obligated to come to the aid of the Soviet forces. In brief, it does not stretch credulity to envision a Communist Italy in the 1950s that would be as firmly in the Soviet orbit as Finland, and ideologically happier with this relationship than was Russia's western neighbor.

THE FOURTH BALKAN WAR

When one looks at the checkered history of Greece and Turkey inside NATO, a first reaction may be to wonder what difference the existence of NATO has made. The mutual antagonism between ancient enemies was not miraculously dissolved under the NATO umbrella. Fear of communism and hope of tapping American resources were the common factors that brought Greeks and Turks into uneasy harmony in 1952. Both nations were admitted into the organization in that year because the newly reorganized military command in Paris believed that Greek, and especially Turkish, manpower was necessary for defense of the southern flank against a possible Soviet attack. Turkey's twenty-five divisions would help fulfill the mandate of the Lisbon conference of the North Atlantic Council in February 1952 whereby NATO would have fifty divisions on hand to contain Soviet conventional forces.

The joint admission to NATO suggested a spirit of collaboration that did not exist between the two neighbors. When the short-lived Balkan Pact (including Yugoslavia) collapsed by the mid-1950s, the conflict between these two NATO members was resumed. Despite their participation in Supreme Headquarters Allied Powers in Europe (SHAPE) assignments, Greece and Turkey were at each other's throats for much of the next forty years over their respective positions in Cyprus and over air and sea rights in the Aegean. Greece left the organization's military wing in 1974, unhappy with American toleration of Turkey's invasion of Cyprus in that year. Turkey in turn denied use of vital bases to the United States and NATO when its military aid was cut off on the grounds that equipment intended for NATO purposes was channeled into an invasion that ended with 40 percent of Cyprus in Turkish possession.

Could an alternative history have been much worse? Very likely. Despite the tensions between them, neither Greece nor Turkey went to war, although not because of any particular act of reconciliation. Greece returned to the organization in 1980 for fear that Turkey would receive benefits by its continued participation that Greece would not enjoy. And Turkey's annoyance with the United States was balanced against continuing concern over the intentions of its Soviet neighbor. Greece and Turkey never went over the brink into open warfare.

Left outside NATO, the histories of Greece and Turkey would have been very different. Turkey would not have found the strength to resist Soviet pressure on its own. Not only would it have had to cede territory in the Caucasus but also its control over the Dardanelles would have been lost. Greece, for its part, might have had to fight over again the battle against communism, and this time it would have had no American partner or Yugoslav defector to help contain the pressure. And with both nations firmly in the Soviet grasp, there would have been no incentive for the Soviets to restrain their satellites from waging war over the Aegean or Cyprus.

FRANCE: 1939 REDIVIVUS

Gloomy as the prospects for Italy and Greece would have been, those of France and Germany, the major continental powers in Western Europe, would have been catastrophic by comparison. For France, the primary concern was always a revived and rearmed Germany, even when this concern seemed to have been subsumed under worry over a well-organized Communist party with 20 percent of the nation's vote behind it. The liberal Catholic party, Mouvement Républicain Populaire, anti-Communist Socialists, and conservative Radicals all saw Communist subversion as the more immediate threat. Even followers of Jean Monnet who looked to a long-term Franco-German reconciliation could not escape the memories of three wars with German Reichs.

As noted in a different context, the Brussels Pact was no solution for

France, although it did combine a program of containment of Communist power with a specific reference to "a renewal by Germany of an aggressive policy." Without American adherence, it lacked credibility to contain a Soviet invasion or, more relevant to the French, to restrain German economic recovery, German rearmament, and the revival of Germany's drive for dominance. France's perception of a German menace was obvious in its desperate attempts within the NATO fold to sabotage the European Defense Community, which would have opened the way for a German army in a European uniform.

In the absence of the Atlantic Alliance, France's paranoia would have been even more evident. What it had failed to do after World War I, namely, to use the Allied military victory to subject an essentially more powerful Germany to France's leadership on the Continent, it achieved after World War II by retaining control of the Saarland and maintaining the division of Germany. France had failed ignominiously in the interwar period to achieve its objectives. Would it have done any better after World War II if Europe and America had failed to effect an alliance? Such a question is easily answered in the negative.

France would have found itself beset by enemies on all sides. From the West, the allies, America and Britain, if they acted at all, would have moved toward restoration of Germany as a bulwark against the Soviet Union. But even if the Anglo-Saxon powers had isolated themselves from the Continent, the only source of assistance in the containment of Germany would have been the Soviet empire. That the American connection was unreliable would have been obvious to the French, either because it would have substituted American for German or Russian domination, or because America would have eventually tired of its military role in Europe and brought its troops home. Such were the concerns that agitated France within the Atlantic Alliance. Witness the efforts of the hapless Fourth Republic to achieve a nuclear *force de frappe*. And, particularly, witness General Charles de Gaulle's none-too-subtle signals to the Soviets that the price for his removal of France from NATO's military organization and his frank acceptance of the Oder-Neisse line was a senior partnership with Germany in his projected *Europe des patries*. De Gaulle sought a revival of the old Franco-Russian entente without removing France from the protection of the North Atlantic Treaty's Article 5.

Without NATO there would have been no American lifeline. And had de Gaulle established his Fifth Republic, he would have been dealing with a Poland or a Czechoslovakia in a Soviet sphere. His only possible partner would have been the Soviet Union. In one sense, this Eastern connection could have been far more effective than France's alliance with the fragile new nations of the East in suppressing German militarism. In this circumstance, the price France would have had to pay for a neutral or a Communist Germany would have been a Communist France. De Gaulle's vision of Europe from the Atlantic to the Urals might have been realized, but not under French leadership.

THE FOURTH REICH

The nightmare of an irredentist Germany unrestrained by a Western alliance was not confined to France. It was never far from the thoughts of other former victims of German occupation. The Dutch and Norwegians had as many reasons as the French to prevent the reemergence of an armed Germany seeking restitution of lost territories. What was lost after World War II was considerably more than had been taken from the Second Reich in the Treaty of Versailles. This pervasive European worry may not have been shared by Americans, but it was recognized in Dean Acheson's repeated testimony before the Korean War that German rearmament was not possible even though German territory would be protected as long as occupation forces remained on German soil. When Germany finally entered NATO in 1955, it was only after its membership was cushioned inside the enlarged Western European Union. Britain's membership provided some reassurance to France, as did the special restrictions on Germany's ability to manufacture nuclear, biological, or chemical weaponry, or even to raise an army independent of NATO.

Without NATO there would have been no means of gradually bringing West Germany into the alliance. Our counterfactual history would have witnessed a Hobbesian Europe in which the powerful consumed the weak, in which there would be no chains to bind an aggressor. True, there were forces in Germany that recognized the ugliness of Germany's past and would make a heroic effort to prevent the reemergence of rabid German militarism. Such was the aspiration of the German Socialists, led at the beginning of the 1950s by Kurt Schumacher and later in the decade by Erich Ollenhauer. Their path was pacifism, which they hoped would appease the Soviets sufficiently to permit the unification of the divided Germanies. This policy's chance of success would have been stronger than that of the pro-Western Adenauer forces, which would have looked to incorporation with the West as a means of taming German expansionism.

But neither the Francophilic Adenauer nor the neutralist Ollenhauer would have been the dominant force in a Europe that resembled the 1930s. In their place, neo-Nazi parties would have had power thrust on them or would have seized control of West Germany. Such parties existed in the 1950s in the Federal Republic (for example, the Deutscher Reichspartei). They received sustenance from the huge influx of Germans expelled from the Sudetenland, Poland, and East Prussia. These displaced Germans played a role in the politics of the Adenauer era that was larger than the size of their political parties. Even with Germany firmly embedded inside NATO and committed to the goals of the Atlantic Alliance, one could find maps that identified East Germany as *Mitteldeutschland* and the lost territories as *Ostdeutschland*. While NATO may have claimed that unification would come from a position of strength vis-à-vis the Warsaw bloc, it did not include the retaking of parts of Czechoslovakia, Poland, or the Soviet Union. In a world without NATO, the irredentist parties would have overwhelmed the moderate democratic elements with promises of the recovery of territory and prosperity.

There would have been only one force that could inhibit the rise of a Fourth Reich, and that would have been the Soviet Union. Given the lively memories of World War II, the Communist empire would have done everything in its power to remove the threat of a neo-Nazi Germany. It would have followed a line attempted in the confrontation between the Atlantic and Warsaw blocs. Unification of East and West Germany would have been part of a package that would have left Germany at best a neutralist nation, without an army or major weaponry. In this scenario, a united Germany would be a Communist Germany, the German Democratic Republic extended to the Rhine.

Yet this is not the most likely history of German-Russian relations. German nationalists would not have been satisfied with a neutral state, even a united state; the lost territories would have been as much on the nation's mind as they were under Hitler. And a subservient role to the Soviet Union would have been even less acceptable. Germany unbound would have found a way to build a nuclear armory and then challenge the Soviet Union in a race far more dangerous than the NATO–Warsaw Pact contest was in its most volatile period. If the Russians had memories of German bestiality in two world wars, Germans remembered the dream of harnessing the resources of the Ukraine, as the Second Reich intended in the Treaty of Brest-Litovsk in 1918 and the Third Reich in its invasion of the Soviet Union in 1941. The image of a Europe under such German domination could be as unsettling as a Europe under Communist domination—and perhaps even more so.

ISOLATED BRITAIN

It has been over a century since Britain, with an empire on which the sun never set, could enjoy a "splendid isolation." The twentieth century witnessed the steady decline of the British Empire despite desperate attempts to maintain the influence it had enjoyed in the nineteenth century. Two world wars left it depleted in funds, resources, and morale. Such hope that the nation had in recovering its leadership rested on a "special relationship" with the United States. An astute British pundit, Alistair Buchan, expressed it in the form of the wise Greek slave manipulating the strong but inexperienced and naive Roman conqueror. America as the daughter of Britain would be instructed in the ways of the world by a wiser and older veteran.

This was the vision that moved Foreign Secretary Ernest Bevin to entice the United States into a European alliance in which Britain would share power with the United States. Britain's position as *primus inter pares* in a global commonwealth offered at least the illusion of substance to its claim as America's partner. When the Atlantic Alliance was forged, Britain appeared to have won its objective. It was soon disillusioned. Paris, not London, became the headquarters of NATO; American commanders, not British, were in charge of military operations. Even its hope for a naval command was denied. As NATO evolved, American concerns centered on France and Germany, forcing Britain to become part of a European rather than an Anglo-Saxon community. Dean Acheson brutally stated the truth of Britain's weakness in deriding its efforts to serve as broker between the Soviet Union and the United States, or as a special partner to the American superpower. In Acheson's words, expressed in 1962, "Great Britain has lost an empire and has not yet found a role."

If Britain's fate within NATO was that it became a middle-ranked nation tied to a European community dominated by Germany, what would have been its future without NATO? Unquestionably, the decline of British power and influence would have been even steeper. In the collapse of an Atlantic alliance, Britain would have clung to the hope that some form of the informal wartime Anglo-American alliance would survive. Those hopes would have been dashed even more quickly than the Greek-Roman model that British leaders had anticipated under NATO. The military collaboration of World War II had little meaning for NATO when the United States helped to abort Britain's invasion of Egypt in 1956 and six years later abruptly canceled a nuclear weapon that Britain had counted on to sustain its position as a nuclear power. Without NATO and with a United States suspicious of all European connections, Britain would have turned to its Commonwealth without success. The rapid degeneration of its empire in the 1950s would have proceeded even more rapidly in these circumstances than it actually did.

After Britain had excluded itself from the Continent, any European policy it could devise would have been a reprise of traditional British alliances designed to keep in check any nation that could control the Continent. Whether that nation was Germany or Russia, a shrunken Britain, its economy in tatters, would have stood no chance of emulating the triumphs of the eighteenth or nineteenth centuries. Belated attempts to join once again with France would have failed in the face of a Communist France or a France under the German Bundesbank. Labor riots would have reduced the national state to anarchy.

If there was a ray of hope in this new world it would not have been in a revival of the American partnership but in a junior partnership with the

Soviet Union in a new common front against German domination. Despite all the economic misery that Britain would have suffered, the British Communist party would have been unable to take over the country as its counterpart in Italy had done. Britain still had resources, and even far-flung friends in Canada and Australia as well as a hard core of Anglophile Americans. It would have survived as it did in World War II and joined the Soviet Union in an effort to keep German power in check. At best the future for Britain would have been an uneasy balance in which it would have played a significant but minor part. The alternative would not have been conquest by Communists or neo-Nazis but acceptance of a position as an offshore island living on the scale of a Third World country. The image of Britain in the Tudor years comes to mind. It was an offshore island of Europe before it became an island empire.

AUTARCHIC AMERICA

All of the foregoing scenarios are based on an assumption that the United States would have turned its back on Europe and reverted to traditional isolationism. This, of course, is not the only path the nation might have followed. One can conceptualize a powerful America with a military machine ready and able to take on any potential enemy and doing so alone. Given the disillusion with the Soviet wartime ally and the concurrent fear of Communist expansion, the United States might not have demobilized after the war. Instead, it might have used the atomic weapon as an instrument of blackmail to deter the Soviet Union from moving beyond its borders with either its armies or its ideology.

Whether or not such a posture would have succeeded is moot. The picture of an aggressive America puffed up by its success against the Germans and the Japanese to the extent that it would assume the burdens as well as the advantages of global supremacy is an unlikely one. Those Americans who had entertained such a notion were few in number and had little influence. Brigadier General Bonner Fellers, for example, hardly spoke for the air force, let alone for the military at large, when he urged America to threaten the Soviet Union with atomic destruction if it did not accede to American supremacy. This would have been an extravagant interpretation of the atomic diplomacy that critics have attributed to American policy toward the Soviets in 1945.

The form that American disillusion with Europe was more likely to have taken would have been to look either inward or to the Pacific. Isolationist tradition never applied to Asia; it had been directed since the end of the Franco-American alliance only to Europe. While bilateral agreements with specific European countries might have been possible after the war, particularly with Britain, the temptation to use such arrangements as buffers against communism would have been diluted by a sense of betrayal once again by an ungrateful Europe. The sentiment that led America to reject the Treaty of Versailles and the League of Nations in 1919 would have risen again, with even greater force than had been manifested a generation before. The massive demobilization of America's armed forces in 1946 was a portent of what would have happened if the United States had rejected an entanglement with Western Europe. Rather than rearming against Soviet communism, the nation would have turned its back on an Old World that would never reform; it would have let the former allies resume their feuds, and let the Soviets extend their reach to the Atlantic. The warnings of such old isolationists as former Ambassador Joseph Kennedy and former president Herbert Hoover would have been accepted instead of being ignored as they were on the eve of the Great Debate in 1951 over dispatching U.S. troops to Europe. In December 1950, Kennedy had claimed that entanglement with Europe—and Asia as well—was suicidal. It would neither win friends nor assure America's security. It would only waste troops and resources in a useless effort. And if communism did succeed in Korea or Europe, what of it? It would be a short-lived triumph, as the West would break loose from the Soviets much as Tito's Yugoslavia did in 1948. Hoover invoked a "fortress America" in a public address, asserting that if Europe should be united under a hostile power, Fascist or Communist, it need not affect America. America, both he and Kennedy asserted, could be autarchic, independent of the rest of the world.

The national euphoria that would have accompanied this divorce from the Old World would have lingered for a decade. Not even the knowledge that the Soviet Union possessed an atomic device, and a few years later, a hydrogen bomb, would have jarred America from its complacency. Only when the limits of its own vast resources began to take a toll on the nation's prosperity and security would the price of autarchy have become increasingly unbearable. Raw materials for American industry, including nuclear weaponry, required imports from abroad while exports were needed to absorb American manufactures. Isolationism in the postwar world would have depressed America's standard of living as well as its spirits.

This new sense of insecurity would have coincided with changes in military technology to induce panic far more severe than Sputnik caused in 1957. Such would be the effect of the Soviets and the Germans possessing intercontinental ballistic missiles that these power shifts could have made America as vulnerable as Europeans felt themselves to be in the 1970s. German expansionist dreams expressed in Operation Barbarossa in 1941 would have become a reality as Russian resources were harnessed to the German economy. In a world made smaller by technology, the Atlantic Ocean was no longer a guarantor of American independence. Even belated attempts to mobilize China or Japan to counter the power of a united and hostile Europe stretching from the ocean to the Urals and beyond would have failed. When not fighting with each other, the Asian powers would have been intimidated by the Eurasian behemoth.

The consequence for the United States would have been a massive military buildup that would have drained the economy and damaged the fabric of democracy. In the 1940s, those who raised concern about America becoming a garrison state under military control recognized that Generals Marshall and Eisenhower were not men on horseback, no matter how high their civilian offices. And if General MacArthur aspired to that role, as some of his critics claimed, he quickly reconciled himself to exile in the Waldorf Astoria when his autocratic style proved to be more attractive in Japan than it was in Washington. An America without an Atlantic alliance, however, might have turned to dictatorship in its struggle for survival.

Whether or not any of these visions of Armageddon—some of them contradictory—bear any resemblance to reality, it is reasonable to assume in any counterfactual historical study that both Europe and America would have faced a more difficult future than they did under the aegis of NATO. With all the stresses that the alliance produced, and almost all were clearly visible to any onlooker, the last half-century of European-American relations reflected no zero-sum relationship. Each of its members profited from the connection.

NATO AFTER FORTY-FIVE: A COUNTERFACTUAL HISTORY

What then of NATO's future? Most counterfactual pundits looking beyond the Cold War have decided that NATO will dissolve, or should dissolve. Judgments have been made, as noted, on the basis that a new world order would make the old alliance unnecessary, that successor organizations would replace NATO's function, or that the United Nations in the wake of the end of the Cold War would fulfill its original peacekeeping expectations. The most frequently mentioned replacement involves at least one or more of Europe's own organizations, ranging from a modest Franco-German brigade to a more satisfying Western European Union serving as the military arm of the European Union. In brief, there is no reason why a unified Europe, whether or not it should be the United States of Europe, should need an American presence on the Continent or in an integrated alliance.

The trouble with these projections has been the turbulent aftershocks of the termination of the Cold War. The breakup of the Soviet Union inspired not only ethnic conflict among the newly independent nations in the former Soviet empire but also new insecurity among the former Eastern European satellites of that empire. A Russia that has been disillusioned by the lure of a market economy and resentful of its loss of status could produce a new czar with imperial ambitions. Would the European Union be able to cope with these problems, offering the psychological as well as military security that NATO gave for two generations?

The answer to this question is clearly negative. Western Europe has not fulfilled the promises of economic, let alone political, union that the Maastricht meeting in 1992 was supposed to bring. Resentment against German domination, particularly the German Bundesbank, has divided the community. It has not been able to make up its mind about extending its membership or deepening its integration. Its vacillation over the Serbian challenge in Bosnia has weakened its credibility as a successor to NATO.

But does the new disarray in Europe, reminiscent as it is of the national relationships in the first half of the twentieth century, mean that only NATO can cope with the current crisis? The alliance's behavior since 1990 favors the views of those who would bury it as a useless relic of the past. The efforts at the North Atlantic Council meetings in London in 1990 and Rome in 1991 hardly inspire confidence. The new strategic concepts developed there, particularly rapid reaction forces for crisis management, seemed to fall apart in 1991 in the face of NATO's failure to deter Serbian aggression. And the offer of a "partnership" to East European nations at the Brussels summit meeting of January 1994 fell short of the security guarantees that those nations were demanding of NATO. Joint field exercises are no substitute for the pledge of Article 5, which the allies refused to grant in Brussels. Division among the allies over Bosnia continues into 1995 even as NATO acts as a UN surrogate.

Despite these negative signals, my counterfactual history of the next few years finds that NATO will not disintegrate. America's refusal to put its troops at risk in Bosnia until the warring parties had come to their own agreement does not necessarily mean that the United States has removed its commitment to defend the allies in the event of attack. The presence of even a handful of American soldiers in the Former Yugoslav Republic of Macedonia (FYROM) suggests otherwise. Article 4 of the North Atlantic Treaty, wherein the allies will consult whenever the security of any of the parties is threatened, applied both to Bosnia and to FYROM. Although NATO hesitated in Bosnia, it will have no choice in FYROM, where Greece and Turkey have interests at stake. NATO as a deterrent force will have more effect in deterring Serbia's Milosevic from intervening here than it did in Bosnia.

But NATO's survival will rest on more than a token presence in the Balkans. Insufficient as the Partnership for Peace may have been, it was a source of some comfort to the East Europeans. As Russia discovers that America's presence in Europe through NATO is a stabilizing force, it will become more accepting of the Western alliance. The unsatisfactory partnership with Eastern Europe will be replaced by membership, including the guarantees under Article 5. This does not mean that Polish or Hungarian armies will be rebuilt or their militaries integrated into a SHAPE command. What will make their membership acceptable is that Poland and Hungary's status would be much like Spain's or Iceland's—outside a military structure but inside a security system. NATO for Poland will resemble the alliance as it existed before the Korean War converted it into a military organization.

Beyond this arrangement, there will be the ineffable matter of the American presence in Europe. This is a symbol of stability that gives continuing significance to the alliance. America's commitment to Europe was also the glue that seemingly replaced the Soviet threat as NATO's centripetal force. The transatlantic bargain had always been the source of NATO's unity, even as it was obscured by the need to build a defense against an aggressive Warsaw bloc. With the demise of the Soviet Union, insecurity emanating from a potentially irredentist Russia and from a united Germany will require the continuation of the NATO umbrella.

Unlike the conditional tense I have used in my counterfactual history of NATO's first forty-five years, here I use an unqualified future tense as a measure of my conviction that NATO has a function for the immediate future: namely, to assure peace and order in Europe. The belief that membership in NATO is vital to their existence explains the desperate efforts of East Europeans nations to come under the protection of the umbrella. It also explains why none of the charter members is asking for the withdrawal of American troops from its territory. Nor is any member, including France, so dissatisfied with the direction of America's current behavior that it intends to leave the alliance. Withdrawal would be a simple matter under Article 13 of the treaty. A country's membership could cease "one year after its notice of denunciation has been given to the Government of the United States of America, which will inform the Governments of the other parties of the deposit of each notice of denunciation."

The day may come when such a "denunciation" is made. Or, if NATO should become irrelevant through impotence, it may dissolve quickly in the manner of the Warsaw Pact in 1991, or gradually in the manner of SEATO in 1977. My counterfactual history of the 1990s may be as mistaken as Fukuyama's in 1990 or Steel's in 1964. But I suspect that my version may have more validity than theirs.

Appendix
The North Atlantic Treaty, Washington, D.C., April 4, 1949

The Parties to this Treaty reaffirm their faith in the purposes and principles of the Charter of the United Nations and their desire to live in peace with all peoples and all governments.

They are determined to safeguard the freedom, common heritage and civilisation of their peoples, founded on the principles of democracy, individual liberty and the rule of law.

They seek to promote stability and well-being in the North Atlantic area.

They are resolved to unite their efforts for collective defence and for the preservation of peace and security.

They therefore agree to this North Atlantic Treaty:

ARTICLE 1

The Parties undertake, as set forth in the Charter of the United Nations, to settle any international dispute in which they may be involved by peaceful means in such a manner that international peace and security and justice are not endangered, and to refrain in their international relations from the threat or use of force in any manner inconsistent with the purpose of the United Nations.

ARTICLE 2

The Parties will contribute toward the further development of peaceful and friendly international relations by strengthening their free institutions, by bringing about a better understanding of the principles upon which these institutions are founded, and by promoting conditions of stability and well-being. They will seek to eliminate conflict in their international economic policies and will encourage economic collaboration between any or all of them.

ARTICLE 3

In order more effectively to achieve the objectives of this Treaty, the Parties, separately and jointly, by means of continuous and effective self-help and mutual aid, will maintain and develop their individual and collective capacity to resist armed attack.

ARTICLE 4

The Parties will consult together whenever, in the opinion of any of them, the territorial integrity, political independence or security of any of the Parties is threatened.

ARTICLE 5

The Parties agree that an armed attack against one or more of them in Europe or North America shall be considered an attack against them all and consequently they agree that, if such an armed attack occurs, each of them, in exercise of the right of individual or collective self-defence recognised by Article 51 of the Charter of the United Nations, will assist the Party or Parties so attacked by taking forthwith, individually and in concert with the other Parties, such action as it deems necessary, including the use of armed force, to restore and maintain the security of the North Atlantic area.

Any such armed attack and all measures taken as a result thereof shall immediately be reported to the Security Council. Such measures shall be terminated when the Security Council has taken the measures necessary to restore and maintain international peace and security.

ARTICLE 6[1]

For the purpose of Article 5 an armed attack on one or more of the Parties is deemed to include an armed attack on the territory of any of the Parties in Europe or North America, on the Algerian Departments of France,[2] on the occupation forces of any Party in Europe, on the islands under the jurisdiction of any Party in the North Atlantic area north of the Tropic of Cancer or on the vessels or aircraft in this area of any of the Parties.

Following this statement the Council noted that insofar as the former

Algerian Departments of France were concerned, the relevant clauses of this Treaty had become inapplicable as from July 3, 1962.

ARTICLE 7

This Treaty does not affect, and shall not be interpreted as affecting in any way the rights and obligations under the Charter of the Parties which are members of the United Nations, or the primary responsibility of the Security Council for the maintenance of international peace and security.

ARTICLE 8

Each Party declares that none of the international engagements now in force between it and any other of the Parties or any third State is in conflict with the provisions of this Treaty, and undertakes not to enter into any international engagement in conflict with this Treaty.

ARTICLE 9

The Parties hereby establish a Council, on which each of them shall be represented, to consider matters concerning the implementation of this Treaty. The Council shall be so organised as to be able to meet promptly at any time. The Council shall set up such subsidiary bodies as may be necessary; in particular it shall establish immediately a defense committee which shall recommend measures for the implementation of Articles 3 and 5.

NOTES

1. The definition of the territories to which Article 5 applies has been revised by Article 2 of the Protocol to the North Atlantic Treaty on the accession of Greece and Turkey (see Part 10, Section 3).

2. On January 16, 1963, the North Atlantic Council has heard a declaration by the French Representative who recalled that by the vote on self-determination on July 1, 1962, the Algerian people had pronounced itself in favour of the independence of Algeria in cooperation with France. In consequence, the President of the French Republic had on July 3, 1962, formally recognised the independence of Algeria. The result was that the Algerian departments of France no longer existed as such, and that at the same time the fact that they were mentioned in the North Atlantic Treaty had no longer any bearing.

Bibliographical Essay

Inevitably any NATO bibliography has to be prefaced with the term "selective." The literature is too vast to be comprehensive. I recognized the future problem forty-five years ago in a first attempt to categorize writings on the Atlantic alliance under the title of "NATO and Its Commentators: The First Five Years," *International Organization* 8 (November 1954): 447–67. Thirty years later I updated my essay on the early years, "NATO and Its Commentators: The First Five Years Revisited (1984)," in my monograph *The United States and NATO: The Formative Years* (Lexington: University Press of Kentucky, 1984), pp. 204–21. While these exercises may be useful, they do not exhaust the first five years of NATO's history, let alone the first fifty years. More recent bibliographies, which are also broader in scope than the foregoing, are Bert Zeeman, "The Origins of NATO: An International Bibliography," *Bulletin of Bibliography* 47, no. 4 (December 1990), and Phil Williams, comp., *The North Atlantic Treaty Organization* (New Brunswick, NJ: Transactions Publications, 1994).

For this volume, I will include samplings of the more important contributions in each of the periods I arbitrarily have identified in the text, emphasizing the most recent work on the United States and NATO. The most impressive memoir on the origins of NATO is Dean Acheson, *Present at the Creation: My Years in the State Department* (New York: W. W. Norton & Co., 1969). Alan K. Henrikson has written an insightful article on "The Creation of the North Atlantic Alliance, 1948–1952," *Naval War College Review* 32 (May–June, 1980): 4–39. For American opposition to the treaty, see E. Timothy Smith, *Opposition beyond the Water's Edge: Liberal In-*

ternationalists, Pacifists, and Containment, 1945–1953 (Westport, CT: Praeger, 1999).

Significant studies of the first generation include Phil Williams, *The Senate and U.S. Troops in Europe* (New York: St. Martin's Press, 1985), which examines the fall-out from the "Great Debate" of 1951. Recent studies of America's relations with its major allies are presented in Thomas A. Schwartz, *America's Germany: John J. McCloy and the Federal Republic of Germany* (Cambridge, MA: Harvard University Press, 1991); Charles G. Cogan, *Oldest Allies, Guarded Friends: The United States and France since 1940* (Westport, CT: Praeger, 1994); and Robert M. Hathaway, *Great Britain and the United States: Special Relations since World War II* (Boston: Twayne Publishers, 1990). Two major issues of the 1950s are well handled in Samuel R. Williamson, Jr. and Steven L. Rearden, *The Origins of U.S. Nuclear Strategy, 1945–1953* (New York: St. Martin's Press, 1992), and Pascaline Winand, *Eisenhower, Kennedy, and the United States of Europe* (New York: St. Martin's Press, 1993).

Henry Kissinger's memoir *Years of Upheaval* (Boston: Little, Brown and Co., 1982) captures the malaise of NATO in the Nixon-Ford years of the second generation. Even more pointedly, Sherri Wasserman, *The Neutron Bomb Controversy: A Study in Alliance Politics* (New York: Praeger, 1983), deals with a special source of malaise in the Carter administration. Nuclear politics in this period was the theme of Lawrence Freedman, *The Evolution of Nuclear Strategy* (New York: St. Martin's Press, 1981), and David N. Schwartz, *NATO's Nuclear Dilemmas* (Washington, DC: Brookings Institution Press, 1983). Conventional defense was the subject of John Duffield, *Power Rules: The Evolution of NATO's Conventional Force Posture* (Stanford, CA: Stanford University Press, 1995). The impending demise of the Soviet empire is the subject of Michael R. Beschloss and Strobe Talbott, *At the Highest Levels: The Inside Story of the End of the Cold War* (Boston: Little, Brown and Co., 1993), and Richard Kugler, *Commitment to Purpose: How the Alliance Partnership Won the Cold War* (Santa Monica, CA: RAND Corporation, 1993).

The third generation found NATO scholars reflecting on the alliance's efforts to find new missions after the Cold War. Stanley W. Sloan projects a positive outcome in *NATO's Future: Beyond Collective Defense* (Washington, DC: National Defense University Press, 1995), as does Charles Barry, ed., *Reforging the Trans-Atlantic Relationship* (Washington, DC: National Defense University Press, 1996). Sean Kay, *NATO and the Future of European Security* (Boulder, CO: Rowman & Littlefield, 1998), sees the United States as a continuing presence in Europe. Jeffrey Simon, ed., *NATO Enlargement: Opinions and Options* (Washington, DC: National Defense University Press, 1995), deals with a major issue in post–Cold War NATO. Less optimistic about NATO's future is Ted Galen Carpenter, *A Search for Enemies: America's Alliances after the Cold War* (Washington, DC: CATO

Institute, 1992). Joseph Nye, *Bound to Lead: The Changing Nature of American Power* (New York: Basic Books, 1990), is convinced that, despite the changed geostrategic environment, the United States has no choice but to remain entangled in an interconnected world.

Index

About the Author

LAWRENCE S. KAPLAN is University Professor Emeritus of History and Director Emeritus of the Lyman L. Lemnitzer Center for NATO and European Union Studies at Kent State University. He is currently Adjunct Professor of History at Georgetown University. He was formerly a member of the Historical Office, Office of the Secretary of Defense. During his tenure at Kent State he was a Fulbright Lecturer at the Universities of Bonn, Louvain, and Nice, as well as a visiting lecturer at University College London.

About the Author

LAWRENCE S. KAPLAN is University Professor Emeritus of History and Director Emeritus of the Lyman L. Lemnitzer Center for NATO and European Union Studies at Kent State University. He is currently Adjunct Professor of History at Georgetown University. He was formerly a member of the Historical Office, Office of the Secretary of Defense. During his tenure at Kent State he was a Fulbright Lecturer at the Universities of Bonn, Louvain, and Nice, as well as a visiting lecturer at University College London.

About the Author

LAWRENCE S. KAPLAN is University Professor Emeritus of History and Director Emeritus of the Lyman L. Lemnitzer Center for NATO and European Union Studies at Kent State University. He is currently Adjunct Professor of History at Georgetown University. He was formerly a member of the Historical Office, Office of the Secretary of Defense. During his tenure at Kent State he was a Fulbright Lecturer at the Universities of Bonn, Louvain, and Nice, as well as a visiting lecturer at University College London.

ISBN 0-275-96418-3

90000>

EAN

9 780275 964184

HARDCOVER BAR CODE